THE FRAGILITY OF EMPATHY
AFTER THE HOLOCAUST

THE FRAGILITY OF EMPATHY

AFTER THE HOLOCAUST

CAROLYN J. DEAN

CORNELL UNIVERSITY PRESS

ITHACA AND LONDON

An earlier version of Chapter 1 was published as "Empathy, Pornography, and Suffering," in *differnces: A Journal of Feminist Cultural Studies* 14 (2003) : 88–124.

Another version of Chapter 2, "Goldhagen's Celebrity, Numbness, and Writing History," appears in *History of the Human Sciences* 17 (February/August 2004).

First published 2004 by Cornell University Press
First printing, Cornell Paperbacks, 2004

Printed in the United States of America

Library of Congress Cataloging-in-Publication Data

Dean, Carolyn J. (Carolyn Janice)
    The fragility of empathy after the Holocaust / Carolyn J. Dean.
        p. cm.
    Includes bibliographical references and index.
    ISBN 0-8014-4162-5 (cloth : alk. paper)—ISBN 0-8014-8944-X (pbk. : alk. paper)
1. Holocaust, Jewish (1939–1945)—Influence. 2. Holocaust, Jewish
(1939–1945—Historiography. 3. Holocaust, Jewish (1939–1945)—Moral and ethical
aspects. 4. National socialism and homosexuality. I. Title.
    D804.348.D43 2004
    940.53'18—dc22

                                                        2004012144

Cloth printing   10 9 8 7 6 5 4 3 2 1
Paperback printing   10 9 8 7 6 5 4 3 2 1

In memory of Brian R. Dean

(1962–2000)

CONTENTS

ACKNOWLEDGMENTS

This book was completed during a residency at the Rockefeller Foundation Center in Bellagio, Italy, and I thank the Foundation, Susan Garfield, Gianna Celli, and those friends who forged the community that proved so supportive there. Omer Bartov provided a gentle reading of several chapters, and David Kertzer has been giving in ways great and small.

Lynn Hunt read some chapters early on and Dominick LaCapra read much of the manuscript at different stages and challenged me to push the argument in new directions. Martin Jay, as always, read and reread every chapter, provided crucial insights, and helped sustain my confidence in the project. And Joan Scott offered countless suggestions about how to improve the manuscript and helped me come to a better understanding of the project as a whole.

I also thank Laurie Bernstein, Marcia Brennan, Deborah Cohen, Ruth Feldstein, Ruth Gutmann, and Maud Mandel for readings and counsel. Dagmar Herzog gave her invaluable expertise, references, and a critical reading. Clare Rogan, Julie Bacon, and Becky Colesworthy provided extraordinary research assistance, and Teresa Jesionowski, Herman Rapaport, Catherine Rice, Nancy Ferguson, Liz Cunningham, and John Ackerman pushed the book through all the various stages from manuscript to publication. I thank Alan Schechner and Mischa Kuball for being consistently generous in response to requests to include their work, and am deeply indebted to Andrea Belag, who allowed me to use her work for the cover. Finally, I drew on the considerable emotional resources of friends and especially those of my family, and am deeply grateful to them all.

C.J.D.

THE FRAGILITY OF EMPATHY
AFTER THE HOLOCAUST

Introduction

In an editorial on photos of lynching exhibited at the New-York Historical Society in 2000, reporter Brent Staples claims that the "modern era takes it on faith that images of suffering stimulate sensitivity to that suffering." Yet now, he says, the effect of these images is more often to brutalize spectators and "normalize" atrocity, turning the "likenesses of these events [into] a form of brutality in themselves."[1] Staples's challenge to the modern era's putative faith in the power of empathy—or what used to be called "sympathy," an important quality of the feeling individual in the late eighteenth and early nineteenth centuries—is a familiar one. "The mind sickens and grows numb," said George Steiner of the effects of simply knowing about so much brutality in the twentieth century.[2] Psychologists and other scholars have defined a new problem in trauma studies they call "empathy fatigue" or "compassion fatigue," in which numbness is conceived explicitly as a form of self-protective dissociation.[3] And those responsible for fund-raising in international humanitarian organizations, including Amnesty International and Doctors without Borders, have claimed that they face a "numb" public.[4]

The essays in this book explore a pervasive conception in the West that defines our failure to stop suffering before it begins or as it is happening: our numbness. They do so by analyzing various ways in which we address our relationship to the genocide of European Jewry. By "we" and "our" I mean the imaginary collective of feeling or unfeeling human beings in the West (though I focus mostly on

1

Americans) presumed or invented by public intellectuals, historians, journalists, and critics more generally who have participated in this discussion since the end of the Nuremberg trials.[5] Assertions that we are numb and indifferent to suffering, that exposure to narratives and images of suffering has generated new and dramatic forms of emotional distance, *however* they are transmitted, are by now commonplace in both the United States and western Europe. The source of such assertions is not only the intensification of visual images and narratives of violence since the 1960s, but also the central role American and European intellectuals accorded the Holocaust of European Jewry in shattering the once secure meaning of "humanity" in the West.[6] Yet the tendency by critics to wistfully hearken back to humane ideals they insist we can now no longer live up to after the Holocaust bears investigation, for this rhetoric takes specific forms and expresses new historical restraints on imagination and feeling.[7]

Discourses about various impediments to empathic feeling have existed since the eighteenth century, when sympathy was first deemed a crucial component of the enlightened self, the feeling individual, and the new social order. In his "Letter on the Blind," for example, Denis Diderot noted that distance inured us to the suffering of others, and satirists from Mandeville to Richardson sought to expose the exploitation and manipulation of sympathetic emotion by do-gooders.[8] In 1769, when sentimentalism was the height of fashion, the witty correspondent Madame Riccoboni wrote from Paris, "One would readily create unfortunates in order to taste the sweetness of feeling sorry for them."[9] In a parallel nineteenth-century narrative that derives from enlightened humanism and yet also pokes fun at its bourgeois proponents, writers from Honoré de Balzac to Karl Marx sought to reveal how the pity that moved the prosperous classes consolidated the very misery they bemoaned. Marx draws an unflattering portrait of a sordid bourgeoisie that professes pity but really revels in the persecution of the weak, so that, for example, wives of prominent bourgeois politicians enthusiastically applaud the "revolting atrocities" to which Parisian Communards were subjected.[10] In response to the images of violated and abused slaves that American abolitionists circulated in the early nineteenth century, several commentators noted that while they were meant to inspire moral action, the drawings often owed their impact to more prurient pleasures.[11]

Efforts to inspire moral action on behalf of the poor and disenfranchised presumed that arousing human compassion required some symbolic proximity to the sufferer. One had to be inspired by the powers of imagination to feel a likeness to the sufferer that images or narratives of violation were meant to generate.[12] These images, however, could also arouse the "wrong" sort of compassion, or insincere forms of sympathy. Denis Diderot, Jean-Jacques Rousseau, and Balzac, among others, each presumed that all natural human compassion has socio-historical limits determined by the extent of our real "likeness" to others. Thus geographical, ethnic, and social distance may preclude or distort compassion. Distance extends across space and between cultures, so that when there are calamities in Japan, says Rousseau, he can't get very worked up about them. Distance is also so deeply embedded in social difference that the poor become but a spectacle for the wealthy.[13] In short, imaginary likeness overcomes the power of local allegiances and renders the concept of suffering humanity possible, but too much distance leads to insufficient or disingenuous sympathy.

The socio-historical context within which more recent anxieties about our ability to feel compassion have been articulated has changed dramatically in the aftermath of two world wars, both in Europe and in the United States. Still, pre-1914 campaigns against the abuse of Africans in King Leopold II's Congo, the well-publicized effects of colonialism such as war and famine, or the awareness of high levels of poverty and hunger at home during that time demonstrate that humanitarianism in Europe or the United States was hardly widespread, however heroic and disproportionately vocal its practitioners.

After the Great War and during the interwar period (1918–39), however, a new middle-class consciousness of empathy's precariousness emerged, and it intensified dramatically after the Second World War. After 1945, the victors prosecuted war crimes literally, by putting perpetrators on trial, as well as symbolically, by reasserting the Enlightenment heritage against the unfathomable collapse of empathy. For the first time a series of international documents enshrined the human rights of individuals in international law, including the Universal Declaration of Human Rights (1948), the Genocide Convention (1948), and the expansion of the Geneva Conventions (1949). In the next decade, and especially after 1960, discussion about the war shifted from war crimes generally to the extermination of European Jewry and genocide more broadly, and the phrase "crimes against humanity," first coined in reference to the 1915 Turkish genocide of Armenians and invoked in the Nuremberg trials, became increasingly pervasive.[14] As Isaiah Berlin wrote in 1959 in reference to the Holocaust, "because the rules of nature were flouted, we have been forced to become conscious of them."[15] Moreover, revelations during the 1961 Eichmann trial about the passivity of the United States and Britain (for example, about the failure to bomb Auschwitz) emphasized moral ambiguity more than the righteous Allied narrative of victory over evil.[16] It was in the context of these discussions that new anxiety about the fragility of empathy developed most self-consciously. Recent rhetoric about numbness and indifference to human suffering, the propriety of displaying that suffering, and questions about how men and women could inflict such agony on others—that is, questions about human indifference to the fates of others—thus signals an important cultural narrative that has yet to be systematized and examined. Of course, many scholars and others approach these questions as philosophical, moral, or even psychoanalytic dilemmas. Instead, I address discussions of our numbness as a socio-cultural and historical problem posed particularly by current representations of the Holocaust, primarily but not exclusively in the United States.[17] These essays, which obviously do not aim to be a comprehensive treatment of "Holocaust representation," focus on four culturally prominent and revealing ways in which scholars (mostly historians), journalists, and high-brow cultural critics have addressed, diagnosed, and explained (or not) what seem to be excessive constraints on compassion. Why are representations of the Holocaust referred to pervasively as "pornographic"? How have historians discussed means of generating empathic responses to Jewish victims, particularly in the debate over Daniel Jonah Goldhagen's controversial *Hitler's Willing Executioners?* How might we understand historians' persistent invocation of "indifference" when addressing bystanders of Nazi crimes? And finally, why did psychoanalysts, journalists, and other intellectuals associate Hitler's cruelty and Nazism with male homosexuality in spite of the Nazis' vicious treatment of gay men, and why might this association resonate today?

Whether or not there has been a real failure of empathy is not my subject.[18] Instead, I investigate presumptions about how empathy sustains collective identity rather than the historical constitution and alteration of emotional states. Moral assumptions, national cultures, socio-economic conditions, and other factors intertwine differently in different times and places to generate widely varied responses to representations of suffering, and to determine why some victims evoke compassion and some do not.[19] I don't address *why* numbness has emerged as a diffuse and pervasive cultural narrative; rather, I try to understand how it coheres and what cultural fantasies that narrative constitutes or leaves wanting in terms of who "we" are.

Indeed, this narrative on numbness may represent something quite new in the history of humanitarianism, for it does not simply suggest that most of us won't disrupt our daily routines for the sake of others near or far without a real or imaginary causal connection to sufferers.[20] It suggests that we are often willing to do so, but to our surprise we feel nothing or are paradoxically immobilized by guilt and even resentful of those who make claims upon us.

Numbness, that is, manifests an important challenge to the liberal ideal that we can empathically project ourselves into others with whom we share a common humanity, whether strangers or neighbors. For numbness is not only a psychological form of self-protective dissociation; it is arguably a new, highly self-conscious narrative about the collective constriction of moral availability, if not empathy, and may thus constrain humanist aspirations in ways we do not yet recognize. Because numbness may also be a necessary dimension of our ability to absorb mass atrocity, it paradoxically confirms ideas about our common humanity—we can only respond numbly to what we feel in excess—while also rendering humanitarian practice increasingly vexed.[21] It may be that numbness merely exposes in new and dramatic terms the limits of the ideally expansive liberal "we." Indeed, one of the main aims of these essays is to demonstrate that complicated discussions about numbness are new ways of working through our own fraught awareness of the boundaries of the human "we," whose very self-constitution has always depended on both animal and human "others."[22]

These four essays fit into a much broader discussion about the sources of our numbness now taking place in a wide variety of arenas. In what remains of this introduction I define the narrative of numbness as an object of inquiry by synthesizing different discussions of the fragility of empathy. The narrative that emerges defines in explicit terms the ways in which we both self-consciously and unselfconsciously think about the problem of empathy's fragility, as well as what is emotionally, culturally, and politically at stake in how we reflect about who we are and what our expectations of our actions and feelings should be.[23] Moreover, as we will see, critical writings about numbness in its various guises make it very hard to figure out whether critics believe that images and narratives of atrocity and violence are the effect of a real diminution of empathy or its cause. Such references also make it impossible to know whether they think the effect of the prevalence of images and narratives of violence is the creation of too much empathy or not enough—that is, does the increasing exposure to images and narratives of atrocity encourage us to identify with victims or with perpetrators? Does it excite us or numb us or both?

Though recent narratives about empathy's decline are in many ways continuous with older humanitarian and sentimental discourses, the newer discussion, which has intensified since the 1960s, begins not with the aim of overcoming insufficient empathy or unmasking hypocritical or disingenuous expressions of it—though it seeks to do those things, too—but with a dramatic and widespread conviction about the "exhaustion of empathy" and thus with numbness.[24] Over the last century, perhaps mostly because of the increasing integration of psychoanalytic understanding into mainstream discourse about self and society—and shorn, to be sure, of its technical context—empathy has replaced sympathy to signify feeling compassion for others (though late eighteenth- and nineteenth-century versions of sympathy also embraced what we now call empathy).

Robert Vischer in 1872 coined the word *Einfühlung,* or "feeling-in," to describe the process of contemplating art objects as a projection of our own feelings, and the American psychologist Edward Titchener rendered *Einfühlung* as "empathy" in 1909. German philosopher Theodor Lipps developed it into an aesthetic theory popularized by the Bloomsbury critic Roger Fry and the English novelist and critic Vernon Lee (the pen name of Violet Paget).[25] In the social sciences empathy arguably expresses Wilhelm Dilthey's effort to imagine the historian as a scholar who relives the past by identifying with the experiences of others (what Dilthey called understanding, *Verstehen*).[26] "Empathy" gradually became a standard part of psychoanalytical and psychological terminology and migrated eventually to American postwar analyses of prejudice and newer approaches to industrial relations and worker management.[27] More recently, analytic philosophers study its cognitive bases.[28]

Now a heterogeneous group of scholars has identified a gap between "representation and responsibility," which they claim has opened up since the end of the Second World War and indicates empathy's depletion. The increasing tension within discourses on human rights between an emotional allegiance to empathy and a sense that this term can no longer capture modern historical experience has been the subject of various commentaries on the exhaustion of empathy. In some commentary, the challenge to humanist ideals presented by the Holocaust suggests that empathic identification remains theoretically ideal, urgently necessary but often unfeasible: George Steiner, for example, calls for a renewal of human feeling, but also claims that there can no longer be any "presumption of a carry-over from civilization to civility, from humanism to the humane."[29] Another group of scholars claims that the recent history of genocide and totalitarianism simply overwhelms notions like empathy and dignity. Thus both Slavoj Žižek and Giorgio Agamben argue that those qualities belong to a moral framework that defines suffering and persecution in tragic terms, relying on themes of heroism and redemption already exhausted by twentieth-century crimes.[30]

All this commentary about the fragility of empathy after the genocide of European Jewry frames the recent discussion about the sources of our numbness, which has two separate and yet interrelated dimensions. The first narrative I want to discuss addresses the effects of new media on human feeling. Discourses about the media explain the failure of empathy by reference to insufficient feeling (the gap between the representation of suffering and our ability to be moved by it) and stress our now highly mediated relationship to the images we see. They go so far as to question whether suffering even has a clear relationship to a discernible reality.

This absence of reference to something we know is real takes several forms and tends to be related to visual culture, or the presumption that knowledge now comes primarily through the eyes. Many accounts simply claim that televised images of suffering shown to millions "merely intensify the silence" about atrocity elsewhere; in other words, our overexposure to suffering "desensitizes" us.[31] Indeed, a plethora of writers, journalists, and reviewers have evoked what Barbie Zelizer calls the "overuse of icons of atrocity" as a way of describing how the mass media redefine our relationship to human suffering. They insist that new visual media generate what Zelizer calls "moral habituation"—you see so much you don't notice it—and in seeing more, you may even feel less.[32] Suffering in effect disappears, or cannot be referenced in any meaningful, empirically discernible fashion. "Moral sensibility," as Arthur and Joan Kleinman argue, becomes "unhinged from responsibility and action."[33]

As Jean Baudrillard famously argues in a more radical interpretation, the line between fiction and reality has been so blurred by new technologies of representation that desire, empathy, and pleasure are media "effects" with no referent to real suffering, so that all forms of affect are paradoxically engineered responses generated by the media's "habitual social control."[34] In a breathtakingly arrogant remark, Baudrillard claims that television "is the perpetuation [of Auschwitz] in a different guise. . . . The same process of forgetting, of liquidation . . . the same absorption without a trace."[35] In a less pessimistic but no less critical argument, Zelizer insists that the first journalistic representations of the Holocaust de-emphasized Jewish pain in favor of an iconography of universal human pain, thereby rendering the Holocaust a privileged symbol of human suffering at the expense of understanding it.[36]

In reference to a Museum of Modern Art (MoMA) exhibit of photos of Cambodians about to be executed by the Khmer Rouge at Tuol Sleng prison, Lindsay French decries the way in which the images were shorn of their historical context. The exhibit rendered them icons of inhumanity but in so doing maintained the distance between them and us by not informing us of who they are and what historico-political circumstances led to their imprisonment and death. The author claims that if they were images with which audiences were familiar (say, American hostages in Iran) the exhibit would be unimaginable, because the victims would occupy a quasi-sacred cultural status that would preclude their being put on display. In the end, French insists that the exhibition of such pictures might "generate a powerful human connection to and empathy for their subjects' suffering." Yet this finally ambivalent assertion reminds us that as images of horror become objects of aesthetic—sublime or beautiful—appreciation, they lose their raw and painful immediacy and may, but don't necessarily always, have anaesthetic effects.[37] In all these narratives, then, noble feeling shades over into numbness as visual images, in particular, transform layers of context and complexity into a message of their own making: emotional response is no longer deeply embedded in a knowable past.

Other scholars, concerned instead with disingenuous empathy as a mode of insufficient feeling, have attacked media representations of suffering as "entertainment." Such remarks are legion, particularly with regard to the Holocaust, and have generated new suspicions of empathy and its motives and purposes. In one strain of this argument, primarily in the works of literary theorists, some representations of the Holocaust establish false equivalences between different kinds of suffering. As both James E. Young and Andrea Liss argue in quite distinct ways, efforts at the United States Holocaust Memorial Museum to facilitate spectators' identification with victims' suffering often end up dissolving the difference between spectators and Holocaust victims and encourage a lazy and false empathy in which we simply take the other's place. Young, for example, cites the identity cards bearing names and profiles of victims by means of which the museum visitor is asked to "become" a Jew from Lithuania, a "gypsy" who perished at Auschwitz, and so on. This strategy of identification distorts and blots out the experience of victims by encouraging a false likeness between them and us. The artist Alan Schechner has expressed this view in visual terms (see figure 1).[38]

In yet another discussion of the "repressive effects of empathy on those who remain beyond the pale," Jonathan Boyarin argues that "in popular culture representations of the Holocaust, the particular horror of the Nazi genocide is emphasized by an image of Jews as normal Europeans, 'just like us.' In fact we can only empathize with, feel ourselves into, those we can imagine as ourselves." "The space of the other," he writes, is therefore not really expanded. The Holocaust survivor and writer Ruth Klüger, in an uncanny reminder of Madame Riccoboni, describes what she calls a "pseudo-coming-to-terms-with-the-past [*Pseudovergangenheitsbewältigung*]" on the part of those who were not victims. This pseudo-engagement is not really concerned with those affected by crimes against humanity, but with "the amusement of fully enjoying one's sensitiveness," of which she argues philo-Semitism may be one manifestation.[39] Such revelations suggest that empathy entails obliterating boundaries between self and other in order to take the victim's place—a *reductio ad absurdum* of empathic logic in which the imagination absorbs and thus annihilates what it

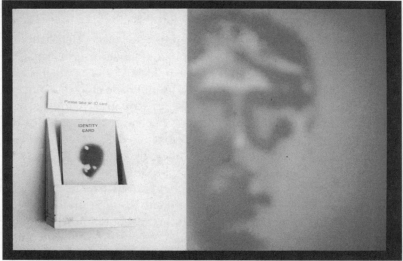

Figure 1. Alan Schechner. *Our Faces, Their Faces.* Video projection and identity cards, 1997.

contemplates.[40] Moreover, in this view, identification with the victim and repression of his or her difference—or unconscious presumptions about the centrality of our own experience—go together, and empathy turns out to be a disguised form of (in this case gentile) hegemony. This discussion links disingenuous empathy to Enlightenment universalism, whose emphasis on our likeness may erase our real differences in the interests of those gentiles who define the standard against which "likeness" or "difference" is measured.

It is hard to make absolute distinctions between various views about the fragility of empathy, but those discussed thus far are different from and yet related to another more mainstream criticism of the role of the Holocaust in American and, to a lesser extent, western European public opinion. This second narrative aims at a recent cultural investment not only in suffering endured but also in feeling victimized, and locates disingenuous empathy not in the psychological and political premises of Enlightenment universalism but in our repudiation of those premises. Its most vocal proponents include prominent historians, journalists, and literary theorists who suggest that universalism premised on compassion and dignity has given way to another false universalism based on suffering.

In the United States this discourse is surely linked to a more general criticism of so-called identity politics, as well as to racial and ethnic tensions and their effects, though it exists in western Europe in a more general form—in particular via criticism of Jews as a privileged "victim group."[41] In his contentious book on *The Holocaust in American Life*, Peter Novick tells us that "nowadays the status of the victim has come to be prized" and refers to a "culture of victimization."[42] In his work on restitution for victims since the Cold War, the historian Elazar Barkan claims that "descriptions of the phenomenon tended to criticize the spread of 'victims culture,' " but elaborates on this insight no further.[43] Tzvetan Todorov, the Bulgarian-born French literary theorist, writes that "until the middle of the twentieth century, the narrative favored by the Western public attributed a heroic role to our own community. But in recent decades there has been a change of paradigm, and the favorite story is now a melancholy tale in which we play the role of the victim."[44] He also notes that "today the victory won has less prestige than the suffering endured." While he doesn't see this as a necessarily bad development, since it has permitted national mythologies finally to focus on the Jewish victims of unspeakable crimes, he bemoans any "permanent identification with victimhood."[45]

The historian Jane Caplan criticizes American "identity politics" by linking them to "the proliferation of victim statuses in U.S. popular discourse" and uses "identification mechanisms"—again, the identity cards at the U.S. Holocaust Memorial Museum—to make her point.[46] Another eminent historian, István Deák, writes in a long review essay about books on modern crimes against humanity, "All the writers under review show considerable courage in treating their subjects with detachment; by so doing they defy those who jealously claim that the suffering of their own people is unique and even morally superior."[47] Jack Kugelmass asks questions about the way in which American Jews are encouraged—in what are essentially pilgrimages to death camps in Poland—to "experience themselves as Holocaust victims." He then ties this problematic demand thoughtfully but without extensive analysis to a claim that "American society increasingly attributes a positive valence to victimhood, and this, at the very least, sets the stage for public displays that in an earlier era would have been scorned or shunned."[48]

In yet another essay, the journalist and writer Philip Gourevitch exclaims that the existence of the U.S. Holocaust Memorial Museum testifies to the "centrality of victimology in contemporary American identity politics."[49] Alvin H. Rosenfeld also accuses non-Jewish victims of Nazism of "universaliz[ing]" and "relativiz[ing]" the Holocaust so that they might be numbered officially among its victims; he says they seek to exploit a "strong" and "growing" movement within American culture "intent on developing a politics of identity based on victim status."[50] So dominant is this frame of reference that the author of a sensitive discussion about how post-Holocaust generation Jews "internalize the status of victim . . . [to] create an alternate Jewishness out of a legacy of suffering" feels finally compelled to distinguish narratives of the Holocaust's "after-effects" on Jews from "narratives of rape victims, domestic or child abuse and war casualties" who have also claimed victim status for themselves.[51]

In this discourse, the sacrosanct status of the Holocaust in American life turns out to be a pretext for the assumption of victim status under the cover of righteous indignation. Here the source of empathy's degradation is not Enlightenment universalism but its perceived collapse, since giving the Holocaust quasi-sacred status means, paradoxically, that we cannot really feel anyone else's pain except our own. Critics conceive the "culture of victimology" as a symptom of the disintegration of normative frameworks of "likeness" that permit the proper and properly outraged assessment of injustice. My point is not that this emphasis on "victimization" should be dismissed out of hand—on the contrary, it constitutes a crucial cultural narrative that begs for analysis—but that it is part of a more general suspicion of disinterested empathy whose rationale is rarely analyzed.[52] Why, after all, should being a victim have become a crucial way of sustaining a sense of self and cultural recognition unless disinterested empathy has somehow lost its cultural legitimacy? However different the sources of the two critiques, on the one hand the *reductio ad absurdum* of the Enlightenment's basic tenets or, on the other hand, the reduction of Enlightenment universalism to a "universalism of suffering," both essentially identify the narcissistic blotting out of the other as a central socio-cultural problem that impedes mutual recognition and thus our ability to empathize with others.

All these critics diagnose the failure of empathy as a social problem whose sources we can pinpoint within a familiar conceptual framework derived originally from eighteenth-century thinkers' awareness of impediments to empathic feeling. Most if not all of these arguments conceive of the revival of empathy as the healthy restoration of the other's wholeness and distinctiveness and thus seek to restore distinctions between victims and perpetrators (between Jews and gentiles, between "real" suffering and false claims to it, and so forth) in a post-Holocaust context in which critics perceive disinterested indignation and thus non-exploitative empathy as unfeasible or compromised. Now, according to some of these arguments, media representations distort historical memory and turn us all into "victims" of their own capacity to fascinate and thus transform atrocities into spectacles. In a world in which heroes are few and "the role of victim, alas, is accessible to all,"[53] we find ourselves not distinguishing perpetrators from victims but engaged in the farcical and yet finally tragic quest to have been the "real" victim, more victimized, more deserving of a memorial, and so on, until even the American President Ronald Reagan could envision SS men as "victims" of Hitler's fanaticism.[54] At its worst, even when we lay no claim to being victims, we need them to be like us to feel for them, or what we feel on their behalf is so entirely bound up with our own pleasure that those feelings are hard to distinguish from narcissistic, cheap sentiment.

There are thinkers who feel that empathy is now simply a shattered and outmoded ideal, or from a far more modest perspective, that survivors' trauma always, necessarily, overwhelms our empathy but that we have a moral obligation to listen. Jean Baudrillard at one extreme suggests provocatively that television and Auschwitz meld into each other, and are simply different modern modes of transforming human beings into dead things: empathy must always be a form of nostalgic longing for a world in which people were living beings that mattered. At the other extreme, Lawrence Langer believes that people matter so much that we cannot reduce their incommensurable experiences to things we can understand. He exhorts us to "work," when we are dealing with survivor narratives, "with limited aspirations, rather than the unlimited ones bequeathed by our Enlightenment and Romantic heritage."[55] Moving as his accounts of such narratives are, in the end he insists that almost all our efforts to make meaning of or explain the Holocaust—whether via psychological elucidation or redemptive discourses that "never again" shall this happen—must necessarily be defenses against the anxiety such narratives generate. In his view, empathic understanding always ends in some basic refusal to confront the real depth of atrocity and agony that most often takes the form of a naïve hope in a future guaranteed by one's own moral integrity: not only "never again," but also "not me, I could never do that to others, ever."[56]

The essays that follow ask implicitly how we have tried to establish normative frameworks suitable for remembering and thinking about the Jewish victims of twentieth-century crimes against humanity. They all address consistent and complex narratives of denial and displacement: denial of our own failure to grasp the pain of suffering others and our own ambivalence, fascination, or repulsion toward representations of them; displacement of our own negative feelings onto "bad" objects, particularly social outsiders. Whether or not we can restore empathy as we still conceive it—as a mode of intersubjective relations implying healthy boundaries and the otherness of others—is difficult to say, but in any case, we have and continue to run up against limits to empathic identification posed by historical trauma and its challenges to the restoration of whole, bounded social subjects.[57] That said, we also see the most startling developments in international law—in particular, challenges to state sovereignty in order to prevent mass atrocities—even as the limits of this new humanitarianism are all too obvious.

Here I wish simply to define the recently perceived precariousness of empathy as a particular cultural narrative and thus to constitute it as an object of inquiry open to interpretation. The essays here take apart self-evident presumptions in mainstream, widely accessible aesthetic and historical debates about Holocaust representation to demonstrate how these presumptions are pervasive and diffuse ways of using rhetoric to control despair, powerlessness, and ambivalence. They try to show how concepts, references, and forms of address that seem obvious or even outmoded turn out to be unacknowledged but crucial to the very formulation of questions central to those debates. This rhetoric—say, the "pornography of suffering"—shapes visual and textual images of perpetrators and victims, determines "our" own relation to those images in ways still barely explored, and reveals that there is still much in our relationship to representations of suffering that remains to be thought.

The consciousness that empathy can no longer be considered a straightforward response to suffering, whether willed or intuitive, arguably represents a dramatic shift in the suffering body's ability to represent humanity's violated dignity, one whose meaning is still unclear. Moreover, as Michael Ignatieff persuasively argues, this development has occurred at the very moment when the "idea that we might have obligations to human beings beyond our borders"—something most Enlightenment thinkers and sentimentalists did not believe was necessarily natural or inevitable—is increasingly based on bodily suffering, on our imaginings of the terror and deprivation to which bodies elsewhere are subjected.[58] If, as the historian Michael Geyer has remarked, "it requires learning to see through the eyes of others," it is important to understand how historians, public intellectuals, and writers have recently sought to account for and address what they perceive to be the collective failure of the empathic imagination and the apparent difficulty of learning.[59]

CHAPTER ONE

Empathy, Suffering, and
Holocaust "Pornography"

According to the curator of a controversial exhibit at the Jewish Museum of New York in 2002, the Israeli media had claimed that one of the artworks displayed "'turn[ed] the Holocaust into pornography.'"[1] How do we begin to understand such an assertion?[2] In what follows, I discuss how we use the term "pornography," often imperceptibly, to make cultural meaning out of increasing anxieties and wariness about our responses to representations of bodily suffering, specifically that of European Jewry during the Holocaust.

A wide variety of critics frequently use the term "pornography" to describe the "marketing" of the Holocaust, presumably to describe the reduction of human beings to commodities and the exposure of vulnerable people at the moment of their most profound suffering, hence re-victimizing the victims. As we will see, critics now are pervasively using "pornography" in order to figure an American collective relationship to the Holocaust; in particular, pornography is invoked to describe a deficit of proper empathy. This is something that has happened especially since the opening of the United States Holocaust Memorial Museum in 1993.[3] What does it mean that critics use this particular term to figure our ostensible loss of empathy? And why has this term been used so pervasively to describe the mind-numbing effects of the marketplace, as well as to refer to Holocaust images and narratives thought to violate the memory of victims' suffering?

I will not focus on the specific formal attributes of narratives about

Holocaust representations in terms of how they have been fashioned by the media. For example, how is information or meaning about the Holocaust transmitted differently in a museum or on television? What constitutes a public narrative about the Holocaust even remotely adequate to the task of transmitting its meaning responsibly? Are those narratives that are accused of being pornographic *really* pornographic? Instead, I am asking how new cultural and ethical problems surrounding representations of bodily suffering—in particular, the purported exhaustion of empathy—are rendered thinkable and discussable, let alone worked through recent claims that Holocaust representations are "pornographic." Instead of asking how new technologies of representation affect concepts of originality and authenticity, or how the media affect the structuring of history and memory, I want to ask how the use of pornography makes sense of, expresses, and even shapes our understanding of what appear to be new historical limits on compassion.

As I mentioned in the Introduction, whether or not there has been a real failure of empathy is not my subject. Rather, I am interested in how we address and work through the perception that "we" as a society have been unable to live up to expectations about our own humanity and how references to pornography are part of that cultural self-evaluation. Pornography has of course been given normative definitions in specific national contexts since the nineteenth century, all of them drawing in different ways on the association between pornography and the degradation of the social body.[4] The aim of this chapter is to discuss how a particular narrative about pornography now works to mask, constrain, and control pain, despair, and ambivalence provoked by the representation of suffering others. This is not to say that there are no representations or objects we might consider and want to analyze as "pornographic"—film and literary theorists have tried to define pornography in generic terms, and states, politicians, and prosecutors have long sought to regulate it.[5]

Unquestionably the most recent high-profile effort to introduce a normative definition of pornography into law has been made by the feminist legal scholar Catharine MacKinnon, who sought to redefine pornography clearly as a violation of women's rights (these efforts were rejected in American courts by reference to the First Amendment and were made law in Canada).[6] I cannot possibly address the complexities of these debates about pornography here, in particular the precise relationship between aesthetically or normatively defined pornographic representations and this other narrative about "the pornographic" that concerns us (which would take us into specialized aesthetic and legal discussions). But I will say that most efforts at regulating so-called pornographic material have many of the same problems of definition manifest in the radically contingent, oddly empty and thus slippery signification of the term that permits the sort of promiscuous usage that this chapter will try to understand.

Critical references to pornography make it hard to know whether critics believe that pornography is the consequence of a real diminution of empathy or its cause. And such references also make it impossible to know if the problem they think pornography presents (say, in reference to images of atrocities) is the creation of too much empathy or not enough. Does it encourage us to identify with victims or with perpetrators? Does it excite us or numb us or both? I argue that the narrative about pornography is a particular allegory of the way in which we lose our feeling: it traces new concerns about the failure of empathy now increasingly being articulated in many scholarly discourses. I address how the concept of pornography traverses varied cultural terrain from museum exhibits to scholarly discussions of "holocaust memory," and thus I do not offer formal analyses of art objects or evaluate the merit of scholarly arguments. Rather, I focus on their reception by a range of critics from academic specialists to journalists writing for a wide audience.[7]

Though pornography has long taken both written and visual forms, for many people its invocation now conveys above all the recent privilege accorded to visual media in shaping our experience of historical events and, more specifically, of suffering. The literary theorist Fredric Jameson argues:

> The visual is essentially *pornographic*, which is to say that it has its end in rapt, mindless fascination. . . . Pornographic films are thus only the potentiation of films in general, which ask us to stare at the world as though it were a naked body. On the other hand, we know this today more clearly because our society has begun to offer us the world—now mostly a collection of products of our own making—as just such a body, that you can possess visually, and collect the images of.[8]

In a similar vein, the human rights activist Jorgen Lissner writes:

The public display of an African child with a bloated kwashiorkor-ridden stomach in advertisements is pornographic, because it exposes something in human life that is as delicate and deeply personal as sexuality, that is, suffering. It puts people's bodies, their misery, their grief and their fears on display with all the details and all the indiscretion that a telescopic lens will allow.[9]

Arguments like these use pornography metaphorically to associate visual cognition with human degradation and violation.[10] Jameson in particular associates perception paradoxically with a state of mindlessness or unknowing, and an eroticized act of visual possession with de-eroticized numbness. But while "pornography" is closely linked to visual culture, its significance and usage are far more complex than this common appropriation (as a metaphor for visual cognition in an age of mass media) intimates. For example, in a brief set of reflections about kitsch and Holocaust representation she wrote in 1994–95, the survivor and author Ruth Klüger links immediate postwar attitudes among American Jews toward the Nazis' Jewish victims to "pornographic pleasure":

In the eyes of those who found it so necessary to fantasize [that they as American Jews would have defended themselves] . . . I belong to those, who had committed God knows what crimes, or conversely, submitted to degradations in order to survive. It was the same as the old, and not yet outdated, attitude to rape: the woman becomes worthless, because she has had bad luck. And something of pornographic pleasure persisted in the interest then in the Holocaust, which was not yet named that.[11]

Klüger also links pornography to moral numbness and degradation, but she uses it to describe the particular, sadistically tinged pleasure implicit in the American Jew's fantasized superiority over the camp survivor. Pornographic pleasure is not a metaphor for universal "numbed" (and primarily visual) cognition but expresses a smug fantasy of being different from others who are otherwise like you, the pleasure of not-having-been a victim.

Pornography in these three accounts draws together commercialization, sadistic self-righteousness, moral numbness, and voyeuristic fascination, all of which have some relation to each other that is not articulated or presumed to be self-evident. Pornography seems to be an infinitely plastic term whose concentration of rhetorical force and explanatory power is such that its meaning is not really held to account. It appears to mean so much and yet its meaning is so hard to pin down that references to pornography do not encourage discussion, but arguably inhibit us from thinking clearly about what rhetorical work the term actually performs.

Finally, that pornography alludes to so-called inappropriate sexuality, and that its current usage transfers these allusions to nonsexual contexts like the Holocaust, is significant and yet remains generally neglected. Historians have certainly traced a long tradition that links pornography and pathological sexuality more generally with pathological (anti-liberal) politics. The French revolutionaries' use of Marie Antoinette's sexualized body in pornographic pamphlets to stigmatize and discredit the French monarchy is only one example.[12] I hope not only to use the discourse on representations of suffering in the Holocaust to address larger questions about the exhaustion of empathy, but also to speculate about this odd centrality of so-called sexual pathology in figuring challenges and threats to normative cultural expectations about our own ability to act humanely and empathetically toward others.

In what follows, I focus on the use of pornography in reference to representations of Holocaust atrocities in a wide variety of areas, but specifically in relation to the integrity of historical memory and its violation by the so-called Shoah business. I will trace how the widespread usage of the term "pornography" seems elegantly to account for the exhaustion of empathy, and yet turns out not to explain anything at all.

Most often the invocation of pornography to criticize recent representations of the Holocaust expresses fears about whether we can sustain the humanist ideal of disinterested indignation and thus of a healthy respect for and outrage at suffering not our own. Pornography, which originally referred to a specific and ever-changing category of specific texts and images, began after the Great War (1914–1918) to represent more generally a potentially objectifying, dehumanizing, and thus morally distorted perception of suffering in particular, and this trend continued thereafter.[13] James Agee, writing in *The Nation* in 1945 about newsreel footage showing the invasion of Iwo Jima, said that he believed "we have no business seeing this sort of experience," and added that he could not explain why he felt this was so except by analogy to pornography: "pornography is invariably degrading to anyone who looks at or reads it"; it creates "incurable distance" and betrays those with whom we are trying to identify. Images of war atrocities, he felt, were thus "pornographic."[14] Ten years later, in 1955, the British anthropologist Geoffrey Gorer used the phrase "the pornography of death" not only to describe the unbearable publicity afforded soldiers' most intimate and painful moments, but also to denounce numbingly violent fantasies he thought represented surrogate gratification in an otherwise impoverished popular culture.[15] After Gorer, who was also a biographer of the Marquis de Sade, the Canadian philosopher Lionel Rubinoff published a book about psychology and politics called *The Pornography of Power,* aimed at analyzing the cool ruthlessness of contemporary culture.[16]

In 1965, George Steiner wrote one of the first essays linking this usage of pornography to the Holocaust of European Jewry. He claimed that "the novels being produced under a new code of total statement shout at their personages: strip, fornicate, perform this or that act of sexual perversion. So did the SS guards at rows of living men and women." To the extent that pornography expresses the "diminishing reserves of feeling and imaginative response in our society" (and so is a surrogate form of sex in an imaginatively impoverished world), it expresses "modern totalitarianism" and oddly not only describes but also accounts for genocide.[17] In the same year, a professor of journalism, Donald M. Gillmor, wrote an essay titled "The Puzzle of Pornography" that also constitutes one of the first references of its kind: "the real hard core of obscenity," he said, "is not the dirty picture or the Anglo-Saxon pejorative but rather the horror of an Auschwitz—the degradation and dehumanization of the individual human being."[18] Indeed, after the 1960s, and in reference to the Holocaust more specifically, pornography seems to be a compressed way of describing a series of links between moral and political failure and moral and political perversion forged by a consistent (and often confusing) bringing together of two main themes: pathological politics and pathological sexuality. Thus pornography invokes not only the objectifying films of the battle of Iwo Jima but the horror of Auschwitz and the SS—"modern totalitarianism."

This early commentary on the genocide of European Jewry, still arguably *the* image of modernity's horrors in the West, illustrates dramatically how pornography links erotic compulsions to perverse political formations and institutions, but also does so via an implicit denunciation of popular culture, the category of material to which "novels of total statement"—sexually explicit books—and dirty pictures belongs. Steiner straightforwardly conflates pornography with moral degradation and Nazism, and Gillmor urges us to focus less on "dirty pictures" than on Auschwitz as an emblem of human cruelty. Both nevertheless rely on a presumed connection between sexuality and violence that is affirmed in one case and implied in the other, between popular, "dirty" images of sexuality and Nazism. The reference to pornography thus becomes a way of making an argument that isn't quite finished, mapping a trajectory from illicit sexuality to Nazism that never makes clear what they really have to do with one another. The link is made by analogy, by suggestion: the sexually explicit book says this, the SS says that; the dirty picture dehumanizes, surely, but Auschwitz was worse.

The recent and pervasive spread of information about the Holocaust through mass media transmission (in films, television, much-publicized museums, and so forth since the Eichmann trial in 1961 and the airing of the Hollywood television miniseries *Holocaust* in 1978)[19] generated a variety of despairing discussions about Holocaust representations that tie obscenity and pornography not explicitly to Nazism, but to the media's irresponsible overexposure of the atrocities perpetrated by Nazism, to "loud, simplified, and vulgarized representation[s]" of the Holocaust, and to the inevitable distortion of memory such popular forms of historical remembrance entail.[20] In a 1978 review of the miniseries *Holocaust, New York Times* critic John O'Connor claimed that when a "historical fact has been put through the peculiar process that is called commercial television . . . that processing [in its more extreme moments] proved to be almost as obscene as the Holocaust itself."[21] The literary critic Alvin H. Rosenfeld said of popularizations of the Holocaust, "in the places where mass suffering once was, prurience has come to be."[22] Even more recently, a film critic referred to *Schindler's List* and other movies about Nazism as "pornograph[ies] of suffering."[23]

In a long 1980 article for the *New York Times Magazine*, the historian Paula E. Hyman summed up the general interpretive trend: "The

Holocaust," she asserts, "has become marketable." She notes that Elie Wiesel "wonders sadly" whether all his efforts have had "any beneficial impact at all," for "the proliferation of sensationalized books and popularized television programs and films has dishonored the victims and rendered the public insensitive to the tragedy." In the same article, Wiesel is quoted as worrying whether or not we have reached a "saturation point."[24] Remarking on this popular consumption of the Holocaust a few years before, the historian Lucy Dawidowicz insisted that "pornography and Nazism have mutually reinforced each other over the decades" and referred to the "pornography of the Holocaust."[25] Ten years later, and two years after his statements to Hyman, Wiesel wrote a piece on "trivializing memory" in which he argued that the vulgarization of the Holocaust recast the memory of the Jews in a context of "total decadence everywhere, debauchery and mockery at every level."[26]

Such sentiments have generally been reiterated by a diverse array of intellectuals who, like some of those I've already cited, haven't always invoked the words "pornography" or "obscenity" but have reinforced the discourse of numbing by oversaturation. Thus the late historian Sybil Milton claimed that the "thoughtless and repetitive overuse of [Holocaust] images has reduced atrocities to an almost commonplace sight in the press and on television"; the literary theorist Geoffrey Hartman warned of a "desensitizing trend" produced by images and narratives of Nazi atrocities; the writer Daphne Merkin noted that in reference to the Holocaust "our receptors for outrage have been dulled"; and the literary critic Andrew R. Carlson remarked: "the Holocaust has been too commercialized and so mythologized in the popular imagination that the message is losing its effectiveness. The shocking reality, the unfathomable sorrow, and the irretrievable loss of the Holocaust are being forgotten."[27]

Ultimately, pornography remains the compressed expression of this relationship now between illicit sexuality and representations of Nazism in popular culture (and thus between sexuality and violence, between "perverse" sexuality and perverse politics, between moral numbness and "perversity" more generally) whose logic is never very clear. In other words, pornography condenses these relationships into one word that never accounts for how exactly a sullied eroticism is related to or what it has to do with mass atrocity specifically, and with the degradation of human beings more generally. Indeed, the use of the term has exploded to refer not only to the Holocaust but also to other atrocities, and its users and readers both deem its meaning self-evident and surely are not necessarily seeking to make the conceptual leaps the term "pornography" does in these contexts. Just a few examples will suffice: in 1977, reviews decried Jerzy Kosinski's novel *The Painted Bird* as the "pornography of violence";[28] the historian Thomas Laqueur referred to a "pornography of horror" in a review of Serge Klarsfeld's book on *French Children of the Holocaust*;[29] the author of a book about Binjamin Wilkomirski's *Fragments*—a Holocaust memoir that turned out to be fake—noted that "many critics have remarked on [*Fragments'*] emotional and brutal aesthetic of violence; some have even spoken of a pornography of violence";[30] the literary theorist Michael Rothberg has claimed that a sexual episode in one of Philip Roth's novels "suggests that there might be something *pornographic* about making images and ultimately commodities out of the Holocaust."[31] Though Rothberg refers here to the episode's sexual allusions, he means something more, which the referent "pornography" is supposed to make clear. Finally, outside the context of the Holocaust, the historian Leon Litwack uses his fellow historian Jacquelyn Dowd Hall's words to describe postcard images of lynching exhibited at the New-York Historical Society (and mentioned in the Introduction to this book): "folk pornography."[32]

The word "pornography" condenses all these meanings and stands in for relationships that are not otherwise accounted for, and that is from whence it arguably derives its rhetorical power, manifest at the very least in the vast and varied references to the term. In sum, pornography continues to suggest a relationship between sexual, moral, and political perversion that it establishes now by reference to "desensitizing" trends, the mass media's assault on historical memory, and its transforming Jewish victims of Nazism into consumable things, all of which undermine healthy empathic identification.

This discourse is itself reiterated by historians, art critics, and others, particularly in reference to various efforts to memorialize or even to reflect upon and criticize how we have memorialized the Holocaust. In many discussions, pornography is invoked to figure the genocide of European Jewry as a fragile body of memory increasingly subject to violation. In *Selling the Holocaust*, Tim Cole writes of his first trip to Auschwitz: "We were tourists of guilt and righteousness: guilt at an almost pornographic sense of expectancy of the voyeurism ahead."[33] Further on, he ponders the "titillation" afforded to concentration camp tourists (titillation camouflaged by "worthy" feelings) and cites psychologist Israel Charny's own reaction to reading about the genocide: "The reading becomes exciting. . . . One murderous incident follows another. . . . My excitement mounts. . . . It is almost a sexual feeling. . . . I flow into the next account of a killing and become one with the murderer."[34] Cole returns again and again to a description of himself and secondary witnesses (whether tourists, historians, or commentators) as voyeurs similarly aware of what, quoting the journalist Philip Gourevitch, he calls the "potential for excitement . . . and even for seduction by the overwhelmingly powerful imagery" in a mostly unselfconscious fashion.[35] And so do many others. In reference to the Holocaust Memorial Museum in Washington, D.C., Victoria Barnett writes that "A major risk of this kind of museum is that it could degenerate into obscene voyeurism."[36] Michael Sorkin declares that "An excess of detail can neutralize and obscure, commemoration can become entertainment, even pornography."[37] And Alvin Rosenfeld also expresses alarm that the Holocaust has been transformed into pornography through the mass marketing of memory. As he claims, "a pornography of the Holocaust . . . may undercut a didactics of the Holocaust" because popular representations of the event might result in an "incipient rejection of the Holocaust rather than its retention in historical memory."[38]

In these examples, pornography refers to the emotionally charged relationship between spectator and representation of suffering as a problem of misplaced or compulsive eroticism and aggression—hence, critics now use the adjective "pornographic" to describe the Holocaust Museum exhibit or a visit to Auschwitz as if its meaning were self-evident. But pornography is so elastic and symbolically versatile a metaphor that in other contexts it also seems to describe the broader "neutralizing" and obscuring of horror and thus of memory so bemoaned by these critics. Pornography has such vast referential powers that the problem posed by "blurred newspaper or television images from the other side of the world," whose sheer volume, according to Victoria Barnett, makes solidarity with victims impossible, can be described as pornographic.[39] For Cole, pornography even signifies the treasonous theft of memory, since at various memorial sites, according to him, the betrayal of memory takes place under the guise of a righteous polemic about the necessity of remembering. "Pornographic expectancy" thus describes the way in which false meaning takes the place of truly meaningful identification with the victims or, as Sorkin puts it, "how will this exhibition secure the purity of tears?"[40] "At the end of the twentieth century," says Cole, "the myths [of the Holocaust] have become more real than historical reality."[41]

Expectancy, excitement, voyeurism—all of these then violate the dignity of memory by taking the historical event out of context, by appropriating it for our own pleasure and rendering meaningful empathy impossible. Indeed, the invocation of pornography expressed the brunt of the criticism not only of Holocaust memorials but of a controversial exhibit that took place at the Jewish Museum of New York titled "Mirroring Evil: Nazi Imagery/Recent Art" from March to June 2002: that it betrayed historical memory and insulted victims by associating the oppressiveness of consumer culture with the oppression exercised by Nazis, and by promoting an identification with perpetrators.[42] The exhibit presented nineteen primarily conceptual art works by young artists from Europe, the United States, and Israel, most of whom were not Jewish and none of whom were alive during the event itself. Among the most controversial pieces in the exhibit were a miniature death camp made out of LEGO blocks by the Polish artist Zbigniew Libera; an image of the British artist Alan Schechner holding a colorized Diet Coke can superimposed on a famous black-and-white photo of emaciated Jews at Buchenwald (figure 2); a set of "luxury products" packaged and marked with expensive logos made to look like Zyklon-B gas canisters by the American Tom Sachs; and an installation by the Israeli artist Roee Rosen that encourages viewers to imagine themselves as Eva Braun having sex with Hitler and dying with him on their last night together. Other works in the exhibit showed stills of Hollywood stars playing Nazi roles in movies and busts of a fantasmic Joseph Mengele, the Auschwitz doctor who was famous both for his cruelty and his charm, and many highlighted toys, from the LEGO blocks to stuffed animals with Nazi insignia. Moreover, the cover of the exhibition catalogue displayed a crucifix metamorphosing via light play into a swastika, which enraged Catholic groups (figure 3).[43]

Menachem Rosensaft, a lawyer and the head of the International Network of Children of Holocaust Survivors, demanded that the ex-

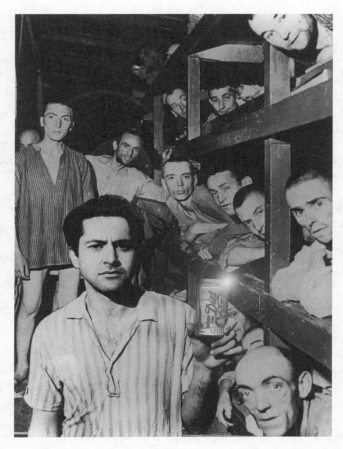

Figure 2. Alan Schechner. *It's the Real Thing—Self-Portrait at Buchenwald*. 1993. Digital still.

hibit be withdrawn from the museum's schedule, claiming that the art displayed was "the functional equivalent of painting pornography on a Torah scroll and exhibiting it as art."[44] Elie Wiesel called the show "obscene" and a "betrayal" because it "distort[ed] the truth and the suffering that several generations had to face."[45] A review in the British news magazine *The Spectator* insisted that the show was "a loathsome mixture of pornography-as-violence, plain pornography, and witlessly repulsive kitsch."[46] Of a hundred or so reviews that took a more measured view of the exhibit and a more or less neutral stance, several

Figure 3. Mischa Kuball. *Hitler's Cabinet*. 1990. Plywood installation with light projection.

describe the work displayed by noting that the artists' intent was to "infuse images of the Holocaust with those of pornography, kitsch, and mass production"; that the work is like "porno art," meaning that it is "sadistic"; that it contains "erotic materials," and that it compares "shopping malls and modern porno to Sobibor and Auschwitz."[47]

Pornography describes the commercialization of the Holocaust as the betrayal of historical memory; the art appropriates the event for narcissistic uses that are part of forgetting its horror. Yet when interviewed by a journalist, the art historian Ellen Handler Spitz, author of an essay in the catalogue, argued that "the artists are ... making analogies between the way we are co-opted by advertising, and the way the Nazis used propaganda. They make us question how we are victims of propaganda in our lives today." She also noted more significantly that "we are used to the old images, and they don't have the power to upset us anymore."[48] Another distinguished art historian, Linda Nochlin, claimed that the artists "make clear that this ostensible subject, already prepackaged and fetishized in 'Holocaust' memorials, local shrines, documentaries, theater, and novels, can now be represented—and thereby distanced—only through the visual apparatus of popular culture: the pop icon, the fetish, most notably, the toy."[49]

According to them, the exhibit *proceeded* from the presumption that Holocaust images have become what the *New York Times* art critic Michael Kimmelman called "respectable pornography,"[50] and have been rendered banal in contemporary North American and European culture. The exhibit looked critically on the cliché that the Holocaust has become commercialized, that we are so saturated by the iconic images of the event that we have become numb to their effects and that what we do know about the genocide of European Jewry is "prepackaged" and fetishized anyway. In the most persuasive defense of the exhibit, James E. Young, who wrote the catalogue's foreword, insists that young artists cannot be expected to represent the Holocaust, but only their own "hypermediated" experience of it—the memory of a memory—and forces us in the process to ask hard questions about the transmission of memory.[51] The exhibit's proponents countered the objection that the art on display insults, betrays, and trivializes memory by insisting that it actually calls attention to the ways in which pop culture itself trivializes memory, and, moreover, that all memory of the Holocaust must necessarily be mediated by our own ambivalence, distance, and contemporary concerns. In this way they challenged the charge that the analogy manifest in much of the art between today's unwitting victims of consumer culture and yesterday's victims of Nazism was facile and offensive.

But there was another objection articulated most forcefully by Michael Kimmelman, and often repeated by other less well-known journalists and art critics evaluating the exhibit. Reviewing the catalogue before the show opened, Kimmelman suggested that the artwork illustrations he had seen sent such a clichéd message that they finally failed to explore crucial questions about "the line between historical inquiry and obscene gaze" and whether or not, as we've seen, "Holocaust images [are] respectable pornography."[52] He seems to argue that art cannot simply point out that the Holocaust has become banal and inaccessible without itself turning into the cliché it condemns. Another, more negative critic said: "It's just too glib, too facile and visually far too underimagined."[53] Even James E. Young asked, explicitly if sympathetically, because he thought the exhibit at least posed the question: "Which is worse? The cultural commodification of victims or the commercial fascination with killers?"[54]

The exhibit's proponents insisted instead that the art shocks us out of mind-numbing clichés by stimulating pleasure and using it as a pedagogical tool. As Norman L. Kleeblatt says in the introduction to the catalogue:

> Earlier, less well-known examples of transgressive art about the Holocaust era place the viewer at the highly uncomfortable intersection between desire and terror. [The artist and Jewish Buchenwald survivor Boris] Lurie appropriates the harrowing, iconic photographs taken by Margaret Bourke-White and others in the weeks following the liberation of the camps. He juxtaposes her images of the piles of victims' bodies and the emaciated survivors clinging to barbed-wire fences with prurient nude pinups. Simply put, as we look at these opposing scenes of defilement, Lurie forces us to confront our own voyeurism. The artist equates our looking at representations of victims with viewing pornography.[55]

As many critics note, the exhibit moves us away from an art that traditionally identifies with victims, to one that "dare[s] to invite the viewer into the world of the perpetrators," and it is this identification with perpetrators that they portray as pornographic.[56] Linda Nochlin says that "the erotic charge of the Nazi uniform, the visual presence of . . . matinee idols . . . has to be weighed against our twinges of guilt at admiring, getting a visual charge out of, well, Nazis." This art "perform[s] the banality of evil with the sting of the outrageous. The horror of the Holocaust, such reasoning might go, has been so often iterated that it has sunk to the level of cliché. What can bring back the original shock? Reviving the corpse of feeling with a salutary slap in the face."[57] That salutary slap takes the form of forcing us to conspire with perpetrators, to—as another critic writes—"taste the juice of our own cruelty" and thereby, through our "spectatorial power (to look) and our powerlessness (in being unable to resist their seduction), we become momentary doubles for both the perpetrators of evil and its victims."[58] This art, writes Handler Spitz, "holds up its unwelcome mirror to our faces and asks us to confront our own disavowed capacities for viciousness, hatred and indifference." She insists: "To the traditional art that creates an empathetic nexus between viewers and concentration-camp victims, these artists would add an art that brings us face to face with the killers themselves."[59] As one of the most elaborate essays in the catalogue, by scholar Ernst van Alphen, puts it: "The visitors of [Ram] Katzir's installations were invited to color in images based on Nazi photography. . . . This making of the Nazis is a convoluted yet real form of identification. In creating the perpetrators, we as visitors become somewhat complicit in the *possibility* of the Nazis—not, of course, with *actual* Nazis."[60]

Thus the metaphor of pornography describes a general process by which bodily degradation and suffering—the indignity of the literal body and the metaphorical body of historical memory it is our responsibility to transmit—becomes a focus of fascination or pleasure of both erotic and aggressive drives. In so doing, it describes a process by which we transform the subjects of our interest into objects of our now corrupted pleasures, and, at least in the commentary on the Jewish Museum exhibit, pornography is used to mean the same thing by the show's detractors and proponents, who merely give the term a different valence. For many former victims and their relatives, calling the exhibit pornographic describes a traumatic reliving of the event: it "repeats" the original violation of their dignity as human beings. For proponents of the exhibit, placing viewers in the position of self-conscious pornography consumers permits a reenactment of something forgotten, repressed, and presumably (at least in the sense of collective historical rather than individual memory) traumatic—the shock of the Holocaust, the violence of industrialized murder, its potential recurrence. Still, it's by no means clear how this artwork moves beyond simulated traumatic reenactment as sublime, ambivalent, and narcissistic over-identification (with perpetrators and victims) that replicates the exhaustion of empathy it is meant to criticize. Thus one may be very sympathetic to the intellectual challenge the exhibit poses, especially its emphasis on the hypermediation of memory. But we must still be interested in unpacking the significance of pornography as metaphor for narcissism and passivity, for eroticism and aggression, and most of all, as a metaphor for being so caught up in pleasurably ambivalent identification that you may remember or forget, but you are never able to feel empathetically for the other as other, because that victim, that perpetrator, is you.

In another twist that is part of the same pattern, pornography describes the process, perhaps unavoidable, by which victims are victimized again, by which the medium of representation—say, photography—"brings with it a concomitant degradation of dying."[61] This discussion takes up once again all the multiple themes with which we've become familiar, including criticism of popular cultural Holocaust representations, commodification, the distortion of historical memory, ambivalent identification with victims and perpetrators: in short, pornography means an erotically charged, ambivalent identification that impedes empathic identification and allegorizes our inability to feel for the *real* victim. Thus survivors expressed this concern about the victims being doubly victimized by the Jewish museum exhibit, and this anxiety has long characterized criticism of both documentary film and photography—photographers are, so some critics claim, "voyeurs" and "trophy hunters," and at the very least the camera is a "weapon" that aggressively consumes and objectifies its subjects.[62]

This logic is, not surprisingly, also implicit in the denunciations of popular representations of the Holocaust, in which it is the more general process of transforming the atrocities into a consumable, commercial product that degrades dying. It was central to discussions about how most effectively to represent atrocities in the U.S. Holocaust Memorial Museum. As Michael Berenbaum, the museum's project director, put it, "We wanted to come as close as possible to desecration without re-desecrating."[63]

In an article on his visit to the U.S. Holocaust Memorial Museum, Philip Gourevitch uses pornography to describe just this sort of "re-desecration":

> Peepshow format. Snuff films. Naked women led to execution. People are being shot. Into the ditch, shot, spasms, collapse, dirt thrown in over. Crowds of naked people. Naked people standing about to be killed, naked people lying down dead. Close-up of a woman's face and throat as a knife is plunged into her breast—blood all over. . . . Naked women dragged to death. Shooting. Screaming. Blackout. The film begins again.[64]

In this passage, Gourevitch excerpts comments from notes he wrote trying to describe one of the video exhibits about the violence of the *Einsatzgruppen* (mobile killing squads) meant to convey Jewish suffering to a presumably ignorant audience. For him, this educational exhibit repeats in other terms the violation of Jews by their Nazi executioners. Peep shows and snuff films are metaphors both for the secondary degradation of the victims—for the violence perpetrated by the exhibit on the memory of the Holocaust—and for the eroticization of violence and the presumed excitement it evokes. Where the concept of "moral habituation" interprets our numbness or loss of feeling as a form of self-protective dissociation that violates victims again, this particular allusion to pornography seeks to describe and account for the way in which our numbness to suffering is itself a mode of feeling or affect that dissociation cannot adequately describe—again, the blurring of the "real" victim, the confusion between our desires and their pain.

For Gourevitch, the problem of how to avoid re-desecration of the victims is not, it seems, a problem that any formal representational strategy such as realism—or context, perspective, accompanying narratives—might remedy. More simply, the reality that is itself being photographed makes these films pornographic, and, from his point of view, there is no escaping the dominance of the viewer over the viewed, identified as he or she is with the perpetrators who (for the most part) shot the films.[65] Here all representation is pornographic in the sense we have been using it thus far: identification with perpetrators or victims, whether as documentary film or as ironic artwork, cannot be useful pedagogy (for example, as Young suggests, in helping us to acknowledge, confront, and interpret our own potentially "pornographic gaze"). Gourevitch's invocation of pornography suggests that realism is somehow rendered pornographic by the *necessary* fascination such images produce, by the way the act of looking in this context inevitably divorces us from our humanity. Images of extreme suffering must also always be "snuff films." Realism can only ever generate a form of rapt fascination, and fascination can only ever numb and pacify, can only transform victims and spectators into things. Here we are back to Fredric Jameson's use of pornography as a metaphor for how looking is transformed into a form of commodity fetishism. It is not surprising then that Gourevitch concludes that the museum is a bad idea, one that testifies to the "centrality of victimology" in American identity politics.[66]

Pornography thus signifies the multiple ways representations of victims themselves degrade their subjects. Critical writing thus uses pornography as a tautology for human degradation as well as to forge a link between bad art and bad politics, between museum exhibits and 'victimology.' Critics of Daniel Jonah Goldhagen's widely read

Hitler's Willing Executioners also testify to the centrality of this tautology in conveying a form of despair and anxiety in discourses about the Holocaust and the recovery of historical memory. Goldhagen not only blames the genocide of European Jewry on an innate characteristic of Germans, but also repeats accounts of atrocities over and over, saturating the narrative with such violence that critics have claimed the text itself becomes a form of brutality as senseless and violent as the events themselves.[67] The book not only offers more than enough evidence to prove its case, but also gratuitously repeats the brutality it describes.

Critics have differently attacked the text's performance of this excess. They mostly refer to it as "voyeuristic" or as a book whose "perverse allure" became increasingly evident as the author proceeded on his German book tour. The sociologist Michael Bodeman wrote that Goldhagen's work "is a pornography of horror" because his book "brings sexuality and murder . . . into indirect or direct association [such] that the pleasure derived from the perpetrators' killing and torturing is brought before our eyes . . . in a voyeuristic narration."[68] Atina Grossmann claims that Goldhagen uses a "pornographic language of witness."[69]

In critical perceptions of Goldhagen, pornography represents how moral habituation takes the form of overexcitement, whether as identification with perpetrators or with victims or both. Indeed, Goldhagen's refusal to spare any detail resembles the visually conveyed history that so horrified Gourevitch in the Holocaust Museum. As Jameson noted, commodities suck the life out of you while keeping you spellbound. Pornography, then, helps us to conceive the affective excess implicit in empathic failure: the deadening of emotions that drives the desire to see more and more; the oversaturation that leads to an obsessive moral concern with subjects such as the Holocaust; and most dramatically then, the desire to be horrified. And it is pornography that historians and critics have used over and over not only to account for the feelings we don't consciously feel but also to explain how our own feelings replace those of victims and thus constitute a violation of the historical memory it is the aim of these books and exhibits to transmit.[70]

Thus Goldhagen's language and even the horror he conveyed is "pornographic," and this adjective helps to condemn the book's affect without explaining how, for example, bad affect constitutes bad history, and how "lurid" witnessing necessarily accounts for why the book violates victims when it might also—as its proponents argued—inspire shame and moral conviction in its readers.[71] Ultimately pornography not only condenses multiple strands of meaning but also manifests a link between sexual pathology and perverse politics without actually explaining or accounting for it. This is why it is always employed as if its meaning were self-evident. Both Lucy Dawidowicz and George Steiner help us by making this obvious. Dawidowicz uses pornography to account for the relationship between numbness, affect, and moral degradation. But now she is interested in the causes of fascism and Nazism more generally. By way of circular reasoning, she argues that

> The antihumanists and sadists were those who helped to create and develop Fascism and Nazism. Those movements, in turn, bred new generations of antihumanists and sadists, providing ever-increasing audiences for the consumption of pornography, plain and political. Today a sizeable population views the Third Reich's terrors and murders only through a prism of pornography. Their loss of moral affect becomes a loss of political affect. Morally dulled, they become more vulnerable to the appeal of antihumanist movements and eventually more receptive to the obscenity of anti-Semitism.[72]

Here, pornography stands in for a cause never otherwise articulated (Davidowicz presumes that antihumanists, fascists, Nazis, and sadists consume pornography more than others not in those categories), and its consumption in turn creates the loss of moral and political affect and a new generation of anti-Semites. The metaphorical slippery slope so often invoked to describe the effects of pornography—"falling" becomes increasingly dramatic, intense, compulsive, and inevitable—thus accounts for the loss of moral affect without, however, specifying its cause or rationale.

George Steiner similarly insists that pornography "has long had an intimate and cruel involvement with sadism" and claims a connection between the "methodical reversion of many political communities to the use of torture," "mass sadism," and the proliferation of pornography. In particular, he argues that "the new barbarism

[Nazism] and the breakdown of verbal and pictorial taboos have co-incided in time," but his most substantive evidence is that the author-ity of print impresses itself most dramatically on the "semi-literate" who is presumed to be particularly vulnerable to its effects.[73] In other words, from Steiner to Dawidowicz, from Gourevitch to criticism of Goldhagen—indeed, in most invocations of pornography in the con-text of Holocaust representations—pornography is an alibi for a rela-tionship between cause and effect that is never anywhere named or explained: it stands in for a framework able to account for the rela-tionship between moral and political perversion, between the loss of moral and the loss of political affect, between the excitement associ-ated with sadism and the numbness associated with fascism, Nazism, and anti-Semitism.

Pornography figures how the desire, identification, and agency intrin-sic in empathic imagination turn into the obliteration of the other; his-torical memory becomes nothing but a reflection of a now spatially in-finite, narcissistic self.[74] This rhetorical operation expresses something quite a bit more complicated than the conventional notion that pornography represents an unspeakable association between sexual-ity and murder, or describes a form of passive, fascinated numbness. Of course, the invocation of the metaphor of pornography explains the destruction of human dignity and its wholeness by yoking an in-ability to feel with overstimulation. Pornography interprets the ex-haustion of empathy as the compulsive wrenching of the suffering body out of its proper historical context and the making of it into the object our own desires and identifications, whether referred to as "en-tertainment," "victimology," or commodification (as in "selling the Holocaust"). But pornography does not just express the loss of equi-librium implied by too much distance or proximity in ways of which we are perhaps not fully aware. It does not only describe the histori-cally specific exhaustion of empathy as a recent dimension of social order—that is, it does not only figure a world in which the normative conditions that make proper feeling possible, thinkable, and attain-able have been seriously undermined, whether by technological transformation or by the excesses of late capitalism. Moreover, pornography, in spite of appearances, is not simply an economical way of expressing our problematic failure to live up to the promise of our own humanist ideals—it is not only a concise way to demand the affirmation of a normative "common humanity" (we affirm that we are all the same regardless of our differences but still tend to objectify and dehumanize different others in spite of ourselves), or to denounce it (we try to empathize with the other, but tend to put ourselves in his or her place).

Pornography figures our relationship to suffering so potently and concisely because it is both full of meaning and an empty category, and thus never only a sexual metaphor for political pathology: it is full, because as we have seen over and over again, its interpretive breadth is dramatic, its explanatory power breathtaking; and it is empty because, as we have also seen, it doesn't really explain anything.[75] Recall that critics use pornography to refer to erotic and aggressive drives that cause us to lose empathy and yet also use the term to describe the general cultural *effects* of those same drives—the paradoxically bureaucratic ruthlessness with which violence was perpetrated, power exercised, and suffering disregarded is "pornographic" (or is "a pornography of violence").

Again and again, pornography accounts for the exhaustion of empathy without specifying how moral perversion produces political perversion: pornography, that is, stands in for a causal relationship between illicit excitement and numbness, between moral and political perversion, one constantly invoked and presumed but nowhere really explained. In the figure of pornography, critics have intertwined the two narrative strands conventionally used to define morally problematic positions relative to the suffering of others: insufficient feeling for the other and disingenuous feeling for the other, who is but a screen for the projection of one's own excitement. In so doing, critics perfectly allegorize the conundrum of bureaucratic ruthlessness, of banal evil, as well as their conceptual and emotional elusiveness. This persistent invocation of a term that no one can quite define yet everyone understands, one that stands in for an argument not made and yet seems to crystallize a particular set of negative associations, suggests that pornography both allegorizes a historical problem we cannot resolve *and* nevertheless presents that problem—how could millions of European Jews have been systematically annihilated—as a matter of recognizable corrupted empathy. In other words, pornography draws a line, both palpably and intangibly, between bad empathy and good empathy, so that Potter Stewart, a United States Supreme Court Judge, was forced to conclude in 1964 that he knew pornography when he saw it, the implication being that he could otherwise provide no substantive definition of its meaning. The eminent historian Walter Laqueur even uses pornography as a metaphor for the intangibility of fascism, arguing that "Fascism resembles pornography in that it is difficult—perhaps impossible—to define in an operational, legally valid way, but those with experience know it when they see it. Does such a subjective, 'impressionistic' approach open the door to all kinds of arbitrary judgments and incorrect interpretations?"[76]

Pornography's stunning symbolic versatility, its astonishing concentration of so much rhetorical force in one term and its ability to name and not name simultaneously, explains why its reach is so extensive, and why it can make analytical as well as symbolic connections between illicit sexuality and politics so self-evidently and concisely. Pornography performs these rhetorical functions, because it "explains" without explaining the shattering of the body's dignity and thus the apparent frailty of empathic identification that affirms another's moral autonomy. In this way, it both contains and points to anxieties associated with the exhaustion of empathy and thereby expresses perfectly how, in democratic societies, we can imagine and grasp ever more refined cruelties and yet remain fundamentally baffled by them.

The invocation of "pornography" is thus an extremely effective way of interpreting and representing the exhaustion of empathy. It projects the problem of empathy's erosion onto inappropriate eroticism, linked to both erogenous and aggressive drives. References to pornography thus pass themselves off for thought and make it easier not to think. Pornography *could*, for example, be a figure for traumatic response, for the way in which (among other things) we might numbly represent what we feel in excess. Instead, however, the term functions primarily as an aesthetic or moral judgment that precludes an investigation of traumatic response and arguably diverts us from the more explicitly posed question: how to forge a critical usage of empathy? This is to say that in spite of all the sometimes deeply troubled, sometimes righteous assertions about the incommensurability and inexplicability of the Holocaust and other atrocities, our capacity for that kind of unspeakable and unprecedented inhumanity to others is being explained and interpreted all the time as the product of a relationship between illicit sexuality and political terror that can be represented though never clearly explained.

I've suggested that the use of pornography to describe cultural degradation has a long history and that this usage is both historically specific and intensifies after about 1960: that pornography is in fact a figure for a relationship between morality and politics that can and cannot be pinned down or explained. Indeed, pornography—as an allegory of empathy's erosion—currently seems to be a predominant way of speaking about threats to empathic identification that are not named as such. Perhaps the current usage of pornography to designate some Holocaust representations reflects a more general trend to use so-called pathological sexual expression and all that it signifies to figure as graspable, comprehensible, and discussable what we do not in fact grasp. That is, pornography is often used along with sadism and homosexuality to describe causes and effects of Nazism and to signal its continuing menace.[77]

This metaphoric use of illicit or marginal sexuality is in fact a widespread and complex phenomenon. Take, for example, the work of Robert Cover, the late legal theorist who wrote a groundbreaking essay in 1992 on the way sadism infused law enforcement. He claimed that judges dispense pain and death in the name of enforcing the law and asserted that the law's formal procedures mask the violence implicit in the very idea of "enforcement." The law, he says, "is transformed into a violent deed despite general resistance to such deeds." Inhibitions on doing violence to others make law possible at the same time that the law is infused with and imposed through violence. And, he continues, "almost all people are fascinated and attracted by violence, even though they are at the same time repelled by it. Finally, and most important . . . in almost all people social cues may overcome or suppress the revulsion to violence under certain circumstances. These limitations do not deny the force of inhibitions against violence. Indeed both together create the conditions without which law would be unnecessary or impossible."[78]

Law thus describes this tension between the prohibition on and the expression of violence. But in a puzzling footnote, Cover writes that there are "varying cultural responses to linking pain and sexuality," and that those people [who enjoy pain sexually] tend to be deviants having a "deeper sadomasochistic attraction to pain or violence."[79]

Cover does not resolve how the attraction to violence can be universal—can infuse the law itself—and yet be particularly profound in so-called deviants who experience a "deeper" attraction to violence than the rest of us. He seems to be straining to account for particular instances that prove the exception to the rule of the "average" person's attraction to violence, and in the process he implies that this "deeper" violence is an aberration that throws the whole productive tension between violence and inhibitions on violence that is the law off kilter. Thus sexual deviance becomes an emblem for some potentially "deeper" threat to the very stability of the law that is otherwise difficult to name.

Indeed, the historian Michel Foucault, seeking in contrast to Cover to criticize the theoretical and empirical bases of liberalism and democratic institutions more generally, places this pleasure for which Cover cannot account—the unassimilable potential at once marked and concealed by sexual pathology—at the center of history, calling it "power." In order to do this, he allegorizes power in sexual terms:

The pleasure that comes of exercising a power that questions, monitors, watches, spies, searches out, palpates, brings to light; and on the other hand the pleasure that kindles at having to evade this power, flee from it, fool it, or travesty it. The power that lets itself be invaded by the pleasure it is pursuing; and opposite it, power asserting itself in the pleasure of showing off, scandalizing, or resisting. Capture and seduction, confrontation and mutual reinforcement: parents and children, adults and adolescents, educator and students, doctors and patients . . . all have played this game continually since the nineteenth century.[80]

Thus, in *The History of Sexuality*, the web-like, abstract, and highly productive force Foucault calls "power" embraces, caresses, electrifies, and has eyes. Though the sexual body is "wrapped" in power's "embrace," power is not sensual but "sensualized." Foucault's passive voice defines power metaphorically as a disembodied pleasure whose force is embodied by persons who consciously or unconsciously thrill to its gaze and its touch. In so doing, Foucault rewrites history so that this unassimilable pleasure is its prime mover, its inexpressible origin. No longer does pathological sexuality represent pathological politics, meaning that, as we've seen, pathological sexuality is antithetical to democratic liberalism: instead, power fashions liberal democracy itself as the expression of sexual "pathology" (or at the very least, as shot through and through with sadomasochistic pleasure). In his account, the qualities that define human agency, including complicity, fragility, seduction, confession, and eroticism, are all antithetical to self-possession. The liberal self is porous, always in thrall to power's whims; Foucault rewrites the openness of democracy and the will of the rational mind as the mysterious but compelling lure of discipline.

Foucault's work thus conflates the acknowledgment of the dark side of empathic identification (its narcissistic, indeed sadomasochistic dimension) in the construction of historical narrative with history itself, so that historical memory is, paradoxically, only comprehensible as an aestheticized self-loss, a pleasurable submission to the self-shattering forces of eroticism and desire. Foucault's work anchors motivation not in the rational mind but in the fantastical longings of a body no longer capable of consenting. These limitations in many ways mirror the limitations of Cover's account: in both cases, tropes referring to pathological sexuality stand in for the impossible transmission of historical memory and the shattering of the dignified body. Is it possible that pornography plays this same cultural and conceptual function? That pornography, as a metaphor of a numbness born of affective excess linked both to death and erotic drives, is in a more accessible discussion playing the role pathological sexuality seems to play in these scholarly discourses? Or that the logic implicit in the current usage of pornography, as an explanatory framework for unspeakable crimes that explains nothing, is replicated in other discourses whose common concern is the challenge posed to democracy by porous, narcissistically wounded selves and whose implicit presumption is the identification of such selves with deviant sexuality?

The notion that we are currently "numb" and inured to suffering is by now commonplace. Similarly, that the tears we shed in response to narratives and images of suffering are no longer necessarily pure surely goes without saying. But what needs to be discussed are the different ways in which we now make cultural sense of this recently fraught conscience, and with what consequences. The vast referential powers of pornography have become indispensable to explaining, interpreting, and constructing the problem of moral habituation to suffering. They are particularly important because they have in addition become a means of addressing complex historical problems in a deceptively simple fashion. The persistent usage of pornography by critics as an explanatory framework both for unspeakable crimes and for our simultaneously numbed and fascinated response to the representation of suffering attributes such crimes to seemingly explicable motives (we know them when we see them) even while insisting that they generally defy any clear explanation. This usage contains in a familiar, comforting, and yet intangible and indefinable category fears, traumas, and fantasies that traverse a general cultural landscape and seem most significantly linked to floating post-Holocaust anxieties about the failure or corruption of empathy. Indeed, the meaning of pornography—so imprecise and covert in its allusions that in its current form it should be abandoned or, at the very least, explored in great depth—is now so pervasive and so self-evident that, among others things, the "pornographic expectancy" before a visit to Auschwitz should be subject to far more inquiry than I have undertaken here.

CHAPTER TWO

Goldhagen's Celebrity, Numbness, and Writing History

The notion that historians of the Holocaust undertake their task partially to restore to victims their dignity—if only not to grant their persecutors a posthumous victory—seems to be embedded quietly but forcefully in the aims of Anglo-American historical scholarship and the historian's mission.[1] This ideal is arguably manifest in some historians' insistence that, say, in contrast to postmodern literary theorists, they write about things that matter. Jane Caplan writes that "it is one thing to embrace poststructuralism and postmodernism, to disseminate power, to decenter subjects, and all in all let a hundred kinds of meaning contend, when *Bleak House* or philology . . . are the issue. But should the rules of contention be different when it is a question, not simply of History, but of a recent history of lives, deaths, and suffering, and the concept of a justice that seeks to draw some meaningful relation between these?"[2] In keeping with this sentiment, some historians address their audience in the name of remembering and preventing a future crime. Thus Omer Bartov writes: "There may perhaps not be any lessons to be learned from the genocide of the Jews; but, all the same, we must know that the killing goes on, and even if we are safe from it today, we may become its victims tomorrow. This is not a memory, not even a history, for the murder is in our midst, and our passivity will be our nemesis."[3]

Though most historians do not employ such rhetoric explicitly, their dual role as both scholars and preservers of truthful, accurate, and verifiable memory against distortion and manipulation—particularly in the traumatic case of the Holocaust and in the face of revisionists who would deny its extremity—invests them with a special responsibility not to reduce victims' lives and deaths to "faceless, abstract, entit[ities]."[4] For most often unarticulated reasons then, historians have by and large reaffirmed the power of dignity and empathy particularly embedded in one redemptive strain of historical analysis driven by a vision of "humanity triumphant"; they have done so in spite of an increasingly large (mostly literary and philosophical) literature which insists that the Nazi extermination of European Jewry has called the universality of humanist concepts like dignity into question.[5]

The restoration of flesh and blood to bloodless categories, this celebration of life, and the insistence that we must actively defend it—this defense of what matters—is thus a defense of humanist ideals that give historical interpretation a universal meaning and raison d'être. Dignity and empathy are so pervasive and self-evident that they do not need to be named, and yet because they are so central to the organization and inspiration of meaning-conferring historical narrative, they are always present in the guise of some name—in the invocation of what matters, in the concept of letting historical actors speak for themselves, in the commitment to accurate historical reconstruction and letting the story generate the lessons it will—the "necessity of civic virtue."[6]

At the same time, the emotional power of these commitments and the force with which a certain kind of historical narrative is thereby animated are difficult to locate in any specific source because dignity and empathy have become nothing less than synecdoches for the properly human. The commitment to these ideals thus imperceptibly frames our relationship to ourselves and to others in both the past and present: it is so profound a presumption that it is hard to discern explicitly even when most forcefully articulated. In this context, the connection between the historian's desire to restore human dignity by way of generating empathic identification and the analytical task of reconstructing events is difficult to identify in any precise manner, all the more in histories of the Holocaust in which the emotional weight of the material makes empathy both necessary and unbearable. Indeed the conscious or unconscious pressure to tell not only an empathic but also redemptive story as a counterweight to the horror wrought by the perpetrators renders historians' efforts to narrate the Holocaust particularly vexing.

In this chapter I examine the way in which the commitment to dignity and empathy defines, enables, and constrains historical knowledge. How, for example, do historical works implicitly sustain the dignity of those whose humanity has been ruthlessly denied and assaulted? More specifically, I focus on the different ways in which some professional historians seek to forge identifications between contemporary readers and the victims of past genocide and with what emotional and analytical consequences.[7] I begin with a discussion of historians' reception of Daniel Jonah Goldhagen's *Hitler's Willing Executioners*, focusing on the way they interpreted his work to have problematically forged identification with victims of suffering. I devote the remainder of the chapter to examining how other historians seek to foster empathic identification in ways less controversial but equally compelling.

Calling something "pornography," as mentioned earlier, is a way of putting aside arguments about the nature of representation in favor of a vague but palpable sense that this image or that text elicits an improper response. Above all, "pornography" shapes and defines a problem in a disarmingly clear moral language whose meaning on closer inspection turns out to be pretty opaque: designating something "pornographic," among its other functions, passes for an argument about the relation between moral and political perversion where there is really no argument and attributes responsibility for Nazism and fascism implicitly to particular sorts of illicit, sexual emotions.

Historians, of course, explicitly reject ostentatious moralism and invoked the word "pornography" to criticize Daniel Jonah Goldhagen's *Hitler's Willing Executioners* because it manifested a surfeit of emotional identification inseparable from various forms of numbness, including shock and voyeurism.[8] Several critics have pointed out that Goldhagen's book was important precisely because its unrestrained moralism enabled the reader to cut through complexity and hold the perpetrators accountable in an emotionally satisfying fashion. Others felt that in so doing it offered too close an identification either with the suffering of victims or with the hatred of perpetrators.[9] Goldhagen's central thesis is that the genocide of the Jews was possible in Germany because ordinary Germans had been conditioned by anti-Semitic rhetoric into becoming a nation of murderers. The "cognitive model of the Jew"—a term that seems to mean perceptions of and ideals about Jews inherent in German culture and "minds"—thus provided a form of cultural conditioning whose impact is as significant as socioeconomic structures. Goldhagen terms this conditioning the "eliminationist mind-set"—the desire to eradicate Jews and "Jewishness"—specific to German anti-Semitism. After summarizing anti-Semitic discourse in Germany, Goldhagen discusses police battalions, labor camps, and death marches: in all three cases, "ordinary Germans" (that is, mostly low-rank non-Nazi policemen and employees of camps) demonstrated themselves capable of gratuitously sadistic behavior toward Jews that was systematic, widespread, and cannot be explained as anomalous or by reference to coercion. He answers the difficult if not impossible question about why so many human beings became murderous in extreme conditions by linking brutality to Germanness, and in so doing focuses primarily on the crimes Germans committed and on how much Jews suffered.

Goldhagen's focus on Jewish suffering was an important corrective to the predominant (if not uncontested) historiographical trend since the 1960s, usually dubbed "functionalist" or "structural-functionalist." This trend generally neglected the experience of victims in favor of explaining genocide in mechanistic terms that emphasized the "cumulative radicalization" of bureaucratic decision-making instead of human agents; it thereby downplayed the role of ideology and stressed the often improvised role of policy-making rather than victims' suffering.[10] Though it downplays the lived experience of victims, this view nevertheless represented a significant development in scholarship on the Holocaust, for it shifted the perspective away from a focus on Hitler and his fanatical anti-Semitism (the "intentionalists") to the complex bureaucracy of the Nazi State.

A second generation of modified functionalists has acknowledged explicitly that the mass murder of European Jewry was not simply a "by-product" of economically motivated and other decisions made by mid-level bureaucrats in the Nazi hierarchy but was mired in the fanatical anti-Semitism of both Nazi functionaries and higher-level SS men. At the same time, they still too often link anti-Semitic ideology "functionally" with other Nazi policies, such as the resettlement of populations to the East and the need to supply the *Wehrmacht* after the invasion of the Soviet Union.[11] Thus, as Goldhagen, a political scientist, argued, while the decisions about the organization of extermination have received a great deal of attention, the fact that the Nazis "had to induce a large number of people to carry out the killings" has been treated "perfunctorily and mainly by assumption." Or he says more bluntly: "[German cruelties] leave no doubt that . . . the Germans were not emotionally neutral executors of superior orders, or cognitively and emotionally neutral bureaucrats indifferent to the nature of their deeds." Indeed, he insisted that neutrality in this context was a "psychological impossibility."[12]

Although it represents an important shift in perspective, *Hitler's Willing Executioners* remains highly unorthodox. Unlike historians whose allegiance to a neutral narrative voice restrains moral judgment, encouraging a cognitive rather than emotive mode of apprehension, Goldhagen inserts himself into the action, asking the reader to imagine in the most vivid terms how a German soldier must have felt as he shot a young Jewish child, and he describes the murder in gruesome detail. Referring to other atrocities, he asks: "How could any person have looked upon these pitiable, sick Jewish women without feeling sympathy for them, without feeling horror at the abject physical condition into which they had been plunged?"[13]

Historians' invocation of "pornography" became a way of speaking about this type of moralism in a book that simply did not subscribe to any serious historiographical conventions about distinguishing clearly between the event and one's subjective judgment of it, between history writing and the evocation of (in this case traumatic) memory. But perhaps the use of the term "pornographic" in this context once again also masks what is really at stake in the criticism of the book and arguably what is at stake in the way historians seek to calibrate both their own and the reader's distance from and proximity to suffering in the representation of extreme events.

In this revelatory because extreme case, historians' condemnation of Goldhagen focused on the problematic aspects of his work and also on its popular appeal. Most reviews and discussions roundly criticized his work for the moralism alluded to above and for a wide variety of analytical failings. Critics accuse him of several serious violations of scholarly research. He does not appear to have mastered the secondary sources in his field and demonstrates little familiarity with Holocaust scholarship and available primary sources. Indeed, he fails to acknowledge most other scholars who have studied related subjects. He demonstrates little respect for competing interpretations with which he is familiar and dismisses them cursorily, especially if they conflict with his own judgments. He resurrects tired clichés about the "mind" of Germany because he takes no account of more recent studies that focus on anti-Semitism and the ideological indoctrination of perpetrators; he focuses so intensively on anti-Semitic ideas that he strips the Nazi genocide of European Jewry of its socioeconomic and political context, and thus neglects the role of the state and the specificity of industrialized murder. Moreover, he fails to place any of his data in comparative historical perspective. He ignores the complicity, even murderousness, of non-Germans. And he also ignores the gains Jews made in Germany before 1933 and the tremendous social and cultural status they enjoyed; thus he implied that they remained willfully blind to the virulent hatred all around them. In short, Goldhagen moves away from recent and sophisticated explanations of why ordinary Germans elected Hitler and followed him to a crude, monocausal cultural account that returns to German exceptionalism at best and to muddled, ahistorical ideas about "national character" at worst.[14]

Historians were incensed by the rather unsurprising revelation that these scholarly denunciations of his work did not have all that much influence on a mass public. They thus blamed the appeal of Goldhagen's book on the publisher's clever marketing strategies (and thus indirectly on the audience for being hoodwinked), on the work's putatively simplistic argument ("people," declared Yehuda Bauer, "don't like complicated explanations. They want simplicity, even mindless simplicity"),[15] on Goldhagen's charisma, and most of all on themselves for having lost touch with a wider public (sometimes blaming trendy scholarship for having alienated the masses, so that Hans Ulrich-Wehler incomprehensibly deems Goldhagen's success a symptom of "cultural studies").[16] There has so far been little discussion beyond these particular themes about the phenomenon of historians' dramatic and emotionally intense condemnation of Goldhagen. The vast majority of commentary focuses either on Goldhagen's problematic scholarship or on his popular appeal in different national contexts and seeks to analyze and understand the gap between historians' views and those of the larger public.[17]

The allusion to Goldhagen's work as pornographic, however, provides a bridge between historians' scholarly judgment and discussions about Goldhagen's appeal to a mass readership. For historians, the text's so-called pornographic tendencies indicated a serious methodological problem and yet also accounted for its popular success. As Hans Mommsen wrote: "Goldhagen's portrayal of sadistic and gruesome violence releases a certain voyeuristic moment that serious Holocaust research has deliberately avoided in its restrained portrayal of the crimes, particularly since it translates at best into mere *Betroffenheit* [affectation of dismay—Trans.] and contributes little toward real explanation. One may assume that Goldhagen is not sufficiently conscious of this effect, which presumably contributes decisively to the mass marketing of his book." And in a telling allusion to Steven Spielberg, Mommsen claims that what Goldhagen seeks—insight into perpetrators' psychic makeup—was already effectively treated in *Schindler's List*. Thus Mommsen blamed the book's affective and moral content for diminishing our capacity to exercise sober judgment, and views the explicit portrayal of violence as antithetical to historical explanation. Moreover, he derides not the book's moral vision itself but the way in which it appeals to the wrong kind of emotion, including voyeurism, and prurience and tendencies associated with pornography.[18] Along the same lines, Norman Finkelstein declares that Goldhagen's commercialization of the Holocaust "breaks new ground with the invention of a new subgenre: Holoporn."[19]

Thus explicit portrayals of violence must produce a disingenuous emotional response (*Betroffenheit*)—what I have referred to thus far as "corrupted empathy"—and the restrained portrayal of violence, by implication, evokes proper feelings, though it is not clear why exactly this is the case or what those feelings would be. Historian Geoff Eley's introduction to the book he edited evaluating the "Goldhagen effect" in various national contexts is exemplary of how historians for the most part presume a relationship between the "restrained portrayal" of the genocide of European Jewry and the transmission of historical knowledge about that event, a conceptual sleight of hand more often than not facilitated by the self-evidence of the appellation "pornography":

There are also genuine issues of taste, strategy, and ethical choice involved in choosing to present this in all its vivid awfulness, particularly given the pornographic discourse associated with the circulation of such images. Raising this issue isn't to argue for censorship, and Goldhagen's option for a graphic detailing of atrocities is certainly legitimate. But it does signal the complexities involved, as against the absolutism and highly moralizing tones of Goldhagen's justification for choosing his own approach, which effaced the ethical seriousness of his predecessors and, not surprisingly, provoked their annoyance.[20]

Eley then quotes Mommsen's words to exemplify this "annoyance" and never returns to the question. Perhaps also because the essay is an introduction to a collection, Eley does not discuss in any more detail why Goldhagen's graphic representation of atrocities is in fact "legitimate" other than by reference to the tautology that to deny its legitimacy would be tantamount to censorship. Atina Grossmann similarly notes that Goldhagen "gained moral authority via . . . a grotesque, lurid, virtually pornographic language of witness," and that he "respected no *Schamgrenze* [shame border]." Grossman believes that Goldhagen transforms sadistic and voyeuristic impulses into a virtuous quest for truth that has a "certain docudrama authenticity," meaning, of course that it is finally inauthentic. She writes that Goldhagen touts the relentless depiction of violence as moral virtue, and his "language of witness" has a murderous, sadistic, "virtually pornographic" quality rendering the virtuous transmission of knowledge inextricable from far more suspect pleasures.[21] The German critic Silke Wenk takes Goldhagen to task for his "pornographic rhetoric," in particular for his musings on the thoughts of Nazi perpetrators. Historians Ruth Bettina Birn and Volker Riess, quoting journalist Jacob Heibrunn, refer to the "almost pornographic" quality of Goldhagen's depictions of murder.[22]

But as Jane Caplan argues eloquently, the real problem with Goldhagen's argument is not that he depicts violence so graphically. Rather, his very questionable efforts to foster empathic identification "constitute the text's core strategy, the logic of how it positions its readers."[23] That is, the book reduces the genocide to a series of "negative and positive identifications on the part of the reader: a repudiation of the motives and choices that underlay the horrifying acts of the killers, and an empathetic identification with the suffering of their victims."[24] Goldhagen's narrative thus reduces the historical complexities involved in explaining and understanding mass murder to the reader's repudiation of killers and identification with victims. But structurally—if my reading of Mommsen, Eley, Grossman, and others is correct—to the extent that Goldhagen's narrative is "pornographic" or "voyeuristic," its logic also identifies the reader with the perpetrator, contaminating any pure identification with victims. It places all readers in the ambivalent position of complicit and yet also mournful bystanders.

Goldhagen's narrative then not only reduces genocide to negative or positive identifications that represent the Holocaust simplistically as a moral struggle between innocent victims and evil perpetrators but also more problematically mobilizes identification with both victims *and* perpetrators. As these critics note, Goldhagen's work "efface[s] the ethical seriousness of his predecessors"—meaning it tries to outdo them on a scale of moral gravity—and yet respects no "shame border." The reader is thereby identified both with the perpetrators' shameless, objectifying, numbing gaze and with the moral outrage proper to witnessing atrocities against innocents. Though these critics tend to use the term pornography to refer to passive voyeurism, prurience (both of which imply moral numbness), and just plain bad literature, it is this dual identification with victims and perpetrators to which pornography seems primarily to refer.[25] The historians discussed here use "pornography" to indicate that Goldhagen's book confusingly and misleadingly incites both moral numbness and moral outrage, and they can't figure out which side of the fence, methodologically speaking, it is really on. His narrative then is not merely "pornographic" and voyeuristic, but also moralistic in intention. It is this (unavowed) ambivalent identification with both victims and perpetrators that constitutes the text's "core" and explains why it was deemed pornographic by its detractors and celebrated as morally righteous by its defenders.[26]

The reference to pornography expresses historians' refusal to confront this ambivalent identification as a problem common to most representations of the horror of the Holocaust and of all mass atrocities. Instead, according to most historians, the work was pornographic because it was just bad history pretending to be good history: it incited the worst sort of voyeurism and yet purported to speak for victims. Historians responded to Goldhagen's insistence on his moral integrity by attacking the book as if he had made a conscious choice to deceive his audience, as if his emotions got the better of him, or even more patronizingly (but importantly) that the only way to make the genocide accessible and meaningful to a mass audience was to play on their emotional needs and to tell them fairy-tales.

Thus those least enamored of Goldhagen accused him, not quite bluntly, of hypocrisy or disingenuousness—of being anything but saintly. They said that he says one thing and does another in order to sell books or amplify his celebrity (as Mommsen implies when he politely but disingenuously notes that Goldhagen must not be aware of the effect his narrative produces). Another, more generous version of this criticism is that Goldhagen is so driven by what Josef Joffe calls "prosecutorial passion" that he can't see the forest for the trees; that is, Goldhagen is not so much a hypocrite as he is so blinded by the force of his own emotion that he mixes things up and confuses different levels of analysis.[27] And finally, there was the more general protestation, best represented here by Grossman and Joffe, that Goldhagen derives moral authority via his lurid narrative, which makes us feel the pain of the victims only by sacrificing analytical sophistication and historical veracity. In Joffe's words, "Goldhagen's was a stark and enthralling narrative, much like the morality tales about heinous queens, wolves, and witches so beloved by children. Why? Because in the end, trembling and terror are but stepping-stones to a morally comprehensible universe. This is the evil that was done, this is who did it; here is why they did it and how they felt."[28] In the end, Goldhagen hoodwinks an audience who, understandably hungry for moral accountability, ends up with something close to docudrama or kitsch (recall also Mommsen's equation of *Hitler's Willing Executioners* and *Schindler's List*). We might conclude from these accounts that Goldhagen's book is closest to the prosecutorial vigilance of the tabloid press (it is "lurid" and "grotesque") or to the naïve enthusiasm (or here too, prosecutorial passion) of the intellectual in the service of a good cause: empathic identification runs amuck, spills over into its opposite, sadism, and seeks to humiliate and destroy its object; the documentary filmmaker who humiliates victims in the name of doing them justice; the seemingly compassionate interviewer who wants to know and tell everything, regardless of the impact on his subject.[29] The more one reads such critiques, the more one wonders how Eley—editor of the collection in which many of them appear— could have named the book's strategic choices perfectly "legitimate."

Finally, Elizabeth D. Heineman, a historian sympathetic if not to Goldhagen, then to the importance of his "speculations," claims that his stories about sexual coupling in the camps are useful at least for drawing attention to the question of sexuality. She notes how some efforts to deal with sexuality and genocide "might serve a pornographic function of simultaneously disgusting and fascinating the reader," especially female victims' stories of sexual humiliation and torture in camps. She rightly insists such stories must be addressed historically to capture the meaning of degradation for the victims and to understand how genocidal regimes include sexual degradation among other tools of humiliation. She also argues, however, that "problematic modes of representation and reception . . . should not be confused with serious attempts to understand the intersections of sexuality and genocide," and aligns Goldhagen's work implicitly with such "problematic modes." Though a relatively straightforward argument, it rests on an a priori assumption that what historians do is "nonexploitative," and while "eroticized images of Nazism in popular culture may appear problematic and even deeply offensive, we gain more if we demonstrate the benefits of a nonexploitative approach than if we simply object."[30] Thus the division between popular narrative and historical research implicitly stands in for thinking through the problem of how to represent sexuality and genocide in a way that will not be exploitative. That is, her argument, however important its insistence on addressing sexuality and genocide, begs the question of what a nonexploitative approach to the subject might be.[31]

To accuse Goldhagen of stirring up the wrong kind of emotions, of hypocrisy, of too much passion, of a general surfeit of emotion or its opposite, extreme cunning, both of which may be personality requirements for saints, dictators, or great polemicists, but not (ideally) for professional historians, is a way of neglecting the intimate, inextricable relationship between numbness and empathic identification that becomes particularly poignant in Holocaust historiography and is central to Goldhagen's problematic text. Of course, historians were naturally loath to see a book that dispenses with the most fundamental of historiographical tenets—"most historians have used more cautious language," notes Jürgen Kocka[32]—feted by press and public alike because, according to them, he used a pornographic language of witness and turned the mass murder of Jews into a spectacle. How much worse then was the elevation of Goldhagen to a spokesman on behalf of victims, as well as his self-fashioning, particularly in Germany, as a courageous young voice in a profession of old, thick-skinned men. Indeed, according to journalist Ron Rosenbaum, so upsetting was Goldhagen's fame that even the most judicious scholars inadvertently revealed a deep repository of unconscious aggression:

in a 1996 symposium at the United States Holocaust Memorial Museum devoted to *Hitler's Willing Executioners*, the moderator called on all participants to respect the "canons of civility" in their discussion, then castigated Goldhagen for running over his allotted time by remarking that when his own students did so, he "often thought of strangling them." The moderator himself does not dispute that he uttered these words, but interprets them differently.[33] Yet in the end (and perhaps this is why the emotion attached to rather petty and patronizing accusations of hypocrisy seemed to exceed the nature of the accusations themselves), whether Goldhagen is a hypocrite or a saint is really beside the point, since the text's real difficulty is that its very logic refuses any simple choice between the moral numbness equated with voyeurism and the moral integrity equated with empathy. Historians who accuse Goldhagen of being a charlatan or an overly vigilant prosecutor demand that we finally take the side of either good or bad history, of moral numbness or integrity when what the book really exposes is the difficulty involved in writing the history of the genocide of European Jewry. Could it be then that Goldhagen's very celebrity became a crucial, indeed indispensable "diversion"?[34] That is, could it be that Goldhagen's celebrity permitted historians to focus on the problems of emotional surfeit—to frame the question at stake into one of restrained versus unrestrained emotion—when the real challenge was more profoundly how to fashion a language at least capable of conveying the difficulty of disentangling moral numbness (generated, as we have seen, even in the most well-intended of Holocaust exhibits) and moral integrity? How else to explain why the aim of discussion was generally to do away with pretense and paradox, to show with absolute clarity that his work was not what it professed to be?

It is as if the venom historians directed at Goldhagen's celebrity was thus a means of disavowing the very difficult question of how best to represent historical knowledge about the Holocaust, a question whose answer was taken to be self-evident—if only by virtue of the consensus on Goldhagen—during the discussion of his work. Thus when Eley noted that Goldhagen's decision to present his material the way he did was "legitimate"—in the face of its near total delegitimation by experts—he seemed to have meant that it was legitimate in the same way that pornography, tabloids, and bad books all have a right to exist (hence the comment that he wouldn't recommend censorship), as if that were a reasonable response to a substantive question about why anyone would write the way Goldhagen did. Caplan insists that survivors were better witnesses than Goldhagen, who claimed to speak in their name. She thus refuses to engage the more fundamental issue that historians usually do not rely on living witnesses, and when they have that privilege, they cannot represent their voices transparently—that is, she does not use the opportunity to discuss the problem of representing trauma.[35] When Joffe claimed that historians saw the "Holocaust à la Goldhagen as Peeping Tom's Paradise," he acknowledged the obscenity of the comparison. But then he grudgingly claimed that you couldn't deny the "perverse allure of the book." In so doing, he summed up how "pornography" became a pervasive accusation because it reduces the really intimate and complicated relation between moral numbness and empathic identification in *Hitler's Willing Executioners* to Goldhagen's hypocrisy: to call Goldhagen's book pornographic becomes another way of saying that under the cover of speaking for the victims, he really seeks celebrity, glory, and riches, or at least some sort of personal familial vindication, since his father survived the Holocaust. Indeed, to the extent Goldhagen's renewed focus on anti-Semitism led to a change in the history of the Holocaust, it led to an emphasis on ideology already under way, and thus on a concentration on the ideological as well as technical components of genocide. Goldhagen's work led to a positivist change of focus rather than theoretical or methodological challenges to the way historians write about the Holocaust.

Thus, we might say that Goldhagen's celebrity distracts or "diverts" historians away from theoretical and methodological questions that might incapacitate historical judgment, and proves correct the dominant and most defensible rationale behind not addressing those questions—they get historians into murky waters by taking them into areas of philosophy and psychology beyond their realm of expertise. Thus celebrity makes it possible to ignore the pressing question about how to represent victims' suffering without too much numbness or too much empathy. Using the term "pornography" in this context became a means by which the frustration about the inadequacy of conventional moral language to address the Holocaust is projected onto a bad object: onto Goldhagen's work in particular, but also onto its commercial success and thus onto all those nameless and faceless readers who apparently can't distinguish between titillation and moral gravity, emotional appeals and serious historical work. The appellation "pornographic" becomes, in its seeming self-evidence, an argument about the superiority of the restrained judgment of historians over the assumed gullibility of the general public.

In what follows, I want to examine the analytical consequences of this sort of projection as it plays itself out in historiography and historically inflected work; or, to put it differently, I would like to examine the ways in which some historians have found their way around the relation between numbing (or the traumatic effects of such disturbingly violent material) and empathy. Thus, just as my interest in why historians and others called Goldhagen's work (or the Holocaust Museum and so forth) "pornographic" was to address the way we figure a set of pressing theoretical, moral, and cultural problems, so my focus here is not on the Holocaust itself—on the event—but on the way some historians have imagined and sought to generate empathic identification with victims in their efforts to convey that historical experience.

Voluminous essays about "Holocaust representation" have addressed the impact of the traumatic nature of the event on scholarship, both literary and historical. They have also sought to interpret the necessary incommensurability of any empirical reconstruction of the Holocaust with its historical meaning. These discussions have thus far focused primarily on three, often overlapping, themes: the historian's traumatic relation to the Holocaust understood as a complicated set of unconscious projections and idealizations and other forms of repression; the difficulty of representing the Holocaust, not only in the sense of its historical singularity, but also in the as yet unfathomable combination of bureaucratic rationality and the mystical, self-shattering union with Hitler; and finally the question about whether the history of the Holocaust can approximate a knowable empirical reality in the neo-positivist sense.[36] These discussions for the most part did not shape historians' response to Goldhagen's book, its reception, and his celebrity, partly because they have participated minimally in such debates, leaving them for the most part to literary theorists and philosophers.[37] Thus the intense projection onto Goldhagen of the role of bad historian may have served both as a diversion from the specific theoretical problem presented by the historian's necessarily troubled relation to his or her material and as a lesson about what happens when historians venture beyond the facts of industrialized murder to larger theoretical or experiential questions. In the context of their assessment of the historian's proper relation to his or her subject matter, both Volker Berghahn and Fritz Stern, for example, assert that the Holocaust was essentially incomprehensible, and express amazement that Goldhagen thought otherwise.[38] Christopher Browning, author of a book on policemen on the Eastern Front, concludes his essay by saying that it would be impossible to venture an explanation of their behavior because the "historians of the Holocaust . . . know nothing—in no experiential sense—about their subject." He offers instead a sensitive and thorough examination of the context that made their behavior possible.[39] Or, as historian Michael Marrus wrote in reference to the difficulty of writing about the Holocaust: "Historians are used to tramping over their fields while suspending judgment on the fundamental human issues that are ultimately at stake. Once pointed in a scholarly direction most of us forge ahead, hoping to navigate safely using the customary tools of the trade. We simply do the best we can, knowing that our efforts are necessarily imperfect, incomplete, and inadequate."[40]

In keeping with this modest approach to historical material, many historians had addressed the causes of inhumanity by employing an argument generally drawn, however implicitly, from Weberian and functionalist theories of modernity and from cognitive social psychologists' emphasis on processes of obedience and conformity in determining collective action: those in which involvement in monstrous acts is a sign not of psychopathological or sadistic tendencies (though they may be present in some individuals) but of socially generated responses among "ordinary men" to particular situations. This emphasis, characteristic, for example, in the famous experimental psychological studies of Stanley Milgram on obedience to authority,[41] informs many cognitive and functionalist historical and sociological accounts of state-sanctioned crimes.[42] The emphasis on socially generated obedience and conformity shares the logic underlying the notions of "moral habituation" and "compassion fatigue" because it describes social processes and behaviors particular to modern forms of technological and social organization and thus depicts new constraints on compassion. Here, of course, it is not the precariousness of empathy generally that is at stake (and for which the Holocaust would be one important emblem) but the specific loss of empathic identification that accompanies modern state-sponsored killing, in particular war and the genocide of European Jewry.

This focus on impersonal social processes is particularly suited to emotionally moderated narrative form and underlies those works on genocide that emphasize the bureaucratic nature of the killing and its relation to "modernity" but also those—such as Browning's, quoted above—that seek to explain face-to-face slaughter as itself facilitated by psychic numbing mechanisms, including ideology, group-bonding against outsiders, and the dehumanization of victims. That is, such accounts indirectly explain the Nazi genocide by analyzing how men in the bureaucratic hierarchy did not bear fundamental responsibility for what they were doing: they were men simply following and placing orders who could not, in Hannah Arendt's most dramatic characterization, even think, or they were policemen, soldiers, or bystanders inured to feeling by the depersonalization of the victims (who are "cargo" for transport or "vermin" to be exterminated) and the "routine" repetition of horrific acts.[43]

In contrast, Goldhagen's work forced historians to revisit the recognition that in many histories of the Holocaust the implicit reliance on some version of this argument about "dehumanization" results in the inadvertent objectification of victims. As many historians noted in different ways, the social processes they elaborate to explain the persecution and finally the extermination of the Jews lead to a focus on perpetrators' minds and actions rather than on victims. As the German historian Ulrich Herbert puts it, "There are almost no studies by German historians that not only describe sympathetically and with regret the fate of the victims but exploit heuristically the victims' point of view; almost none that do not present and analyze events merely from the perspective of German policemen, bureaucrats, and officers . . . almost none that break the perpetrators' interpretive monopoly that derived from the surviving documents."[44] Moreover, these events are often recounted in a minimalist style that reiterates the impersonality and objectification intrinsic in those processes on the level of narrative form. "In many works," Saul Friedländer writes, "the implicit assumptions regarding the victims' generalized hopelessness and passivity, or their inability to change the course of events leading to their extermination, have turned them into a static and abstract element of the historical background."[45] Or, as Friedländer suggests elsewhere, the analytic framework must somehow bear the weight of the historian's own necessarily difficult engagement with such material; he claims historians need to keep some balance in their work, for "in fact the numbing or distancing effect on intellectual work on the Shoah is unavoidable and necessary; the recurrence of strong emotional impact is also often unforeseeable and necessary." Even when the historian is sufficiently aware to measure his or her responses to these unforeseeable reactions, "the full impact of this emotion has on occasion been deflected toward overcritical comments on the behavior of victims."[46] It is perhaps for this reason that many have preferred not to focus on victims (except as distant and finally dehumanized objects of murderous goals) or have ascribed to them more power than they may have had. Moreover, while the emphasis on social and psychic disengagement moves beyond simple analyses of human barbarism to assess under what historical conditions barbarism may be bureaucratically organized, indeed industrialized, it was Goldhagen's rejection of this analysis that proved able to satisfy the public's demands for moral accountability.

Thus historians' alternative to Goldhagen's own logic has mostly been a mirror inversion of it. For Goldhagen's strategy of getting close to his subject exploited victims; historians' alternative strategy of suspending judgment (or trying not to let it get in the way) portrays victims only at a great emotional distance and generates empathy via a cognitive apprehension of the event. As much critical writing has pointed out, the latter strategy can only be fully assessed by attending to questions of historical representation: for the material provided by state-sponsored crimes so exceeds extant analytic and moral categories that it challenges and can overwhelm not only the analytical task of historical work (and its demotion of a narrative mode of representation more suited, like Goldhagen's, to the production of affect) but also the power of traditional narrative style and the pedagogical aims of historical writing, which Christopher Browning claims is "to instruct about the frailty of the human condition and the necessity for civic virtue."[47]

In what remains of this chapter, I am interested in how other historians self-consciously restore to victims the dignity Goldhagen was believed to have diminished in his own emotive reconstruction of their suffering. In particular, how do they seek to avoid reproducing cognitive numbing both as cause and effect of Jewish suffering and, on another level, in the content and narrative form of their work?

How then do these historians maintain the imperative to instruct about the frailty of the human condition while remaining faithful to the evidentiary standards and narrative conventions of mainstream historiography, and this despite the difficulties intrinsic in "Holocaust representation"? Or, to put it differently, how do they mobilize empathic identification without also generating numbness?

I focus on two very different historians who ponder the horror of the Holocaust in synthetic narratives meant to reflect on that event's larger meaning: Inga Clendinnen's *Reading the Holocaust* and Omer Bartov's *Mirrors of Destruction*. Clendinnen's book is, remarkably, written by an insider-outsider for outsiders and is significant for that reason: a professional historian of the Spanish Conquest, a historical ethnographer of Aztec civilization, she turns her hand to the Holocaust as a professional who is nonetheless not in the field. Bartov has established himself as a military historian of Nazi Germany and recently began reflecting on industrialized murder and its aftermath. He focuses on the blurry line between Jewish victims and Nazi perpetrators in postwar Western Europe and Israel and its impact on the construction of what he calls "modern identity."[48]

I choose them both because their texts have been generally well reviewed and well received by historians, in contrast to the reception of Goldhagen's book, and because they implicitly or explicitly want their readers to come away particularly aware of victims' suffering. They also represent a genre of synthetic essays that is as much self-conscious cultural commentary as history, and for the most part they favor a narrative mode and yet keep their subject anchored in its historical particularities. I will argue that their ability to represent the Holocaust in universalizing terms even as they stay close to the events of that genocide itself is crucial to their ability to represent victims' suffering in emotionally compelling and yet bearable terms. Negative reviews of Bartov not surprisingly tend to come from historians who expect him to be illuminating the extermination of European Jewry when his subject is really how war and the Holocaust are crucial historically specific points of departure for the construction of modern identity, which has shaped more recent ethnic and religious conflicts.[49] One review of Clendinnen wonders why Cambridge University Press should have published the book since it relies exclusively on secondary source works in English and therefore can have little to contribute to Holocaust scholarship.[50] In short, their analytical and emotional power and appeal seems to derive paradoxically from the way in which they use the history of the Holocaust to dwell on questions that transcend the particularity of that event.

Inga Clendinnen's account of the Holocaust is marked primarily by her desire to avoid the emotional and analytical paralysis with which historians have for so long regarded the Shoah. "The primary aim of these essays," she writes, "is to challenge that bafflement and the demoralization which attends it. I want to dispel the 'Gorgon effect'— the sickening of imagination and curiosity and the draining of will which afflicts so many of us when we try to look squarely at the persons and processes implicated in the Holocaust."[51] In taking up this formidable challenge, Clendinnen insists on the importance of not treating Nazis as monsters to whom we bear no resemblance, preferring, for example, the unflinching, yet nonjudgmental gaze of Gitta Sereny (the Austrian-born journalist who interviewed both Franz Stangl and Albert Speer). As Clendinnen sees it, "truth wears no shudder marks in Sereny's vision," and her approach is thus preferable to Hannah Arendt's overly "burnished" ideas about Adolf Eichmann, for whose muddled thinking Arendt has nothing but contempt.[52] She insists that ideally we avoid moral judgment and approach these events dispassionately and with an eye for the telling detail. In this approach there is thus no speculation about the nature of the self, no search for "higher" truth apart from what careful scrutiny of the facts reveals, and thus no explicit invocation of or appeal to dignity or empathy. Indeed, Clendinnen eschews empathy explicitly as the stuff of wishful thinking.

The book nevertheless marshals this chilly pragmatism unexpectedly against those who would judge victims for having not sufficiently resisted, attributing such attitudes to an unfortunate penchant among scholars to entertain ideas about how human beings should behave that have no place in historical inquiry. The narrative is arresting and thought-provoking, moving thematically through "chapters" of the Holocaust: "Beginnings," "Witnessing," "Resisting," and so forth; moreover, it addresses the experiences of both perpetrators and victims (the "Auschwitz SS," "Leaders," "The Order Police in Poland," "The Auschwitz *Sonderkommando*").

Clendinnen proposes to read Heinrich Himmler's famous 1943 Posen Speech against the grain and thus in an entirely new light. In so doing she situates herself opposite the Holocaust historian Saul Friedländer, whom she accuses of overreaching the facts—an inevitable consequence, she thinks, of his overtly moralistic vision. In the oft-quoted speech, Himmler scandalously and incomprehensibly exhorts his SS to be proud of maintaining their "decency" in the midst of the mass murder they had committed and were continuing to perpetrate. He tells them that their deeds are "glorious" but must "never be written" because others would not comprehend their necessity. According to Clendinnen, Friedländer interprets the invocation of secrecy not only as evidence of the "horror and the uncanny" residing in the speech but also of the SS's mystical bond with Hitler, without which, he insists, Himmler's words would be incomprehensible. "Precisely at this point—the elation created by the dimensions of the killing—" Friedländer writes, "our understanding remains blocked at the level of self-awareness." Consequently, "the greater the moral sensitivity of the analyst, the stricter the repression will be of a subject deemed too threatening to both the individual and to society." To this, Clendinnen responds: "Here at last comes the nub of Friedländer's argument. . . . Unlike Himmler and his SS, *we* [my italics] have not renounced human morality. We are therefore unable to participate in emotions such as *Rausch* and the 'bond with Hitler.' " And: "Friedländer . . . sees Himmler's secrecy as indicative of something far more sinister and metaphysical than a pragmatic interest in keeping dark things dark."[53]

Clendinnen is surely right that Friedländer here emphasizes the shock and incredulity the historian feels when confronted by Himmler's words—in this case Friedländer analyzes a "block" that precludes the analyst from grasping the perpetrator's motives or feelings (a block that manifests consciously as the incomprehension we feel when confronted by the elation that characterizes the speech). Clendinnen argues instead—as has the historian Yehuda Bauer only recently[54]—that we can understand the Holocaust if we simply retain our faith in rationality and the explicability of all things, however unfamiliar and mind-boggling they may seem. Himmler's insistence on secrecy was thus not necessarily indicative of some mysterious, elation-producing bond with Hitler forged in and strengthened by its exclusiveness, but a means of "add[ing] terror to the silence" that the Nazis had imposed on all those involved in the genocide. Many people " 'in the East,' " she notes, "must have been aware that something grave and terrible . . . was going on somewhere out of sight," and official secrecy only exacerbated these fears.[55]

However commonsensical, Clendinnen's approach seems insufficient to capture the meaning of Himmler's speech, for what exactly would it mean to understand the Posen speech, as she suggests, on its own terms, literally rather than as a rhetorical performance of *Rausch*? Isn't it precisely the delivery of this speech as a means of moral inspiration—this heady celebration of the decency and glory of mass murder—that renders it so uncanny and in need of an explanation? Isn't the conceptual problem presented by the (poorly maintained) "secret" of mass murder not its pragmatism but the pride of those who sought proudly to be one of an elite "bearer of secrets" who understood the necessity of murdering millions of human beings?[56] Friedländer seeks to express precisely the limits of reason before such an overwhelming subject. For we could only understand this speech in its own terms if we were to completely revise and expand our conventional moral frameworks to include a definition of mass murder as a finally decent means to a glorious end. Indeed, Clendinnen suggests that in order to grasp the Holocaust, we extend the parameters by which dignified and rational behavior may be defined so far that such behavior is meaningless by any normative standard. She so normalizes this behavior in the name of not seeing the Nazis as monsters that she cannot explain, locate, or define it except tautologically, as what it says it is. In the absence of any attention to the level of fantasy, rhetoric, or affect in Himmler's speech, Clendinnen renders the SS so purely rational, pragmatic, and affectless that they become the automatons she insists they are not, and portrays inhumanity as so normalized that killing becomes normal, and thus not conceivable as a crime.[57]

Clendinnen's insistence on staring straight into the horror of the event thus paradoxically expresses a desire that there not be any horror, a desire manifested in the text's unusual normalizing of horror. And yet, though *Reading the Holocaust* consciously sets itself against demonizing the perpetrators or detecting anything inexplicable in their behavior, it nevertheless turns them into monsters. Thus in the midst of this exceedingly banal world in which killing has become routine, there appears the pathology of anti-Semitism: "The anti-Semitism enacted inside Auschwitz was pathological. It bore not the least resemblance to the pallid antagonisms, the weary jokes, and unwearying condescension we might associate with the term. Rather it was the active expression of the conviction that Jews were not human at all, but *Untermenschen,* vile creatures whose one aim was to contaminate everyone in their proximity."[58] But it's not clear from what vantage point anti-Semitism could be deemed pathological (since she argues that all phenomena are potentially reasonable and must be understood and interpreted as such). That is, from what normative perspective can we imagine this pathology as pathological? For our ability to conceive the difference between the "merely" wearying aggression directed against a minority group and its eventual extermination, between anti-Semitic jokes and the mass murder of Jews, and between "weary jokes" and Auschwitz, requires the recognition of some normative framework of behavior in which telling jokes might be substantively differentiated from killing those who are their targets.[59] Moreover, our ability to conceive the *connection* between telling jokes about Jews and their murder, one which Clendinnen does not seem to acknowledge, requires an understanding of what non-Jewish bystanders and Nazi perpetrators have in common.[60]

The problem of "ordinary monsters" has plagued commentators on Nazi Germany from Hannah Arendt (the "banality of evil") to Goldhagen's "ordinary Germans," and Clendinnen confronts it here again, for she asks essentially how the most monstrous deeds are perpetrated by otherwise "normal" and "decent" people. Clendinnen finally focuses so exclusively on the ordinariness of perpetrators that their monstrosity appears as an afterthought for which the analysis has simply not made sufficient conceptual room. The Nazis' deeds are somehow not of this world but of Auschwitz, which is the only place "pathological" anti-Semitism appears.

Clendinnen ultimately tells this otherwise untenable story of perpetrators and victims on the level of a metanarrative of triumphal humanity that appears to confer meaning on genocide and with which it is emotionally hard to argue. The *Sonderkommando* at Auschwitz (in this context, camp inmates responsible for the disposal of murdered bodies) display, she notes, a remarkable "*ésprit de corps*" particular to groups of men, and in so doing sustain their humanity in the midst of unthinkable inhumanity: "Fifty is a good number for a work group, large enough to accommodate individual quirks, small enough for the development of *ésprit de corps,* especially if the teams are male, the work physical, the bosses reasonably benevolent, and there are other teams with whom to compete."[61] Clendinnen keeps the narrative flat in order, presumably, to emphasize how the grotesque cruelty of death-camp labor was normalized. Thus, she claims, for the *Sonderkommando*, "outside working hours, the living was easy," since the men were materially better off than their starving comrades although they suffered from "acute nervous depression."[62]

Yet the narrative is not, after all, designed to effectively and quietly showcase this grotesque normalization of horror, but to infuse it with some sort of "normal" meaning, to render the inhuman surprisingly humane and thus to give the monstrous a human dimension. She invokes Primo Levi's angry response to a survivor's account of an impromptu football match between the SS and the *Sonderkommando* at Auschwitz—Levi "heard the echo of 'Satanic laughter' in this game played 'as if on a village green and not at the gates of hell.'" She goes on: "We can see what he means, and why he feels it. It is possible, however, to read the game differently—as men allowed to recognize each other, however briefly, as fellow humans. Both teams knew that at some unspecified time in the future one would eliminate the other, but in Auschwitz the future had little reality."[63]

Here again we perceive a surreal disjunction between "normal" human feeling and the monstrosity of knowing that "one team would eliminate the other." As we read, we begin to realize that Clendinnen's highlighting of this disjunction is not really intended to convey the extreme, uncanny, ungraspable violation of humanity in something as apparently banal as a football match, but to depict camp life finally in meaningful terms commensurate with some sort of redemptive humanness. This desire to salvage human feeling and thus humanity itself from the wreckage of human relations that was Auschwitz, the desire that the "team spirit" triumph over anti-Semitism, appears throughout the book, over and over. Clendinnen recognizes the importance of making us aware that in spite of these moments, the SS was in control:

> Preposterous as it must sound Müller's account suggests that until the general reorganization of May 1944 the majority of SS men working with the *Sonderkommando* at Birkenau did not conduct themselves as virulent anti-Semites to the Jews who worked with them. I do not want to exaggerate the ease of relations, to deny the vileness of the men's tasks, or to minimize their absolute vulnerability before their masters.[64]

My point is not that some SS men were capable of occasional acts of humanity but rather to question the investment in and the consequences of focusing on these acts over and above the context in which they took place. Indeed, this narrative is finally about the triumph of humanity against overwhelming odds, for Clendinnen not only insists on the unexpected "fellow human" feeling emerging in the *Sonderkommando*'s relation with the SS, but on the towering humanity of the victims more generally, who nobly suffer their surroundings.[65] The victims not only play football with the SS, they also look straight into hell without losing their composure, and they carry the most profound and wrenching knowledge humbly and discreetly.

This knowledge of man's incomprehensible inhumanity to man thus manifests itself as a moral lesson about humanity's quiet heroism in the face of extreme cruelty. Our inability to account for why human beings do unspeakable things to others is rewritten as a tale in which humanity's extraordinary resilience triumphs over adversity because the victims behaved and died with dignity, and perpetrators often acted humanely. Our inability finally to know the perpetrators' motives, and thus the incomprehensibility of the Holocaust itself, appears as a tragic form of knowing embedded in the agonizing eloquence of the victim's sacrifices great and small—knowledge both lost and found, dying with the victims and redeemed as a morality tale. The perpetrators' motives thus appear as a minor part of the story much in the same way that "pathological anti-Semitism" finally seems incidental, the exception rather than the rule. Looking straight at the perpetrators thus becomes a tale of humanity's triumph over adversity that gives meaning to the event and transports the victims, intact, to a secular heaven—the family of man. Clendinnen makes two apparently different but necessarily related strains of argument: she provocatively normalizes and banalizes death-camp work and benignly describes SS murderers as grudgingly paternal "bosses"; she treats their anti-Semitism as pathological, as something absolutely in contrast to the human relations that are, for example, sustained in SS-*Sonderkommando* relations. In the end, however, the tension between these two strains of argument is not sustained (one thinks, for example of Tadeusz Borowski's irony)[66] but resolved by transforming the incomprehensible "pathology" of Auschwitz into a story of secular redemption. Indeed the motive behind mass murder is so unspeakable that its recognition is not only "blocked at the level of self-awareness" but appears to be wholly beyond the author's conscious grasp: numbing, shock, and nonrecognition themselves undergo a process of sublimation and thus repression, appearing in altered form in a comforting, familiar narrative about humanity's triumph over adversity.

This book oddly fuses the images of victim and historian by way of a charged identification in which the victims see for the historian but suffer for their knowledge in a way she does not and cannot. Indeed, she allegorizes History as the humble, sacrificial visionary who gives up her (psychic) comfort in the interest of a greater good, who flinches before that which she cannot abide but goes on looking anyway: for historians "are the foot soldiers in the slow business of understanding our species better, and thereby extending the role of reason and humanity in human affairs."[67] Historians thus ideally follow (her construction of) victims' example: Is this not what looking into terror straight on and moving beyond bafflement is really about? This gloriously redemptive tale thus constructs such an idealized and ideologically constrained image of what it means to be a dignified human being in the face of incomprehensible tragedy that the eloquence with which Clendinnen sees beauty in the context of ruined and dying bodies appears as an investment in redeeming such experiences at the cost of understanding them. The moral rhetoric of dignity and the religious rhetoric of sacrifice merge imperceptibly, for this particular restoration of dignity to victims reinterprets tragically shortened lives as secular sacrifices—they died so that we might know—and envisions only extraordinary courage and eloquence where there is also terror.[68] In short, however good her intentions—and it is, again, hard not to feel that any celebration of humanity's great and small triumphs against the odds must be a good thing—Clendinnen's invocation of dignity is nevertheless insensitive to the uncanniness evident in that banalized and disturbingly pastoralized image of the *Sonderkommando* with *ésprit de corps*. The invocation of humanity in this book limits our ability to assess and analyze the experiences of victims by sending them symbolically to heaven. It is perhaps the odd insistence that Nazi perpetrators must be stared at directly and without flinching as if they were but another band of criminals that leads Clendinnen to conclude that hard as she tried she still could not understand the Holocaust. For in the end, the Nazis are just another bunch of bad guys, some of whom prove to have soft hearts and yet—

and here is where the analysis loses its way—they are also incomprehensible, monstrous, and finally "pathological."

Unlike Clendinnen, Omer Bartov takes the uncanny nature of the Holocaust as his point of departure rather than as an argument to be refuted. Indeed, he agrees with Saul Friedländer's argument that Himmler's Posen speech represents "a redefinition of ethics and decency."[69] Whereas Clendinnen perceived that the perpetrator had to be looked at without flinching, Bartov recognizes the complexity of doing so and seeks instead to understand the historical context within which persons capable of perpetrating such crimes might emerge. How, he asks, "do we come to terms with the realization that it is often people like us who are often the first to join the ranks of those whom we now describe as the scourges of humanity?"[70] As he writes in *Murder in Our Midst,* an earlier collection of essays: "All soldiers who kill in war are motivated, at least in part, by precisely this fear [of death]. . . . We may say that in war many soldiers *discover* the pleasure of killing; some will rebel against that pleasure (and become pacifist); others will yearn to perpetuate it (and become fascist)."[71] For Bartov, war provides the context for this discovery, and the Great War explains how, after 1918, the discovery was given its modern meaning. World War I produced a new individual who represented a "readaptation" to the machine age of the warrior-hero of the past: "The machine had forced the individual back into the mass and it was the machine that enabled him to rise again from the multitude. Paradoxically, precisely by achieving that apparent liberation from mechanization, men rapidly learned how to turn other multitudes, to which they themselves did not belong, into anonymous masses that could this time be physically destroyed without presenting any threat to the perpetrators' sense of individual humanity."[72] This reliance on machines transformed war into a highly technical affair whose leaders were bureaucratic manipulators of machines now often distanced from actual killing. Industrialized warfare thus created a new technocratic elite prepared to wage war, and it de-individuated persons so dramatically that different sides could claim to have been "victimized" by a war whose perpetrators were elusive because they themselves could only be distantly if at all implicated in killing.

This elusiveness is replicated in the structural-functionalist paradigm used by historians of Germany to understand Nazi perpetrators:

The functionalist interpretation ... ended up by drawing a highly de-politicized picture of the Third Reich where no one was actually responsible for, let alone guilty of, anything, since everyone was involved as a smaller or bigger cog in a monstrous, faceless, and ultimately uncontrollable machine. The structure, rather than being the reaction of human agents, was thus presented as having molded and dehumanized the men who worked for it.[73]

Bartov turns to this problem of assigning responsibility to perpetrators in *Mirrors of Destruction*, a later collection of essays that takes up themes merely hinted at in *Murder in Our Midst*, of which it appears to be an extension. In *Murder in Our Midst* Bartov sought to explain why the line between victims and perpetrators blurred after the Great War by reference to the postwar relationship between man and machine. In this other book he focuses again on that compromised boundary in another context: the creation of new enemies that facilitates the appropriation of "victim" status by German and French perpetrators after the Second World War. This book charts the fantasmic creation of enemies and victims in rhetoric that manipulates both categories of meaning in accord with the nation's need to affirm sovereignty or expand borders. Thus, a nation defines inner enemies in order to consolidate its own identity, or it plays "victim" in order to escape responsibility for its actual aggression against others. For example:

The new enemy of postwar Germany, "the Nazi," is ... both everywhere and nowhere. On the one hand, "he" lurks in everyone and, in this sense, can never be ferreted out. On the other hand, "he" is essentially so different from "us" that he can be said never to have existed in the first place in any sense that would be historically meaningful or significant for "us," namely for contemporary Germans. ... Hence "we" cannot be held responsible for "his" misdeeds.[74]

Here Bartov seeks to move beyond the "bafflement" to which Clendinnen refers by locating it within this fundamentally apologist discourse whose terms he applies to a broad temporal and conceptual field, stretching from the interwar period to ethnic cleansing in Bosnia. For in the context of this discourse it is difficult to comprehend the perpetrators among us, or to assign them responsibility, not only because so many were bureaucrats or because the event itself is beyond understanding. It is difficult to assign responsibility because we cannot locate the perpetrators, who have successfully transformed themselves into victims. Most important, by acquiescing in this logic, we have also erased the identity of the victims and thus continue the perpetrators' work by other means. For the perpetrators' power lies in their ability to define the victim in their own terms by transforming him into an enemy and thinking of themselves as the "real" victims. "[R]evolutionary situations are highly fertile breeding ground for fantasies and distorted perceptions," Bartov claims, generating an "enemy . . . whose very persecution would serve to manifest the power and legitimacy of the victimizer, while simultaneously allowing the persecutor to claim the status of the 'true' (past, present, and potentially future) victim." Thus, for example, ideas about Jewish power became increasingly fantastical: Jews were everywhere but invisible contaminants capable of mutating surreptitiously and hiding behind otherwise benign appearances—Germany was "a society of doppelgängers, where each individual might discover in himself an unknown Mr. Hyde or be metamorphosed overnight into a repulsive insect. . . ."[75]

From Bartov's perspective, the perpetrator has successfully rewritten history in the image of his own fantasies, and the loss of boundaries between the identities of perpetrator and victim represents a form of perpetrator psychosis—a fluidity born of efforts to "cope with trauma." "[I]magination and metaphor are crucial in liberating people from the perceived stranglehold of uncontrollable, invincible forces . . . the aftermath of disaster may have fewer devastating psychological and physical consequences for survivors if they can, in turn, victimize their real or imaginary enemies."[76] Moreover, this logic is so ubiquitous that it describes a sort of universalized victimhood— a pattern in which the perpetrator sees himself as victim—that ultimately transcends differences in national contexts and applies to both France and Germany as well as other recent narratives involving ethnic and national conflict, including Palestinians and Israelis, Hutus and Tutsis, Serbian Christians and Bosnian Muslims. Bartov thus defines the fantasy of the "enemy within" both as a "distorted perception" particular to a given context and as so ubiquitous that it shapes the form of all social conflict since the Great War. That is, the enemy within is both the symptom of social crisis *and* it is constitutive of polities in post-1918 regimes of all forms. Everyone wakes up fearful he may metamorphose into an insect, meaning that old models of surface and depth—the benign appearance that masks the monstrous, criminal soul—have given way to a different, terrifying construction of selfhood in which boundaries between the two are difficult to distinguish.

In other words, Bartov associates imagination and metaphor with images of perpetrators overwhelmed by a catastrophe whose power they project onto the victim. Jewish identity thus either inverts characteristics perpetrators attribute to (in this case, male) victims (the Jew is tough and manly, as in Zionist imagery), or internalizes them (the Jew is effeminate, sickly, protean). The victim is thus a projection of the perpetrator's fantasy, and it is the historian's job to restore victims to their proper place in history: "In a world obsessed with defining enemies and making victims, historians should remind those who would listen that there are other ways to view reality."[77] But if fantasies about enemies and victims are so ubiquitous that they appear to be embedded in the very structure of modern polities and are thus indistinct from "normal" perception, if the border between perpetrators and victims is so mutable that perpetrators easily transform themselves into victims, how do we know there are other ways of viewing reality? Where do we locate the victim's reality? Here Bartov focuses on the process by which fantastic, distorted perceptions are so normalized that they seem real to those who possess them and, most potently, he focuses on the difficulty of maintaining an undistorted position "outside" these fantasies, which engulf entire populations.

In contrast to Clendinnen's narrative, perpetrators' distortions were and are so powerful and prevalent—"murder," Bartov writes, "is in our midst"—and the idea of humanity so fragile that it is never a question of normalizing perpetrators but rather of understanding how to hold onto reality. In this account, perpetrators are abundantly human precisely by virtue of their very distorted, defensive response to perceived threats to identity, but the question of their "normality" is neither here nor there, since they are and are not so clearly "normal." Bartov contrasts the perpetrators' distorted fantasy world with the writings of victims (Holocaust survivors in particular) that counter the perpetrators' fantasies with the suffering of real victims. He recasts victims' suffering as a lesson, not about human resilience and nobility but about human frailty and the fragility of human dignity. His assertion that "our own time, too, contains gaping black holes" might be interpreted to signify both what the historian cannot really know in the sense of empirical knowledge but nevertheless must convey: the "fragility and precariousness of the idea of humanity and the need to preserve it with utmost care. . . ."[78] The lesson of the Holocaust, he remarks, glossing Alain Finkielkraut, is that the very ideal of humanity and human dignity is mortal. The historian's struggle to "provide a picture of the past as a model for the future," and thus to determine "what will be remembered and what will recede forever into oblivion" is then above all a struggle to keep the ideal of human dignity alive once living witnesses to crimes against humanity have perished. Human dignity stands in for what we cannot know about the victims, and it links us to one another such that "their" murder is not only a distant memory but is also present in our lives as it was in theirs.

Bartov thus insists that perpetrators' fantasies constitute the distorting mirrors through which enemies are defined and through which, indeed, much of "modern identity" is refracted; he also draws a boundary between the perpetrators' fantasmic victimization and the sufferings of real victims, and in so doing, emphasizes the "distortion" intrinsic in perpetrators' perceptions of victims and tries to contrast them to reality. Bartov's book thus treats the mutable boundaries between enemies and victims proper to the Great War, the Holocaust, and postwar national conflicts as (distorting) mirrors in which we "see ourselves," and it claims that there are other, more truthful ways of seeing. Yet Bartov explains modern genocide and modern identity finally in terms of a distortion so generalized that in the end it is virtually impossible to preserve undistorted truth and thus the normative division between fraudulent and actual victims. He does so finally by transfiguring the suffering of specific victims (those survivors to whom he refers again and again) into universal suffering humanity: he generates an agonized identification with their suffering, a longing that victims had not suffered, and thus invokes in us a commitment to the idea that humanity should not suffer ever again. That is, in this world where perpetrators have so successfully turned themselves into victims, the suffering of real victims is only audible as we read the memoirs over and over, and again at the memorial service, as we remember the horror of things past and dream of a future in which good triumphs over evil. Unable to normalize perpetrators but having so generalized their fantasies that they are (conceptually if not literally) inescapable, Bartov does not, in marked contrast to Clendinnen, sublimate the unspeakable shock of victims' reality into a tale of secular sacrifice, but tells it as a story about humanity's *unfulfilled* potential to do good.[79] Thus this history of how the sociocultural dislocation wrought by war shaped modern identity is also a drama of tragic longing. In this bleak world it is only a constantly renewed identification with victims' suffering that confronts distortion and stands in for the specific suffering of different people at precise times and places.

The historian in both Clendinnen's and Bartov's very different works fuses symbolically with victims and yet is also always a proxy (recall that Clendinnen sees through their eyes), guarding against an over-identification in which the historian would take the victim's place. At the same time, the figure of the historian in these texts represents a relation between past and present either as tragic redemption, the frailty of civic virtue, or the need to be forever vigilant. The violation of human dignity appears as the necessity of restoring dignity; the destruction of moral community achieved by the Nazis is conveyed as a challenge to us to make the right moral choices. What we cannot know about the victims' reality (those "gaping black holes" to which Bartov refers), Bartov and Clendinnen in different ways recast as a tragic knowing: we are too late. This shattering but nevertheless necessary and safe—because temporally and emotionally deferred—identification with the victims' suffering shocks and agonizes but, I would argue, never numbs: it simultaneously represents shattered and restored dignity and makes an otherwise meaningless loss of life meaningful by giving us a role to play in the here and now, for, to recall Bartov once more: "we must know that the killing goes on, and even if we are safe from it today, we may become its victims tomorrow. This is not a memory, not even a history, for the murder is in our midst and our passivity is our nemesis." Or, as one writer remarked, Clendinnen's work is so powerful and important because it "links collective memory—a disciplined and critical remembering—to the production of civic virtue here and now, and to the proper and vigilant exercise of choice."[80] Too much proximity to the victims, too much horror and thus too much numbness—the exhaustion of empathy—is always mediated by our ability to act in the present, and it is the historian who implores us, who carries the weight of tragic knowing and conveys it to us.

This powerful restorative mission imperceptibly defines discussions of what good history is as well as the mission of historical scholarship. In order to mobilize empathic identification, the historian renders the victims' deaths meaningful in the end by turning them into symbols of universal suffering and thus the Holocaust into a metaphor for evil.[81] In the process the particular suffering of the victim is both absorbed into the shattering experience of universal victimhood (in this case they happen to be Jewish, but they could be others and perhaps you) and experienced as the reader's shame, which increases in proportion to the victims' innocence: Bartov, sensitive to the specific question of Jewish identity and suffering, forges that identification through his moving calls to action on behalf of all victims in all times and places, and Clendinnen does so in her troubling transformation of the *Sonderkommando* into a pastoral image of "laboring men," and thus through the problematic construction not only of innocent, but of "noble," "tragic" humanity.

These narrative strategies are moving and defend against numbness, whether in the form of voyeuristic pleasure or emotional deadening, because the historian rhetorically sustains our intense but sufficiently distant identification with victims—though as I have argued, Bartov is ultimately far more successful in achieving an accurate portrayal of victims. In this sense such history is the opposite of Goldhagen's work, which was perceived to be all numbing in the form of excessive emotionalism and moralism. The commitment to human dignity and empathy that motivates many historical accounts and in the name of which we are implicitly exhorted to remember, necessarily repeats the elation and anxiety present in the historian's relationship to the suffering he or she studies—the elation attached to being a guardian of memory, the anxiety produced by the responsibility for lives, deaths, and suffering, but now does so in a way that tempers Goldhagen-like emotionalism in favor of a charged but tempered empathy. At the same time, the vigilance and even action in the name of humanity to which we, the readers, are spurred, this agonized but also deferred identification with a "common humanity," must be necessary compensation for the persistent shattering of that commonality again and again.[82] This identification defends against numbness by mobilizing an identification with a normative ideal of humanity to which (in Clendinnen) few victims actually live up or which potentially (in Bartov) must be necessary compensation for humanity's real frailty.[83] Both are complex defensive functions in relation to traumatic material.

In conclusion, efforts to draw on dignity and empathy are not necessarily bound to fail, for not all efforts to interpret the Holocaust historically, ethically, or psychologically, as Bartov's work demonstrates, prove to be facile forms of redemption that seek "humanity" where normative frameworks for ethical, humane action have been utterly destroyed.[84] We might seek to analyze which narrative strategies are more effective or more problematic than others and insist on reworking such concepts to make historical explanation as well as an identification with victims possible (through, for example, a deferred connection that defends against self-shattering or over-identification). It is, of course, difficult to avoid the self-indulgent nostalgia for a past in which "we" would have made different choices. These accounts of the Holocaust try to grasp the ordinariness of monstrosity but must ultimately fail, whether via the (defensive) refusal to grant monstrosity sufficient conceptual development or by (the equally defensive) granting monstrosity so much power to shape our world that we are left merely to long for a better one. The goal of making us long for a world in which genocide would not occur is thus remarkably elusive, weighted with too much confidence or resigned hopefulness, both of which turn out to be different forms of anxiety. Though defenses against anxiety must be part of any historical narrative about mass murder, I've tried to suggest here that we should nevertheless be suspect of works that make us too comfortable, and explore in more depth our responses to works that make us squirm.

CHAPTER THREE

Indifference and the Language
of Victimization

Amnesty International informs human rights workers that "Many people make a conscious effort to not know some of what is happening in the world so they will not be forced to make moral choices. These people hesitate or refuse to confront the personal consequences of social injustice or the violation of fundamental rights of various kinds, believing it is best to remain ignorant or keep silent."[1] In an essay on human rights, Michael Ignatieff writes: "The history immediately antecedent to the Universal Declaration of Human Rights provides abundant evidence of the natural indifference of human beings. The Holocaust showed up the terrible insufficiency of all the supposedly natural human attributes of pity and care in situations where these duties were no longer enforced by law."[2] In his study of victims' claims for restitution, Elazar Barkan argues that although international morality has expanded dramatically since 1945, empathy is never automatic and depends increasingly on how one makes one's case and who is willing to listen.[3] British political theorist John Keane simply tells us that "empathy with the violated happens, but no one knows how, why, or for how long."[4] And I've noted that many Enlightenment thinkers conceived indifference to (literally or symbolically) distant others as a normal human response.

At the same time, this response is considered as ethically irresponsible as it is normal. After all, the role of the Amnesty volunteer is to persuade people that they have a moral obligation not to hide their heads in the sand, and while no one quite understands empathy, everyone agrees that it should be cultivated and that—Michael Ignatieff has spent a career fostering the idea—we ignore suffering others at the cost of our own humanity. As these examples make clear, the tension between our "natural indifference" and the ideal of empathy is manifest in both the real and rhetorical struggle *against* indifference, and is most obvious in the emotionally forceful if now standardized calls for eternal vigilance against discrimination, violence, and persecution.

Student rebels, intellectuals, and humanitarian organizations since the 1960s have perpetually paraphrased and adapted German Protestant Pastor Martin Niemöller's lines about the consequences of turning the other way during the Third Reich—first they came for the communists and I did nothing, then they arrested trade unionists and I looked the other way, then they hunted Jews and I did nothing, and then when they came for me there was no one left to help out.[5] These lines may now seem overly familiar, even self-evident, but their invocation actually represents a pretty recent and dramatic shift in the construction of responsibility for crimes against humanity, in particular away from the perpetrator-victim dyad to a special emphasis on prospective or potential "bystanders"—distant observers or passive eyewitnesses to crimes against humanity, whether persons or policymakers. Thus calls for vigilance against indifference assume, as does Amnesty's pamphlet, a "we" prone to avoidance who must be reminded of the cost of ignorance again and again.

The new preeminence of "bystanders" first developed as a self-conscious discourse about collective social responsibility in the 1960s, though the reasons for its emergence are beyond the scope of this chapter. It is surely related, among other things, to the recognition, some decades after the Holocaust and in the midst of the Vietnam War, that citizens of democratic nations had a responsibility to prevent injustice being perpetrated in their name. It's worth noting that Niemöller's words became particularly famous during the period of protest against the U.S. debacle in Vietnam, and that young German students rebelled against parental authority both by identifying with and feeling shamed by Jewish suffering.[6] Indeed, this rhetoric is now so pervasive that it can be found in a wide variety of sources as well as in phrases so self-evident that their sources need not be remembered or their meaning elaborated: after all, when Omer Bartov claims that "murder is in our midst"[7] in the title of a book grappling mostly with the legacy of industrial murder, we know exactly what he means, as we do when we hear that "we are all German Jews" (as French students cried in the mid-1960s to protest against the expulsion of their Jewish student leader Daniel Cohn-Bendit)[8] or even, as Le Monde's headline bellowed two days after the September 11, 2001 attacks on the World Trade Center in New York, "We Are All Americans."[9]

Here, however, I want to focus on how the rhetoric of "we are all potential victims" by definition expresses not the voices of victims themselves but manifests a collective "we" or "us" redefining values and priorities to take account of victims' voices in new ways.[10] This construction of collective responsibility for crimes against humanity thus incorporates the reality of past indifference and the presumption of our potentially indifferent future behavior toward victims into the struggle against the violation of others. In other words, it places bystanders—the once and now potentially indifferent "we"—and their responsibility to act at the center of the fight against injustice and, in so doing, stresses collective responsibility for those crimes committed in one's name (the Nazi struggle for the "German people," the American defense of "freedom" in Vietnam, the struggle to maintain "French civilization" in Algeria, and so forth). Thus the terms of this struggle extend moral responsibility for crimes against humanity to humanity as a whole.

But this rhetoric also represents another dimension of that recently diagnosed precariousness of empathy, this time embedded in a narrative of empathic identification rather than its failure—hence my references to Amnesty's and others' familiar efforts to teach us to be morally accountable while acknowledging that taking on such responsibility goes against the grain of our generally indifferent natures. By emphasizing the potential fragility of empathy at the heart of this narrative of global empathic identification, I do not mean to say that its 1960s proponents were in bad faith or manifested false consciousness—to the contrary, they created a new form of collective responsibility that is of central importance for humanitarian thought and action. In civil rights struggles in the United States, for example, many who were not themselves the targets of racist discrimination refused to be bystanders. The history of Black-Jewish relations in the United States and the French Jewish philosopher Alain Finkielkraut's ambivalent feelings about French students' identification with German Jews show that this rhetorical strategy was fraught for minority groups, and that it was but one strategy, however predominant, of overcoming indifference.[11]

Though these phenomena must be taken into account, I nevertheless wish to explore the surprising rhetorical effects of the substitution of "we" for "them," of bystanders for victims and perpetrators, both grammatically and conceptually, from the objective "them" to the subjective "we." In what follows I explore the effects of this rhetoric by analyzing how historiographical discussions of bystander indifference during the Holocaust may themselves substitute "we" for "them" and with what consequences. I try to show that in this literature the fantasmic, retrospective identification with suffering humanity from the bystander's perspective may blur victims' identities in its effort to underscore their anguish, and may be an unwitting defensive strategy against numbness.

This blurring of victim identity is distinct from (though it often seems continuous with) other discourses prevalent until the early to mid 1960s in which victims' identities also slipped out of focus. This narrative is thus different from the more carefully cultivated confusion of Jewish victims with other victims of Nazi terror by Allied and Communist governments, resistance groups, and others, including passive civilian bystanders, for reasons deemed legally, politically, or culturally necessary: the need to secure conviction of Nazis at the Nuremberg trial by rendering all humanity symbolically the victim of Nazi crimes; the U.S. strategy of rebuilding West Germany as a bulwark against the Soviet Union during the Cold War (so that German postwar reintegration was accompanied by relative silence about Nazi crimes); the Soviet Union's own interest in forging a universal, heroic memory of war, martyrdom, and Communist resistance (so that the antifascist struggle took precedence over Jewish suffering); the effort, in postwar France, to shape a national memory of heroism under occupation, which led to an emphasis on French valor over the facts of collaboration; and in postwar Italy, the need to forget national complicity, humiliation, and defeat. Finally, U.S. and British self-portraits as morally righteous "liberators" glossed over their relative negligence of Jewish persecution during the war.[12]

The narrative on which I want to focus is also distinct from those accounts that have a similarly confusing but far more apologetic purpose in which perpetrators have often transformed themselves into victims, whether the German postwar reconstruction of their national identity as Hitler's "victims,"[13] Austria's identity as Hitler's first victim, formalized by the Allies' 1943 Moscow Declaration, or Italian fascist POWs' sense of themselves as equally if not more victimized by Nazis than Jews—a hardly exhaustive list. And it comes closer to but finally avoids the difficult question, posed most forcefully in studies of Poland, Ukraine, and Japan, of how victims can also be victimizers.[14]

Instead, much of the historical scholarship on bystanders to which I will refer replaces the victim-perpetrator dyad, however blurred its boundaries, with a fantasmic "we" of common humanity figured variously as powerless, numbed, or passively complicit witnesses to suffering they did not themselves directly cause. I argue that this work affirms human solidarity *retrospectively* in a lesson about the consequences of human frailty: this is what happened, this is what was not done to prevent it, and this is what "we," frail humanity, must make sure does not happen in the future.[15] It affirms human solidarity not—as historian Michael Geyer has argued so persuasively about the historiography on the German resistance to Hitler—by making "whole what had fallen apart in life."[16] The historiography on bystanders does not "bec[o]me the posthumous act of inventing communities [and] creating fictitious solidarities,"[17] but mostly defers redemption to a future when lessons will have been learned. Thus this historiography generally replaces the real failure of human solidarity and its consequences with "our" human frailty and, however unwittingly, blots out victims' experiences (whatever those might have been) in its very effort to move us to tears.[18]

In the now famous exchange of letters between historians Saul Friedländer and Martin Broszat about the particular difficulty of writing the history of National Socialism, Broszat declared:

> The ease with which the centrality of the "Final Solution" was carried out became a possibility because the fate of the Jews constituted a little-noticed matter of secondary importance for the majority of Germans during the war; and because for the allied enemies of Germany, it was likewise only one among a multitude of problems they had to deal with during the war, and by no means the most important one.[19]

Historical work has begun to nuance the rather astonishing notion that the German population did not notice and cared little about what was happening to their Jewish neighbors, a point that Friedländer, in his response to Broszat, contests. Indeed, beginning in the 1970s and early 1980s historians used memoirs, diaries, and as yet unmined archival material on popular opinion, including polls taken by the regime, reports filtered to the SPD press in exile (Sopade), and records compiled by the Gestapo and the SD, the Security Service of the SS, to complicate analyses of the German response to Nazi policies, especially concerning the "Jewish question."[20] They ceased to emphasize the monolithic nature of Nazi terror, which tends to exculpate the fearful non-Jewish population, and began to document the multidimensional response to Nazi policies, including local variations in support for the regime, resentment of excessive indoctrination, conflicts over the state's policies toward the "euthanasia" of the mentally ill and disabled, resistance to Nazi anti-church attitudes, and even some disapproval of pogroms against Jews. This approach began to move narratives of victims and perpetrators beyond abstract invocations of "the Germans" or "the German people" to more particular accounts of perpetration and responsibility. In the end, however, most of these works concluded that despite diverse views, a majority of Germans were "indifferent" to the fate of the Jews.[21] Thus Marlis Steinert wrote that regardless of the diversity of opinion in Nazi Germany, "Given all this discrimination and the beginnings of 'evacuation' . . . the average German's lack of reaction and general indifference towards his Jewish neighbors is conspicuous, especially if one recalls the emotions and unrest produced by the crucifix campaign, the expulsion of monastic brethren, and above all, euthanasia."[22] In his 1983 study of "nonconformist, dissenting strands of" popular opinion in Bavaria that devoted a chapter to what Germans know about the fate of Jews, Ian Kershaw concluded, "Most people in fact probably thought little and asked less about what was happening to the Jews in the East. The Jews were out of sight and literally out of mind for most."[23] Even Sarah Gordon's 1984 study of anti-Semitism conceded: "Apparently anti-Semites and determined opponents of anti-Semitism were polarized around an indifferent or apathetic majority."[24]

Increasingly, most historians concur—albeit with different levels of intensity—that while diverse groups of Germans didn't know all the details, they knew generally what was happening to Jews as well as to other persecuted groups and may best be described as having tacitly consented to Nazi policies.[25] In keeping with this interpretation, they focus even more self-consciously on how bystanders were never merely indifferent but often ambivalent, sometimes complicit, occasionally heroic and mostly not.[26] Otto Dov Kulka and Aron Rodrigue write that the "term 'indifference' may be more confusing than helpful," and argue that "what was actually reported to the regime should not be understood to be 'indifference' but as an attitude that might best be characterized as passive complicity."[27] David Bankier asserts that one can't assume that Germans were indifferent, for "there is conclusive evidence that on the whole the population consented to attacks on Jews as long as these neither damaged non-Jews nor harmed the reputation of the country, particularly its reputation abroad."[28] Nathan Stoltzfus, in an analysis of why intermarried German Jews generally survived the war, states bluntly that the evidence of spouses' solidarity with their German partners "suggests that the regime's ideology might never have developed into genocide had the German people not achieved for the regime the social and economic isolation of the Jews, a prerequisite for their deportation and murder."[29] Here Stoltzfus most explicitly holds "the German people"—an empty category, but nonetheless rhetorically effective—responsible for the Nazis' ability to carry out mass murder, if only by reference to what those few willing to protest had managed to accomplish.

In spite of Kulka's criticism of the concept "indifference" itself, the word and all its synonyms—apathy, resignation, complicity, self-centeredness, and so on—still describe the general population's response to the persecution of Jews, but in many works a more nuanced version of "indifference"—as passive or tacit complicity—is now the beginning rather than the end of the story. Robert Gellately claims: "What is at issue is no longer whether or not Germans knew about the camps, but rather what kind of knowledge they had and how it was conveyed,"[30] meaning that the population may have been indifferent, but that indifference must be explained as well as asserted. Of course, none of this literature aims to diminish the extent of the terror that permeated civil society, and all of it credits those Germans who helped victims of the Nazis in ways great and small. But in order to understand how the population came to consent to murderous policies, historians now explore the dynamics between state and society central to consensus building, and thus focus on how the regime courted and sought to manipulate popular opinion, the manufacturing of the "Hitler cult," and how the population in turn sustained, aided, and abetted the regime and its violence in various ways.

The state engaged in anti-Semitic indoctrination in the army, the police, and among the general public, in the latter by subtly minimizing the viciousness of its anti-Semitic and other racist fantasies and intentions. Nazi Party propaganda deliberately sought to detach Hitler's image from the brutal violence of Nazi thugs, used his cult-like status as the nation's supreme leader to attract and consolidate popular support in spite of often contradictory political positions expressed by Nazis themselves, and planned boycotts and pogroms in such a way as to offer acceptable if not always persuasive explanations of violence against Jews.[31] It also presented a theatrical and spectacular image of unanimity in rallies and parades whose popularity waxed and waned.[32] Indeed, the regime monitored public opinion so carefully that historians have claimed that the Nazis sought to normalize the dramatic measures they initiated against Jews: they introduced policies gradually, avoided persecuting those populations with closer ties to "average" non-Jewish Germans, such as intermarried Jews (mostly Jewish women married to non-Jewish men), shrouded the murder of the disabled in secrecy, and kept the public as isolated from the foreign press as possible.[33] They cultivated the "gradual habituation"[34] of the population to brutal and bloody policies. Thus the public got "used to" the violence around them, displayed "sullen apathy and resigned acceptance," and developed "dulled" senses.[35]

In spite of local variations in attitudes to the regime, the Nazis garnered support from vast segments of the population. They received support from Germans who gave Hitler credit for the economic recovery and ignored or endorsed the violence and persecution that accompanied it. Indeed, many Germans supported the concentration camps in their midst because the regime presented them as an effective antidote to lawlessness. Before the war, there was ample and open evidence both of concentration camps and their severity in newspapers and magazines, where the regime advertised its struggle against "enemies of the people."[36] As camps mushroomed all over Germany after the war began, they became integrated into German society in many regions, and most ordinary people could not help but see inmates at hard labor or paraded through their villages on their way to factories, construction sites, or bomb-clearance duty.[37]

The notorious concentration camp Mauthausen, in annexed Austria, was only three miles from the center of a town, and residents often witnessed beatings and shootings. In Gordon Horwitz's account of the necessarily permeable relations between the camp and the townspeople, he quotes a farmer saying, "I myself saw countless times how inmates were mistreated. I also saw how inmates were shot." But, he continued, "All the SS officers . . . bought milk at my place." Horwitz concludes that town residents were "cognizant of the terror in the camp [but] they learned to walk a narrow line between unavoidable awareness and prudent disregard."[38] Similarly, Ian Kershaw and many others have claimed that after the war began, people had access to information about mass shootings of Jews and other atrocities against Jews in the East in spite of the regime's efforts to hide its must murderous dimensions. Kershaw concedes that "there is incontrovertible evidence that knowledge of atrocities and mass shootings of Jews in the east was fairly widespread, mostly in the nature of rumor brought home by soldiers on leave."[39]

The general population also seems to have greeted the Nazi persecution of groups including not only Jews but homosexuals, Communists, habitual criminals, and later Roma and Sinti ("gypsies") and Poles with relative indifference and even enthusiasm, for many believed it to be part of a positive campaign of moral purification to regenerate the national body. Others simply didn't care about the treatment of such social "outsiders" as long as they were not themselves affected by it.[40] In any case, we've seen that the Nazis were far more careful about violence directed at groups with ties to the "ordinary" German population, whereas Jews, Roma, criminals, and homosexuals—either because they were isolated sub-groups or aroused little sympathy—could be treated with relative impunity, especially after the war began. Indeed, even among the so-called general population, the regime was dependent on local populations who denounced their Jewish and non-Jewish neighbors for infractions of the law.[41]

In yet another important interpretation of public attitudes, many historians explain ordinary Germans' seeming complicity in the regime's persecution of Jews and others not only in socioeconomic and political but also in psychological terms—the German population welcomed anti-Semitic measures and did not generally oppose attacks on Jews and yet also did not want to know these things, says Israeli historian David Bankier, or what was worse, it did not want to know what it actually knew because "knowledge generated guilt."[42] He continues, "This deliberate escape into privacy and ignorance did not save the public from being aware of the Third Reich's criminality."[43] We've seen that Ian Kershaw insists that the Germans were really indifferent to the fate of the Jews because they were just getting on with their lives, but he too indulges the psychological explanation that "there was, it seems clear, much deliberate or subliminal exclusion of the treatment of the Jews from popular consciousness—a more or less studied lack of interest or cultivated disinterest, going hand in hand with an accentuated 'retreat into the private sphere' and increased self-centeredness in difficult and worrying wartime conditions."[44] Ulrich Herbert argues that many ordinary Germans banished politics to areas beyond their awareness and retreated to private lives in order to live and to survive.[45] Even the expatriate writer W. G. Sebald speaks of how Germans' postwar shame at their indifferent response to the Jewish plight under Hitler led not, as one might expect by gleaning the surface, to more sensitivity to anti-Semitism but to more "indifference."[46] Knowledge generates guilt, which generates repression.

Another version of this "retreat" is that intensified Nazi brutality shocked most Germans into self-protective indifference. They were not particularly receptive to anti-Semitism and drew the line at explicit violence against Jews, but the "continual propaganda" and "terror" nevertheless gradually generated distance between Jews and non-Jews.[47] Or, in Sarah Gordon's account, legalized anti-Semitism was "acceptable to many, probably a majority of Germans," but "the physical violence and brutality of *Kristallnacht* were clearly rejected by the same majority" (though other historians have argued that the revulsion against violence had less to do with sympathy for the Jews than with a dislike of disorder).[48] Kershaw sums up mainstream response to the pogrom as "Anti-Semitism,—o.k., but not like that," and in the end claimed that *Kristallnacht* extended Germans' indifference toward the fate of the Jews.[49]

Finally—though I've only covered the most well-known accounts—the eminent German Holocaust historian Hans Mommsen shares these notions that Germans who did not want to know found ways of avoiding knowledge.[50] He also insists that the Germans "shared certain prejudices against Jews but would not support direct action against them and did not show any interest in their persecution."[51] Indifference, he claims, was not really evidence of anti-Semitic bias but of an authoritarian mentality that determined subservience to the State. Moreover, those who were enriched by the expropriation of Jewish property necessarily repressed or simply did not care about the fate of the Jews from whose persecution they profited. But for the "bulk of those citizens who took an indifferent attitude to the 'Jewish question,' it was psychologically difficult to give the rumors of mass executions and the threats in the Nazi press too much weight."[52]

Much of the scholarship thus renders so-called indifference the product of a complex variety of local and national concerns and the symptom of a slow but steady emergence of tacit consent with the regime, reinforced by Hitler's economic triumphs on the one hand and the increasing dehumanization—gradual expropriation, segregation, and total isolation—of the Jewish minority on the other. Moreover, it is crucial to remember that all Germans lived under a regime that makes the line between indifference and being terrorized into consensus hard to draw in bold strokes, regardless of the voluminous examples of the general population's complicity and even enthusiasm. Hence historians often use the term "tacit consent," which implies passive complicity rather than indifference or general and active collaboration, or they emphasize a retreat into the private sphere, which also suggests that people were neither simply indifferent nor Nazi enthusiasts.

Yet in spite of this introduction of complexity into questions concerning the role of so-called bystanders, in spite of all this subtle and judicious historical labor that helps us understand the variety of experience masked by any simple reference to indifference, the concept has not been dethroned. By this I mean that most of this work does not give sufficient content to indifference to make it historically meaningful as a phenomenon that transcends commonplace notions of self-interest or self-centeredness, ignorance, envy, resentment, nastiness, or small-town life, all of which in the end add up to "indifference" to the fate of one's neighbors or compatriots short of a really sinister desire to be rid of them. Thus Robert Gellately, in an account of German complicity with Hitler, remarks that "for the most part . . . good citizens did nothing, either out of fear for their own lives, or because they had grown apathetic or indifferent."[53] In a synthetic history of the

Holocaust, Doris Bergen insists clearly that most Germans knew what was happening and were generally complicit: "Many of them stood to gain from the measures it introduced and others were apathetic. What did any of it have to do with them?"[54]

Dov Kulka argues that there are now two different strains of argument in the literature on German public opinion under Nazism, both of which will be familiar. One, in his view the least apologetic, interprets Germans' apparent indifference as a form of tacit consent generated by the "gradual internalization and assimilation of the claims and content" of propaganda against the nation's so-called internal enemies.[55] The other argument to which he refers stresses Germans' self-protective dissociation, the "retreat" into the private sphere in which they chose "not to know." Kulka emphasizes a difference between "passive complicity" which holds Germans accountable because it implies tacit consent, and this other guilty retreat, which involves a tortured refusal to know what you know and suggests profound discomfort and a troubled conscience. But are these responses really so distinct? David Bankier, who argues that most Germans tacitly consented to the regime, also claims that day-to-day contact with indignities toward Jews "dulled people's sensitivity" and that "indifference and apathy" prevailed. He says "these attitudes derive[d] not from concern over everyday needs, but from a diminished capacity to identify with others' suffering. They resulted from conscious decisions."[56] But how does a conscious decision to repress what disturbs you go together with a dulled sensitivity, which implies you are no longer disturbed? Is complicity a form of numbness or is it numbness that finally accounts for complicity? Is the lack of empathy for others' suffering a condition of tacit consent or does tacit consent generate, as others have argued, a lack of empathy, since when no one else seems to be protesting, only particularly heroic and unusual people tend to raise their own voices? In other words, is tacit consent at least partially a symptom of the regime's terror—which all these accounts acknowledge but also take great care to nuance—or is terror aided and abetted by tacit consent?

This chicken-and-egg problem reveals a more profound conceptual one. Tacit consent is certainly not, in any of these arguments, simply separable from indifference, because it's not clear at all what tacit consent to a murderous regime means except by reference to selfishness, self-centeredness, prejudice, repressed powerlessness and fear, and their consequences—the myriad forms of empathic failure to which "indifference" finally refers. Thus passive complicity or tacit consent are not necessarily so distinct from other ways of thinking about indifference, and this conceptual difficulty may explain in part why "indifference," for all that it has been nuanced, remains central to accounts of bystanders' responses to persecution. It may explain why, in spite of Kulka's claim that indifference cannot capture the emotional density of popular attitudes, historians use it again and again.

Perhaps the stubborn persistence of indifference may be attributed to how many of these various arguments about bystander indifference retrospectively naturalize indifference in their effort to understand it historically and thus critically. In order to address finally how it is that the population, however diverse, "consented" to Nazi policies with knowledge of what was happening to victims and with enthusiasm for their "leader" well beyond the coercion that was necessarily part of living under a dictatorship, historians offer numerous responses that render indifference a matter of course: victims are predictably perceived to be "others," prejudice is of course unacceptable but in this case, at least explicable (given Hitler's economic success, traditional anti-Semitism, ideological indoctrination, human nature, psychocultural patterns) in its nonmurderous forms, and indifference is finally a sorry but enduring fact of human relations—whether as a defensive psychic strategy or related to human self-interest. A passionate and powerful analyst of the German population's complicity, Robert Gellately surprisingly concludes that those who fought for the regime until the bitter end "apparently could not afford to let themselves see the situation, including the brutalities, for what they really were, and could do nothing more than be for Hitler or at least for Germany."[57] Thus he implies that finally fanaticism—whether clinging to illusions of a final victory or continuing to advocate the murder of dissidents—was a matter of not seeing what was there, was an illusion to which many clung, and thus a mode of seeing without seeing, rather than of seeing and not caring, perhaps even deriving pleasure from the pain of others. Deborah Dwork and Robert Jan van Pelt throw up their hands and remind us that while some witnesses to Nazi crimes were "convinced anti-Semites," "most people . . . simply did not know what to do." The real difficulty of understanding "indifference" leads them to ask a series of rhetorical questions to get at the motives of "most people": Were they cowards? Did they act out of an "instinct for self-preservation"? Did their imaginations "rebel at grasping" the truth?[58] Indeed, most historians repeat sociologist Milton Mayer's sense that, given human psychology ("men should not be that way but they sometimes are") and people's own material needs, indifference was a natural response to Nazi anti-Semitism and Nazi policies toward social outsiders in general.[59]

At its best the work to which I've referred carefully documents public opinion, the effects of ideological indoctrination, and how Germans weighed the advantages and disadvantages of the regime to explain how they arrived at a consensus with Hitler. In so doing, it seeks to expose the dangers of prejudice and indifference to it. At its most troubling—one thinks back to Broszat's remarks about Jewish suffering being a secondary concern for most Germans—some of this scholarship treats anti-Semitism as a complex, predictable if tragic response to others' suffering. That is, the notion that the fate of the Jews, according to Broszat, was "a little noticed matter" does not treat indifference as a historical problem requiring investigation, but as a particularly sad chapter in the story of man's inhumanity to man, as the inevitable result of tending one's own garden. Such works inadvertently or defensively diminish the impact of bystander anti-Semitism on the Jewish minority.

Though it is impossible to create any absolutely neat divide between sets of historians working on this problem, we might establish an unsteady but coherent one by reference to the way they interpret the fact that Germans knew what was happening to Jews. Thus, as we've seen, some historians seek answers to German complicity by analyzing how the population made political decisions based on what advantages they derived from Hitler's regime regardless of its murderous intentions. Others emphasize that the Nazis targeted groups already marginal or disliked by "law-abiding citizens" and that terror and coercion mostly impacted these populations to which others were indifferent if not hostile. And others underscore a "not wanting to know," a "retreat into the private sphere" based on a decision not to be exposed to things that disrupt everyday life and not to get into trouble. Most if not all of these historians acknowledge the anti-Semitism of the German population and yet, again, indifference—when it is not an actively self-interested decision to profit from the persecution of others—remains a conscious or unconscious mode of self-protection, of "numbing," that lets you get on with your life and even to profit from things you might otherwise find morally objectionable.

Yet another group of historians tends to reject the coherence and stability implied by this "we" that constitutes the indifferent German population and renders anti-Semitism compatible with numbed complicity. They seek to define indifference by reference to the "difference" anti-Semitism necessarily asserts and generates (and by implication, the difference that the ideally expansive "we" erases). But they are also not content to assert somewhat contradictorily that German propaganda made people comfortable with camps even though many who lived near camps knew better than to believe the propaganda. That is, if many Germans really did know— if not necessarily of mass murder by gassing, then certainly that Jews were persecuted and dying in other ways—indifference isn't just a matter of ideological indoctrination or self-protective numbing in the context of a dictatorship. Rather, indifference requires a more complex explanation that takes into account German susceptibility to Nazi propaganda and German knowledge of what was happening. Indifference was not a calculated retreat in one's own self-interest, but a more active form of uncaring; it wasn't a matter of not-knowing, but the difficult-to-comprehend fact that the population actually did know. It wasn't just tacit consent to policies that remained abstract, and brutality that remained out of sight, but support for a regime whose criminality they were well aware of. In other words, while holding carefully to the necessity of historical explanation and documentation, these scholars insist on a dimension of indifference that cannot be explained by reference to self-interest, risk-calculation, or even unconscious (but self-protective) dissociation. If most Germans were not dissociated, if many knew, then indifference cannot be explained only by reference to Hitler's restortion of "normalcy" to a country rent by hyperinflation, unemployment, and street violence. For this explanation begs the question of what a return to normalcy means under conditions in which you know that many people are being denied rights, arrested and sent to concentration camps without trial, and rumors abound that there are bodies shot in the woods.[60] Nor can indifference be explained by a retreat into the private sphere, which itself begs the question not only of what Germans saw when they went shopping, to work, listened to the radio, and avoided and even denounced their Jewish neighbors, but how exactly they "repressed" that knowledge.

These scholars have sought to call a spade a spade without getting themselves tangled up in the tautology that tacit consent generated indifference, or making the assumption that the anti-Semitic attitudes which tolerated or even supported legalized anti-Semitism have little relationship to extralegal actions against Jews (the argument that "Germans drew the line at violence"). In a remarkable study of Jewish life in Germany focused mostly on the period before deportations began, the historian Marion Kaplan questions the usefulness of indifference as a conceptual construct. She argues that the crucial analytical problem presented by German-Jewish relations in Nazi Germany is "how endemic prejudice becomes epidemic, how bigotry turns into massacre. Simply because so many Germans wished for the Jews to disappear does not mean that we can leap to the conclusion that genocide was inevitable in the 1930s."[61]

As Mommsen implies, when an anti-Semitic regime comes into power even if that is not the reason it was elected, it renders anti-Semitism a matter of state policy.[62] But the radical transformation of the state apparatus undertaken to achieve anti-Semitic ends makes our understanding of why and how the population came to consent to those policies all the more significant. Indeed, the frequent references among many historians to the way in which most Germans "drew the line at direct action," whether explicit, as in Mommsen's claims, or implicit, as in references to the general population's disapproval of the Kristallnacht pogrom or to the regime's care not to advertise its most vicious feelings about Jews except to true believers, however true, are problematic. After all, such references to "line-drawing," however unwittingly, cast anti-Semitic prejudice short of outright murder, destruction, and lawlessness as explicable in the context of constrained political, social, and emotional choices, though of course also regrettable. And this peculiar if implicit boundary between explicable and inexplicable prejudice makes it impossible to use investigations of bystander indifference to "examine," as Kaplan puts it, "the meaning of these 'disappearance' wishes for people on both sides of the 'racial' or ethnic divide."[63] She notes that of course not all Germans wished that Jews would disappear or wanted them murdered, but she warns us that we must acknowledge the relationship between explicable anti-Semitism and genocide if we are to begin to examine such wishes.

More in line with Kaplan's point of view, Saul Friedländer asks why we should bother with all the questions about what Germans did or didn't want to know. Basically, they knew, and they didn't care enough to do much about it, whether they were themselves preoccupied or they weren't. As he puts it, "the widespread indifference of the German population does not demand any unusual interpretation. The basic divergence in attitudes toward the members of the community and 'others' suffices."[64] That is, the privilege of non-Jewish Germans makes them blind to Jewish suffering as well as to their own relative fortune; and the gradual social death of Jews before deportation makes anti-Semitism an essentially "Jewish" problem that they as a community or as individuals have to solve with little help from those privileged enough to be "ignorant" of their plight. Friedländer rejects overly complicated, somewhat apologetic notions about Germans' not wanting to know what they knew in favor of a basic and straightforward recognition of the structural difference between majorities and minorities.[65]

Thus Kaplan and Friedländer, among others, not only provide ample evidence that Germans generally "knew," if not all the details, then enough, and stress their passive but often also active complicity and anti-Semitism. Unlike Friedländer, who nuances his assertion delicately with examples of Germans who resisted anti-Jewish measures, Daniel Jonah Goldhagen refers sarcastically to the "indifference" thesis, which he declares "psychologically implausible." He suggests that "pitilessness" would be a more accurate description of German attitudes but also notes that indifference "must be more than a label slapped on the German people" if it is to have any meaning.[66] Philippe Burrin claims that the war's length "buttressed the widespread moral indifference which perhaps was the most effective facilitator of the Final Solution."[67] Raul Hilberg insists that Germans and others mostly did not care about the fate of the Jews with few exceptions.[68] And Bankier, though more ambivalent, insists that "the absence of comment [on the Nuremberg Laws] was not a result of indifference to the Jewish question . . . [but] a silence of tacit consent to the Nazi solution, based on a deep identification with the spirit of the law. . . ."[69]

Though these constructions of indifference don't clarify Kaplan's question about how endemic prejudice becomes epidemic, they have the benefit of being straightforward and confronting German anti-Semitism head-on. At the same time, they naturalize indifference not from the bystander's but from the victim's point of view. Thus while Bankier, Mommsen, Kershaw, and others render bystander indifference an enduring (and therefore naturalized) fact of *human* relations, Kaplan, Friedländer, and others instead naturalize indifference by making it an enduring fact of *Jewish-gentile* relations. Or rather, as Friedländer frames it, indifference results inevitably from the structural blindness of majorities. This latter argument emerges quietly in the absence of any other persuasive empirical explanation about how an entire population consents to the disappearance of a minority in their midst: its advocates assert at once that gentile indifference and thus anti-Semitism is self-evident, and yet, with the exception of Goldhagen, they all recognize that its particular and systematic brutality, especially after the promulgation of the Nuremberg Laws in 1935, remains beyond our grasp.[70]

Thus Kaplan's question, with its profound moral import, remains unresolved because acknowledging German anti-Semitism and its genocidal potential unapologetically cannot explain how it became epidemic any more than rendering indifference an "understandable" response to historical crisis can. Indeed, the failure of Goldhagen's untenable thesis about "eliminationist anti-Semitism" only emphasizes the difficulty of the question, for we know that indifference cannot simply be conflated with or replaced by German murderousness. And Friedländer's stress on the real division between Germans and Jews cannot account for the very complicated process by which this experience of division is constituted and rendered chillingly normal, to paraphrase Friedländer.[71] As such, it can't account for the way in which anti-Semitic prejudice becomes not only explicable or conceivable but also normal and therefore—to the extent normalized prejudice by definition contains genocidal potential—can't examine how wishes for disappearance come to make sense to those who harbor them. It is perhaps no surprise that the historian David Engel, in a recent introduction to the study of the Holocaust, writes that the behavior of non-Jews (here he refers to non-Jewish leaders) toward Jews, complex and varied as it was, "remains a largely unfulfilled task in contemporary Holocaust research."[72]

Tony Kushner, writing of the British response to Nazi Germany at all levels of British society, notes in the context of work on the

Allies that "'indifference' does not do justice to the complexity of popular and policy makers' beliefs. Sympathy, antipathy and, most frequently, ambivalence were present, but all represented a confrontation and interaction with the Jewish disaster: not the lack of interest that indifference suggests."[73] The problem of indifference might be understood, as Kushner and Kaplan (less explicitly) suggest, as a relationship between (in this case) Jews and non-Jews rather than the tendency to hide one's head in the sand, whether by the not-seeing-but-seeing of tacit consent or the not-seeing-but-seeing of self-protective dissociation.[74] For in spite of what Friedländer says about indifference not requiring any unusual interpretation, his own work on Jewish estrangement focuses particularly on the strained interaction between Jews and gentiles. He describes the wrenching everyday life of Jews under Nazis not only as traumatic. Instead, as he demonstrates, the indignities of everyday life were traumatic because they had been normalized. Thus Friedländer begins to challenge both the expansive "we" that naturalizes indifference and the minority "us" for whom indifference is explained by reference to the long history of Jewish difference.

He documents Jews' social death and seeks to link Nazi elites' and German indifference more generally to what he calls "redemptive anti-Semitism." By virtue of his narration, which zigzags back and forth between Jewish and non-Jewish lives, ordinary people and high-level policy-makers, he describes differently than others a complex relationship between a non-Jewish majority and a Jewish minority in which the most horrific treatment of other human beings—including expropriation, dehumanization, and isolation of a minority group—becomes banal and eventually so normal that murder is not entirely out of the question. The desire that Jews disappear is neither unconscious nor the first thing on every non-Jew's mind. Friedländer thus captures how this semiconscious erasure of Jews becomes so deeply embedded in social reality—becomes structural—that no one but Jews notices it, not just because anti-Semitic legislation doesn't affect gentiles or they somehow get "used" to it, but because it comes to make sense, to be part of the way things should be. This argument already begins to define indifference by reference to a series of dynamic psychic operations that current constructions of indifference, from whatever perspective they are asserted, fail to capture.

Reviews have emphasized Friedländer's erudition, powers of synthesis, and analytical focus on "redemptive anti-Semitism" as motivating Nazi attitudes.[75] Friedländer's concept of redemptive anti-Semitism defines a sacralized but secular struggle against Jews that must be fought at all costs to salvage the national body. It is the analytical purpose of his work to get at what accounts for the shift from "traditional" anti-Semitic prejudice to a belief in the necessity of murdering the entire Jewish population. It rests uneasily alongside his stunning portrayal of Jewish estrangement, which arguably comes as close if not closer—albeit by an indirect route—to helping us understand how endemic anti-Semitism becomes epidemic than references to redemptive anti-Semitism. Yet reviewers have addressed this portrait as a remarkable exercise in empathy rather than as an analytical treatment of the relationship between banality and horror, except to note that Friedländer too insists that "the bulk of the population . . . did not object to the disenfranchisement and segregation of the Jews."[76]

In the rest of this chapter I focus on ways in which we might address indifference differently, taking cues from the process I believe Friedländer describes. Here I will ask about indifference by reference to what one anthropologist has called "small wars and invisible genocides."[77] By this phrase, she means the institutionalized forms of everyday violence that normalize the dehumanization of specific groups of people in ways mostly invisible to others: these "small wars" then define the targets of mass atrocity and genocides when and if they occur and bridge a gap between peacetime discrimination and mass murder. Here I want to use the concept of invisible genocides to refer to how persecution, discrimination, and finally murder become invisible to those who are not its targets, even when they take place right in front of them.

In what follows I will try to avoid interpreting anti-Semitic phenomena (the literal and symbolic disappearance of the Jewish minority) and bystander responses to them by reference to the enduring fact of indifference, with the risks of de-historicization and displacement (the rhetorical substitution of "us" for "them," the inevitably eternal division between "us" and "them") such references so often entail. In order to do so, I analyze a representative selection of some famous memoirs and journals by Victor Klemperer, Mihail Sebastian, and Marcel Reich-Ranicki on Jewish-gentile encounters during and after the war. Clearly there are differences between the experiences of assimilated German Jews and others in countries invaded, occupied, or allied with Nazi Germany, and yet most striking is the similarity of obviously privileged German, Romanian, and Polish (bourgeois, literate, polyglot) Jews' accounts of their relations with non-Jews. Naturally, I don't presume to supply some new understanding of Jewish identity or a new theory of indifference. I mean only to use Friedländer as a point of departure to speculate about how we might approach bystander "indifference" in a way that avoids emptying it of its real dynamism as well as its tragic banality. Through a complicated psychic operation that matches their empirical segregation and isolation, assimilated Jews disappeared before they were really deported. Through another equally complex reconstruction of collective responsibility after 1960 with which we are familiar, the same Jews disappear even as they are enfolded into a renewed moral imagination.

Hannah Arendt once noted in reference to European Jews generally: "The deciding forces in the Jews' fateful journey to the storm center of events were without doubt political; but the reactions of society to anti-Semitism and the psychological reflections of the Jewish question in the individual had something to do with the specific cruelty, the organized and calculated assault upon every single individual of Jewish origin, that was already characteristic of the anti-Semitism of the Dreyfus Affair."[78] If we look at indifference from this general perspective, but not in the same psychocultural terms within which it has thus far been conceptualized, we might at least begin to think about its meaning differently. Moreover, doing so from the victim's perspective, as Friedländer and Kaplan do, necessarily renders indifference no longer a passive retreat into the self or simply a form of erasure (though it can be these things too): in other words, we might focus not on distance, but on estranged proximity, not on repressed guilt or envy, with its sense of quiet rage, but (to invoke Friedländer's words again), on a "chilling normality" which captures well the cold reality of lives literally subjected to other people's repressed or newly liberated desires.

Indifference then is not only a blanket of quiescence, as if an entire population had muffled its envy, rage, and guilt, or had been muffled (as it has so often been portrayed). The image of a quiet and numbed population whose precise relationship to the persecution of Jews is otherwise hard to grasp mirrors the imprecision and intangibility of the concept "indifference" when it is used to describe bystanders (since most persecuted Jews experienced the indifference of friends and colleagues as tangible and acute cruelties). This image predominates because many historians have so naturalized indifference, rendering it a static, timeless concept, that it is hard to explain it as a historical rather than natural phenomenon—petty jealousy, self-absorption, self-interest and the like are, after all, references to the "way people are" even as they may also be precise descriptions of how some people behaved. But as Arendt noted, there is some relationship between society's reaction to anti-Semitism and its impact on individuals and the particularly sinister and psychologically complex historical form anti-Semitism took in Western Europe after the Dreyfus Affair. That particular relationship is very difficult to capture, but the concept of indifference as a quiet retreat surely is not up to the task.

In Victor Klemperer's now widely read war-time diaries, one of the most dominant motifs is how much Germans do or don't know about what is happening to Jews and how they interpret what they know.[79] In the earlier years, Klemperer quietly accommodates ignorance and treats anti-Semitism sometimes angrily and sometimes with resignation. He reports many incidents in which Germans prove to be completely unaware of the measures being taken against Jews, including a woman who doesn't realize that Jews are forbidden from hiding the mandatory star, a man who doesn't know that Jews aren't allowed to ride in trams but must walk, and another who has no idea that Jews cannot buy and sell property on the same terms as gentiles.[80] Moreover, the anti-Semitic sentiments he reports mostly involve quietly muttered references to "they"—the presumably rich Jewish businessmen as well as politicians held responsible for the war, the state of the German economy, and sundry other things.[81] Indeed, the entire diary is rich in instances of small cruelties and records the prevalence of everyday anti-Semitism, the methodical brutality of the Nazi leadership, as well as Germans' occasional acts of generosity.

But what prevails in Klemperer's diary is the quiet cruelty manifest in what were (or once appeared to be) "normal" relations with non-Jews, as well the annihilation of German-Jewish selfhood these relations now entail:

"The SS [says Klemperer's acquaintance Richter] is really a force for a civil war." He was appalled—"The swine! The dirty dogs!"—when I told him about our fate; he wanted—I refused—to give me a piece of shaving soap . . . "And yet I must strictly keep my distance from you!"—"Of course, Herr Richter, you have a wife and child, you are quite innocent."—"No one in Germany is innocent. Why have we tolerated this regime for so long?" I told him that I was as certain of a collapse in the not too distant future as he was, only I feared a general pogrom before the debacle. He did not contradict me; he bade me farewell with a kind of emotional solemnity, as if I were departing for the Russian front.[82]

This exchange constitutes and is recorded as a "normal" encounter—it is a conversation in passing in which two Germans exchange opinions about the course of the war and in which both are convinced and pleased that all will soon be lost. It records an act of kindness—the German offers his German-Jewish friend some shaving soap—and an expression of solidarity, since Herr Richter not only calls the SS swine but also declares all of Germany guilty. The conversation, however, is also obviously surreal and characterized by a quasi-comic normalcy.

Richter, after all, speaks to Klemperer with the pity (the gift of shaving soap), regret (we are all guilty), and rage (they are all swine, the dirty dogs) reserved for those dying too young, too cruelly, and perhaps unnecessarily—young men sent off to war. The acknowledgment that Klemperer is a condemned man thus takes the form of a standard dialogue between a dying man and those taking leave of him: of absolution (you are innocent, Herr Richter, as if to say "you did all you could"); solemnity (he did not contradict me when I told him of my fate); and even a dose of compulsively asserted self-protective realism lacking the requisite gravity and politeness but which often can't be helped (I need to take distance), as if Klemperer were dying not of Nazi persecution but of a war wound or a contagious disease doctors might have prevented. Also manifest in the episode is the inevitable discomfort implicit in the imbalance of fortune—between another's sufferings and one's own relative privilege. Thus "our fate" is met with an offer of shaving soap, and at the mention of a possible pogrom, Richter solemnly shuffles off. It is Klemperer, of course, who slyly supplies the metaphor of the soldier going off to the Russian front and who goes along with the ritualized, normalized form in which his own dying is being discussed. But it is also Klemperer who, by virtue of recording this scene in the role of acute observer, renders its "normalcy"not simply banal but finally unimaginably surreal, tragic, and murderous, for Herr Richter appears in the drama as an unlikely though not unwitting executioner who politely regrets his duty but performs it anyway.

In this context, what has been called bystander indifference is hardly a retreat, a refusal to know, or mere unconcern with the fate of a man one doesn't know well, though Richter seems guilty and a bit afraid: instead, indifference represents active complicity with the murderers, for Richter normalizes Klemperer's impending death and thus erases him as a human being and a German citizen. It is not surprising that in the end Klemperer refuses to forgive this sort of performance because he knows that his friends know better. Thus he claims that because some non-Jewish Germans don't see "what might be embarrassing" they are complicit or because they see but pretend not to that they are guilty. ("Is this true not-knowing," Klemperer asks of a group protesting their innocence at the very end of the war, "or has it come into being only now?"). Or finally and most generously, he permits that perhaps some Germans simply could not imagine what was done in their name and labels this failure of imagination "not knowing."[83] In Klemperer's diaries there is no indifference as such: there is generosity and there are small heroic gestures, but mostly there is complicity, there is knowledge, there is moral failure, and there is "not knowing" understood—and remember this is 1945 before Klemperer knows not half of what we know now—as the inability to imagine such crimes. There is then anti-Semitism so normalized that the disappearance of Jews was not out of the question except for those lacking imagination.

Indeed, what stands out in accounts of relations with non-Jews, in Klemperer's and also in others' stories, is not indifference per se but the uncanny banality with which extraordinary cruelty is manifested. In most camp and other memoirs, the brutality of SS men and others aligned with them—whether they were Nazi true believers or not—is unremittingly and predictably brutal. The quality and nature of this cruelty has been the subject of most studies of Nazi anti-Semitism, because its psychic brutality defies imagination—from laws that prohibited Jews from owning pets so they were forced to euthanize beloved dogs and cats to the more well known savagery of shooting squads and death camps. But the quieter cruelty of one's friends and colleagues, teachers and students, is also remarkable, even though it is more easily enfolded into narratives of indifference on the one hand or anti-Semitism on the other—indeed, Kaplan, and Friedländer have most forcefully documented such cruelty using unpublished sources, including memoirs and police files.[84]

In the following scene from the Romanian writer Mihail Sebastian's *Journal* on August 6, 1941, we find, as in Klemperer, the same parodic and yet chilling portrayal of the brutality infusing Jewish-gentile relations. Since Jews have been denied normal medical care, he visits a wealthy gentile friend to ask if she might get him an appointment with a heart specialist:

> The upstairs lounge is red. And everywhere the colors are strong and overpowering. She herself, Marie, was wearing a long dress or wrapper in the same shrieking violet as the armchairs downstairs. . . . She had never seemed so mad, and this time she did not have her old childlike ingenuousness. She is for Pétain and the Germans, against the British, against the Russians, and against the Jews. If the Germans do not win, there will be a total disaster that does not bear thinking about. Anyway, a German victory is certain. Exactly as in a lunatic asylum, where it is forbidden to contradict patients, I kept nodding my head in agreement.[85]

In this conversation between old friends, Marie has no particular consciousness of what a German victory would mean for Sebastian and that she speaks poorly of Jews with a Jew. This scene strikes one as anything but the quiet and colorlessness of indifference, yet it is not a straightforward anti-Semitic erasure, though her narrative is anti-Semitic. Instead, Marie "shrieks" her "indifference" to murder (just that week, indiscriminate round-ups of Jews in Bucharest had Sebastian wondering if the Germans and their Romanian allies were really going to exterminate the Jews), and more incomprehensibly, to the potential murder of an old friend whose literary skills she admires. Thus indifference is difficult to pin down historically not because it is "natural" behavior, but because its expression in this context, as in the scene drawn by Klemperer, is both so straightforward and so hard to grasp, so patently banal—she is just talking to an old friend while helping him out—and so surreal, since she is condemning him to death.

In this scenario Sebastian is not permitted to be himself, meaning Jewish and Romanian. Sebastian can only be identified as a non-Jew, the "we" she enfolds him in when she includes him in her anti-Semitic diatribe, or the Jew who needs help finding a doctor. Marie's indifference to Sebastian's suffering is not only a matter of indifference as we have learned to understand its meaning—of self-interest, unconscious protective ignorance, or guilt avoidance (though perhaps she helps him out to ease her conscience). Nor is it only a manifestation of anti-Semitic cruelty (though she may derive some sadistic gratification from his disenfranchisement). Instead, all these possible speculations about Marie's psyche aside, her anti-Semitic cruelty takes the form of an everyday ritual. In other words, Marie's indifference might instead describe how "lunacy" passes itself off as normal, how a necessarily failed effort to reconcile Sebastian's dual identity as Romanian and Jewish—her fundamental erasure of his life experience—performs itself as chitchat about the course of the war. Marie's cruelty thus lies in her loudly proclaimed matter-of-factness, in the way she discusses the world around them. Anti-Semitism then only looks unusual to the person who is not permitted to be "himself," to him whose distance from the collective "we" is marked by thousands of gestures great and small, conscious and not.

Indifference does not require an unusual interpretation—no fancy psychology or undue complexity—because it is nothing more and nothing less than anti-Semitism. But indifference isn't only anti-Semitism, respectable or vulgar, fashionable cocktail party conversation or unspeakable sentiments kept to oneself. The indifference recorded by both Klemperer and Sebastian more accurately describes how this anti-Semitism manifests itself as a normalized prejudice. Thus it describes not only the sinister anti-Semitism that became so predominant, but also how society assimilated it, learned it, performed it, believed it, and thus came to conceive it and live it as normal.

There is plenty of Nazi cruelty in Marcel Reich-Ranicki's memoirs, as well as a few minor heroes—the teachers who performed the *"Heil Hitler"* with little enthusiasm—and other "dutiful civil servants" who were "no more and no less," and who were generally indifferent and met with indifference.[86] Reich-Ranicki is a Polish-born Jew who goes to Berlin as a child, is sent back to Poland in 1938, and with his wife

Tosia survives the Warsaw Ghetto. They had no children. Most of his family perishes. He returns to Germany from Poland in 1957 after a falling out with the Communist Party, to which he initially credited his salvation from the Germans, and makes an astonishing career for himself as a book critic. Indeed, he becomes the most well-known book critic in Germany.

Ironically, in Reich-Ranicki's account the two cruelest episodes that involve German bystanders occur long after the war: one in 1963, when he goes to a school reunion (for the class of 1938), and another a decade later, when he attends a party to celebrate the publication of a recent biography of Hitler. Though Reich-Ranicki insists rather banally that millions of non-Jews "looked the other way"[87] during the war as Jews were increasingly singled out for persecution, his description of what that means is far more telling.

In the reunion, everyone becomes a bit awkward at the mention of Jews, and his old comrades politely ask how he survived the war, though he understands it to be no more than a polite question and answers accordingly. But his curiosity gets the better of him, and he finally asks them why they had not been more manifestly anti-Semitic at school given the attitudes and hatred all around them. The response comes, hesitatingly, but as if the question itself were absurd: "Good Lord, how could we believe in the theory of the inferiority of the Jews? Our star pupil in German was a Jew and one of our fastest one-hundred-metre sprinters was also a Jew." Naturally Reich-Ranicki is a bit taken aback, "baffled," since he is forced to ask himself if the persecution of Jews was only "despicable" because some Jews were smart and agile. Here again we find the difficulty his comrades have in treating Ranicki as "himself," that is, as a German-Jew. And again, the very erasure of his identity takes place as a performance of *politesse* involved in the rhetoric of the reply and the apparent generosity with which his comrade expresses the executioner's logic. Indeed, as Reich-Ranicki puts it, "I felt that I had sufficiently upset the genial atmosphere and let it pass."[88]

That this scene takes place more than a decade after the war only marks the continuity between then and now in spite of the different context, in which Jewish suffering, which first provoked awkward silence, now gives rise to philo-Semitism and guilt but never neutrality. In 1973 Reich-Ranicki receives an invitation from the publisher Wolf

Jost Siedler to go to a party celebrating the publication of Joachim Fest's new biography of Hitler. Fest is his colleague at the *Frankfurter Allgemeine* and has arranged for him to be offered a position at that paper. Reich-Ranicki and his wife go happily and notice upon arrival "an impressive gentleman probably in his late sixties" to whom everyone is talking. At once, "Tosia turned pale. I too suddenly did not feel very well."[89] But before they can decide what to do, their host whisks them over to meet the gentleman who, it turns out "was a criminal—one of the worst war criminals in the history of Germany. He had caused the deaths of countless human beings. . . . I am talking of Albert Speer."[90]

Speer is pleasant and Reich-Ranicki notes that he kept nodding his head in agreement, "as if to say: the Jewish fellow citizen is right, the Jewish fellow citizen is welcome." But then Speer, gesturing to Fest's book on whose cover the title *Hitler* was emblazoned in a monumental Gothic script, says: "*He* would have been content with this, *he* would have liked it."[91] Reich-Ranicki is, naturally, horrified. Shall we call Speer's response, let alone the insensitivity of his friend Fest and the publisher, an indifferent one? Reich-Ranicki diagnoses Fest's insensitivity as a symptom of his egocentricity or perhaps his cynicism and predictably has nothing to say about Speer's. Yet the entire meeting with Speer actively erases Reich-Ranicki's German-Jewish identity, as does the fact that Siedler and Fest invited him without thinking. Moreover, these erasures take place in a world in which Reich-Ranicki is a famous and touted German Jew, and in which he graciously chooses to keep up appearances not as a matter of coercion or necessity but as a matter of course—he only wreaks vengeance after the fact, in memoirs (as Klemperer and Sebastian only could in their private diaries).

These erasures, particularly Speer's, demonstrate powerfully how empathic failure, or indifference, can be intrinsic to the very spectacle of showing one's self to be a sensitive person, but more, show how cruelty can take the most banal forms: an offhand, even artificially intimate comment to a man whose family had perished in "his" ovens; your friend forgetting that you might not feel honored in the presence of Albert Speer. Though such observations may appear obvious, my point is that these episodes describe indifference far more effectively than numbness, human nature, or an unconscious refusal to think, and that cruelty is manifest not only in the best intentions but also in the most banal ones. In Reich-Ranicki's anecdotes, indifference actively makes someone else disappear. Though guilt (Speer's), knowledge (Fest's), and anti-Semitism (Speer's references to Hitler), are all modes of *not* thinking (not knowing is no longer an option),[92] Reich-Ranicki demonstrates how not being thought about is itself a violent erasure. In his memoirs, not thinking—indifference, as it were—is depicted as a self-conscious desire to reach out that excludes him from the category "we" in which his friends try to imagine he belongs.

Indifference is thus a symbolic erasure whose brutality is palpable to those who disappear, whether or not bystanders feel good or guilty, whether they are ignorant or knowledgeable or concerned to help but regret that they cannot. To delineate indifference as an active form of complicity that is a form of symbolic rather than literal murder restores the particular responsibility and agency of the bystander rather than attributing to him an "understandable" and predictable because all-too-human response. It doesn't transform bystanders into perpetrators but warns against the retrospective identification of ourselves with bystanders who could not do otherwise, and thus warns against the reconstruction in history writing of a fantasmic "we" who might have done something differently if not constrained by natural human inclinations that we recognize as regrettable and condemn. This retrospective identification with those who were not Nazis, opportunists, and thugs but "normal" people who watched indifferently or helplessly and therefore numbly or guiltily, is apologetic even though it is accompanied by sincere hand-wringing, and unwittingly repeats the self-protective numbness into which some have argued onlookers must have retreated. But most important, this identification with bystanders once again "forgets" the victims except as those "we" could not help or against whose pain we would naturally protect ourselves. In so doing, it unwittingly performs a similar symbolic erasure of the victim—albeit with far less dire consequences—whose own experience of bystanders' grace or cruelty is hardly discussed at all.

The point here is not to hold bystanders responsible for cruelty often carried out in their name, even if they approved from a distance, but to try to understand the problem of indifference from the point of view of the victim: not to make arrogant assumptions about how bystanders *should* have acted, but to be conscious about how "we" may project our own fears and longings onto the past; not to deny that we are all perhaps capable of genocide, but to understand how rhetoric may be mobilized in surprising and contrary ways that facilitate if not mass murder, then a propensity to "forget" victims, to put ourselves in their place, and thus in the end to erase the very historical memory we wish to safeguard—of past atrocity, past crimes, past violence. Saul Friedländer remarks that "In a world in which such choices have all in all disappeared, the memory of the Shoah is paradoxically linked to a simplified, watered down, yet real and probably deep-seated longing for the tragic dimension of life."[93] Historians' works on the Shoah are far from simple or watered-down, but they do raise the concern that bystander indifference still has not been sufficiently historicized, as do Friedländer's own comments about contemporary longings for clear moral choices and sacrifices. Thus it is worth pondering how much the predominant construction of bystander indifference derives from a longing that "we" would have done or will do something differently when the time comes, accompanied by an equally powerful fear that we will not.

CHAPTER FOUR

Who Was the "Real" Hitler?

Sebastian Haffner, a prominent German journalist, made a career seeking to understand Hitler's peculiar charisma. In one of his later books, he asked again:

> Hitler lived from 20 April 1889 until 30 April 1945, i.e. almost exactly fifty-six years. The difference between his first thirty and the following twenty-six years seems to be inexplicable. For thirty years he was an obscure failure; then almost overnight a local celebrity and eventually the man around whom the whole of world policy revolved. How does that go together?[1]

Though Haffner finally decided Hitler's statesmanship had been overestimated, his question about Hitler's journey from "obscure failure" to powerful statesman has undergone many elaborations and provoked studies, commentaries, fiction, and histories that aim to understand not only the mystery of Hitler but also the perpetration of unspeakable crimes in his name. During the war itself, dissident and exiled German writers wrote stunned and angry accounts of how a man of such middling stature managed to enthrall millions of Germans. The writer Kurt Tucholsky claimed that he didn't really exist and was "only the noise he makes," and Bertolt Brecht called him a "nobody."[2] After revelations of Nazi atrocities circulated in the United States, American publications of all sorts also sought to analyze why a democratic society had proven so vulnerable to the persuasion of this undistinguished man "without background, without companions, without occupational or social status, without any acceptable group identification" and a draft-dodger to boot.[3] Many of these were written by German exiles, and some drew on Freud's libido theory.

Commentators in many biographical, dissident, and popular accounts of Hitler and Nazism in the 1940s as well as in the voluminous scholarly studies of totalitarianism and anti-Semitism that flourished in the 1950s and 1960s explain Hitler and fascism by referring to what the British psychoanalyst Ernest Jones called "the psychological position of the homosexual"[4] or, to put it less subtly, latent homosexuality.[5] In this chapter I address this recurring theme. I do not and cannot, of course, aspire to an exhaustive account of postwar American or German interpretations of Hitler's life and career in one chapter. I also can't possibly cover all the variations of the long association between male homosexuality and fascism first established in the mid-1930s by the German antifascist press. Nor do I trace the adventures of the psychoanalytic construction of male homosexuality, from which many premises of that association and much of its intellectual legitimacy derived. And I do not seek to demonstrate that Hitler was or was not a homosexual, though Nazism certainly drew on earlier, homophilic associations in *völkisch* culture.[6] Instead, I map the contours of that "homosexual position" in a select but diverse number of accounts of Hitler and Nazism—a psychic landscape of repressed aggression, passivity, fear of weakness and inferiority that some men occupy consciously and others don't know they inhabit. In so doing, I seek to understand the symbolic significance of this equation between Nazism and homosexuality by tracing a multilayered discourse in which American and German writers forged a powerful link between a pathological politics and a pathological homosexuality. How, then, did this complex narrative about the "position" of male homosexuality explain how men—women almost never figure—come to commit or are complicit in, even indifferent to, unspeakable crimes, first in reference to Adolf Hitler and Nazi Germany, and then in democratic societies?

Many critics since the 1930s have sought to indict fascism by equating it with male homosexuality. As a few historians have noted, the antifascist German (Socialist and Communist) Left, in spite of its stand on decriminalizing homosexual acts, sought to discredit the

Nazi party through newspaper smear campaigns and caricatures that painted it as a hotbed of homosexual activity and therefore dangerous to the nation's youth.[7] In particular, they used the well-known homosexuality of SA chief Ernst Roehm not only to foster doubt about the Nazis' moral credibility but also to expose the hypocrisy of their opposition to sodomy laws. After the Reichstag fire on February 27, 1933, which provided Hitler with a pretext to round up political dissidents and left-wing activists, the Nazis arrested former Dutch Communist turned anarchist Marinus van der Lubbe and made much of his purported part in a Communist conspiracy against the State.[8] The German Communists in exile, however, used his homosexuality and his connections to known homosexuals in the Nazi party to argue that the Reichstag burning was not a Communist conspiracy but a homosexual conspiracy within the Nazi Party to permit the persecution of Communists. The Comintern printed a pamphlet in Paris, translated into twenty languages, elucidating this perspective.[9] Indeed, the association between fascism and homosexuality was so much a part of the cultural landscape that as early as 1934 Klaus Mann, an antifascist gay writer and a son of Thomas Mann, felt compelled to criticize what he conceived as a pernicious and false association between a sexual preference and an ideology: homosexuals, he remarked, had become "the Jews of the Left."[10]

Between 1930 and 1970, the association of male homosexuality with Nazism was well established in high and low culture on both sides of the Atlantic. The most powerful theoretical justification for this view was first established in extensive psychoanalytic accounts authored by left-wing and neorevisionist Freudians such as Wilhelm Reich and Erich Fromm in Germany in the 1930s and later elaborated by Americans and German exiles in the United States, who often incorporated psychoanalytic insights into postwar studies of totalitarianism.[11] That association was also forged in other settings: in the 1945 treason trial of French fascist writer Robert Brasillach, for example, the prosecutor used Brasillach's homosexuality metaphorically to imply that he had perversely "desired" Nazi Germany; and popular postwar Italian neorealist films by Roberto Rossellini and Gillo Pontecorvo most often pitted an idealized working-class heterosexual protagonist (the irresistibly tough resistance fighter who won't break under repeated torture) against a coterie of homosexually coded or homosexual Nazis (the bespectacled, limp-wristed SS colonel).[12] So diverse were the commentaries that in 1949 Arthur Schlesinger Jr., an American historian who later became a Presidential adviser, equated totalitarianism generally with male homosexuality, and in 1951 Marxist philosopher Theodor Adorno wrote that "homosexuality and totalitarianism belong together."[13]

Historians have diverse approaches to this basically fantasmic relationship between Nazism, Hitler, and homosexuality. A few psychohistorians during the so-called Hitler boom of the 1970s, in particular Peter Loewenburg, wrote speculative accounts of Hitler's life and of the Nazi generation,[14] and, as we will see, sought to explain Nazism by reference to the psychological consequences of material deprivation and "fatherlessness" in interwar Germany.[15]

Mainstream historians were uncomfortable with the marriage of history and psychoanalysis. Of these, some have instead detailed the persecution of homosexuals under the Hitler regime and argued that the association of homosexuality and Nazism was a historical fantasy that originated on the Left to discredit National Socialism.[16] Some have merely reiterated the assumption about the congruence of Nazism and homosexuality, both male and female. Joachim Fest, for example, alludes to the "homosexual stamp of the SA [*Sturmabteilung*]" to explain the fervent devotion of its members to leaders rather than programs, as if homosexuality alone might account for this tendency. In equally questionable logic, Gisela Bock notes that the women most likely to work in a concentration camp were "unmarried, childless, tough and efficient," as if the gratuitous addition of "tough and efficient" somehow accounted for why these women were unmarried and childless.[17]

The vast majority of historians of Nazi Germany, however, refuse to engage explicitly in speculation about Hitler's alleged homosexuality, his sex life, or to address the topic of sexual practices among both elite and rank-and-file Nazis. Sometimes they do not mention such matters except in passing by references to rumored "debauched" practices better left unspoken—that is, silence prevails as a matter of good taste.[18] Or they repudiate the accusation, as does Brigitte Hamann in her study of Hitler's years in Vienna: there is not, she insists, "the slightest indication that Hitler displayed homosexual tendencies."[19] Hitler's biographer Werner Maser dismisses rumors of such tendencies as "hoary tales."[20]

More frequently, historians argue that much of the biographical information we have is based on hearsay and speculation, and thus they refuse to engage in an apparently fruitless discussion. Michael Burleigh's history of the Third Reich notes that Hitler's "own emotional life consisted of a menacing cloud of deviancy" that was "publicly rationalized as the . . . cost of duty." But he offers no further discussion, concluding that "the sexual hypocrisy of politicians is unremarkable, of interest merely to the prurient."[21] In his magisterial biography of Hitler, Ian Kershaw goes further; he states that such details don't in any case tell us very much about the sorts of political and social questions historians usually make it their business to answer.[22] Unfortunately, such reasonable (if not wholly persuasive) arguments neither stop the publication of books about the subject nor explain why the specter of Hitler's alleged homosexuality looms so large.

A book by the German historian Lothar Machtan titled *The Hidden Hitler*, which was published simultaneously in German and English in 2001, claimed to provide sufficient evidence that Hitler was homosexual.[23] Reviews were decidedly mixed. The historian Geoffrey Giles denounces the book as "hugely speculative." He claims that Hitler's homosexuality cannot tell us much about "the driving forces of Nazi Germany" and argues that Machtan's work replicates the "insidious charge of . . . extremist . . . groups in this country [the United States] today: that the Holocaust was essentially perpetrated by a group of homosexuals, and therefore any toleration of homosexuals now will one day lead to a similar cataclysm."[24] In another review that testifies to the strength of Kershaw's and Giles's sentiments among historians but also to the power of the claim about Hitler, Richard Bessel, a well-known historian of modern Germany, assures us that most would judge such books as "sensationalist," "suited to a tabloid press concerned more with profiting from stories of sexual deviance than with maintaining historical accuracy"—the good taste argument. Moreover, he says, "there also may be an understandable reluctance to emphasise Hitler's allegedly deviant sexuality for fear of appearing homophobic." He insists that "suggestions that Hitler was a homosexual may not, at first glance, appear to have much in common with responsible history"—the-what-does-sex-have-to-do-with-history argument. Having thus carefully covered his tracks, he goes on to praise the book for having "shed new light on a turning point in the history of Nazi Germany" by offering a novel way of understanding Hitler's bloody consolidation of power after 1933—the dictator sought to cover up his gay allegiances.[25] Surprisingly, only one of the reviews bothered pointing more than casually to the long and fantasmic history of the association between Nazism and homosexuality, though Giles's reference to the responsibility of a "group of homosexuals" for the Holocaust implies it.[26] But surely the assessment of Machtan's book is not comprehensible without an understanding of that history. Thus historians generally do not ask why the topic has so much resonance beyond the reasonable assumption that such books sell, nor do they ask why the books are reviewed in the most prestigious journals and newspapers. The perfectly credible argument that Hitler's sex life isn't fundamentally important to larger questions about Nazism simply does not answer the pressing question of why, if most of the sources that might provide evidence have been discredited, there is still so much interest not only in whether or not we can speak of a gay Hitler but also in what that information might reveal about Nazism.

The most obvious answer—that for a lot of people the idea of a "gay Hitler" is reassuring because it identifies clearly the source of his evil—simply cannot account for the elaboration of the accusation over time.[27] Moreover, the association between Nazism and homosexuality just doesn't seem to have the cultural power it once did—one historian has even dismissed it as that "old canard"[28]—partly because the link between them by now is more diffuse and intangible, no longer a presumption (though more widespread than one might imagine) nor for the most part an open secret that everyone "knows" and no one utters. The association between Nazism and homosexuality remains an oddly persistent question that many people don't want to take seriously and yet which somehow refuses to go away.[29]

I want to try to understand the stubborn persistence of that question in spite of "our" sense that we have moved on by addressing how anti-Nazi critics constructed male homosexuality as an allegory of threats to empathic feeling. What follows explores the different ways in which German exile and Anglo-American writers, critics, biographers, psychiatrists, and journalists used effeminacy, "perversion," and homosexuality to stand in for the sordid, concealed underside of Hitler and the Nazi leadership. The narrative evolves chronologically through a variety of mostly psychoanalytically inflected texts from the late 1940s through the 1970s—most forgotten, some known, a few very famous. It moves away from a direct to an indirect identification of homosexuality and Nazism, and then to an even more indirect and yet oddly *more* powerful identification of homosexuality with the threat of a potential Nazism, this time in the United States. The narrative begins with that (still) compelling question about how a man who was such a "nobody"—an "obscure failure," coarse and absolutely undistinguished in every way—could move an entire nation to unprecedented destruction.

In most accounts of Hitler before and during the war, effeminacy and accusations of implied or overt homosexuality sought to degrade and mock his charisma by attributing it to some hidden, unsavory cause. Hitler's personality somehow is not what it seems: he is naturally seductive, and yet there is something sinister about his charm; he is a model of self-discipline, and yet his restraint seems excessive and unnatural. Thus critics sought to bare the other, concealed half of Hitler to expose him as a fraud. Rumors spread that when Hitler was upset, he chewed the carpet.[30] Other rumors insisted that he was impotent and had only one testicle. Still others claimed that although he condemned homosexuality he wasn't averse to consorting with homosexuals, might even be one himself, and in any case thrived in a "perverse" environment. Hermann Rauschning, ex-Nazi president of the Danzig Senate who went into exile in 1936, said that Hitler liked pornography and that "most loathsome of all is the reeking miasma of furtive, unnatural sexuality that fills and fouls the whole atmosphere around him."[31] Hitler's brutality, said Rudolf Olden, exiled political editor of the *Berliner Tageblatt,* "is simply a feint—deception and self-deception. Even in top-boots, with his . . . whip in his hand, he is soft, hesitant, the 'Austrian.' "[32] Rauschning too says that Germany's leader was "brutal and vindictive" but also as "vain and as sensitive as a mimosa."[33]

Accusations of homosexuality that emphasized Hitler's hidden self were particularly widespread. They were sometimes hinted at and just as often baldly proclaimed: American sociologist Clifford Kirkpatrick wrote discreetly that "in regard to virile heterosexuality, the Nazi 'doth protest too much' "; and the scholar Frederick L. Schuman, while not focusing on Hitler's proclivities, notes diplomatically that Ernst Roehm's homosexuality "was (until many years later) an asset rather than a liability in the NSDAP [the Nazi Party]."[34] The psychoanalyst Walter Langer, writing a now infamous report on Hitler in 1943 for the Office of Strategic Services (America's World War II intelligence agency and the forerunner of the CIA), claims that Hitler probably was not a homosexual himself: "the belief that Hitler is homosexual has probably arisen because he does show so many feminine characteristics." But, he continued, the dictator "derives pleasure from looking at men's bodies and associating with homosexuals. [Otto] Strasser tells us that his personal bodyguard is almost always 100 percent homosexuals. He also derives considerable pleasure from being with his Hitler Youth, and his attitude toward them frequently tends to be more that of a woman than that of a man."[35] Hitler was also said to be a masochist who liked to be degraded by women (indeed, he is supposed to have demanded sexual favors of such a shocking nature that he drove at least three women to suicide).[36] At the same time, he and the Nazis more generally were also supposed to be sadists. According to the American journalist George W. Herald, "Brutal Nazi excesses against Jews . . . are easily recognizable as a species of sadism." The American intellectual Lewis Corey wrote, indicating just how easily one perversion begat another: "The Nazi elites were adepts in the practices of Sadism, from homosexuality to lust-murder."[37]

These speculations about Hitler's private life and person generally tend to come from mostly fictionalized sources authored by ex-Nazis such as Otto Strasser and Hermann Rauschning, who held particular grudges against him, or from his political opponents. They were circulated apparently because accusations of effeminacy (which was often a coded way of speaking about homosexuality) and homosexuality seemed to capture something essential and essentially critical about Hitler.[38] But the most insightful accounts do not just use gender and sexual deviance to reveal something eccentric about his body, behavior, or psyche unbefitting a world leader. They don't stop short at emphasizing that Hitler has two apparently irreconcilable halves but instead employ "sexual pathology" to convey a dimension of Hitler's personality that escapes meaning.

Thus in July 1932, writer Klaus Mann, observing Hitler at a Munich tearoom eating sweets, wrote in his diary: "At the very next table: Adolf Hitler in the most doltish company. His positively conspicuous mediocrity. Extremely ill endowed; the fascination he exerts the greatest disgrace in history; a certain sexually pathological element cannot account for everything."[39] The great man up close is an unbecoming petit bourgeois stuffing himself with pastry. Mann, however, doesn't simply try to show Hitler up, to ridicule the fascination he exerts by attributing it to some sordid "sexual pathology." Here sexual pathology holds the key to Hitler's magnetism but finally cannot account for "everything"—it signifies both Hitler's charisma and the difficulty of explaining it.

Mann's interpretation fits together with a variety of others that implicitly refuse to divide Hitler's character in two and thus to insinuate that the sordid side is the real Hitler.[40] Some fragmented and allusive accounts, such as those of the British modernist writer Wyndham Lewis and the American journalist William Shirer, more or less explicitly use effeminacy now to represent not only the contrast between a respectable and an unsavory Hitler but also to indicate the limits of trying to capture the "real" Hitler. Thus, for example, in contrast to Hermann Rauschning, whose image of Hitler as a "mimosa" merely documents that Hitler has two distinct and seemingly incompatible sides, Wyndham Lewis—in 1939, after he renounced the Nazis whom he had originally admired—writes:

Whenever I think in the abstract about Herr Hitler I think of a flower— the violet. This sounds absurd. He is a human violet, however: his bashfulness is real if nothing else is. He is almost a monster of shyness: and to account for the brazenness of my strange violet—for its pushing itself forward so rudely, as if it were a sunflower or something, and absorbing the attention of the world, in its struggle for a "place in the sun" requires some accounting for. A paranoiac violet! But this male Joan of Arc is a strange man.[41]

Like sexual pathology in Mann's account, Lewis's violet is a metaphor for Hitler's shyness but also for something in his character that "requires some accounting for" but cannot finally be held to account. Lewis continues: "The 'strong man' label in Western politics generally covers something very soft. Hitler, with his epileptic eye, keeps pointing to his label."[42] The epileptic eye thus points to something but does not quite give away the strong man, who remains, in the end, "strange."

Shirer, stationed in Berlin during Hitler's consolidation of power, shares Mann's disdain for the dictator. Watching Hitler meeting Chamberlain on September 22, 1938, he writes that he had not previously noticed Hitler's "ladylike walk." The somewhat bemused

Shirer says the Nazi leader takes "dainty little steps." He also notes that Himmler too seemed like a "mild little fellow" and that "Freud, I believe, has told us why the mild little fellows or those with a trace of effeminacy in them, like Hitler, can be so cruel at times."[43] But some two years later, just after the fall of France in July 1940, Shirer observes Hitler's speech before the Reichstag with undisguised admiration:

> The Hitler we saw in the Reichstag tonight was the conqueror . . . so
> wonderful as an actor, so magnificent a handler of the German mind.
> [. . .] I've often admired the way he uses his hands, which are somewhat
> feminine and quite artistic. Tonight he used those hands beautifully,
> seemed to express himself almost as much with his hands—and the
> sway of his body—as he did with his words and the use of his voice.[44]

Hitler's dainty steps make his leadership slightly embarrassing and mark the contrast between Hitler the man and Hitler the world leader. Yet in the oratorical conquest described here, the conqueror's graceful hands do not seem to be of the same body as his dainty feet: in this case too femininity signifies not only some squalid or soft side of Hitler—the cruelty of the "mild little fellows"—but also some magnetic quality that cannot be accounted for.

In other accounts, gender and sexual deviance remain metaphors for the dimension of Hitler's personality that escapes meaning, but now critics find a way to account for his "strangeness." In the years after 1940 another, parallel discourse insisted that Nazism was a defense against socially and sexually specific unconscious longings. This psychoanalytic narrative in both popular and scholarly variations ranged from the popular self-exculpatory memoirs of an ex-Nazi to scholarly psychiatric accounts of perpetrators that self-consciously sought to understand Hitler's pull beyond those arguments proffered by extant analyses of Nazism.[45]

Popular Freudian-inflected accounts of Nazism attributed sexual deviance to the general effects of sexual repression. In 1934, for example, in an essay titled "Hitlerism as a Sex Problem," the British journalist Rodney Collin wrote that the symptom of repression, "sex starvation"—which manifested in increased homosexuality, promiscuity, and perversion—accounted for the attractions of "Hitlerism" and showed itself in "Jew-baiting, persecution, [and] ultra-puritanism." "More innocuously," he says, "these frustrations were in many cases sublimated into extreme patriotism, loyalty, and a certain disciplined idealism."[46] In 1942, another American journalist, George W. Herald, wrote, "There is an impressive support for the theory that the whole Nazi movement arose in large measure out of the sexual frustrations of some groups in the German population," and noted that Hitler himself was a "sexual abnormal."[47]

Other writers developed more elaborate accounts of Hitler's homosexuality for a general audience. In 1945, the German émigré Samuel Igra concluded that "homosexualism" explained an "attitude towards human life which expresses itself in that seemingly ineluctable life-destroying urge manifested by the Germans towards helpless persons who have come under their wrath."[48] Homosexuals, he wrote, are natural murderers and destroyers of civilization because they spurn "the essential virtues of loyalty and truth, love of children and respect for women, kindliness and justice to one's neighbour as a fellow-being of equal right and equal natural status." But while they hate Jews in particular because "Israel has taken an uncompromising stand . . . against practices that poison the sources of life itself,"[49] they don't know that in attacking Jews they attack themselves.

The most dramatic collapse of empathic recognition and thus the failure to recognize the natural and equal rights of others are derived therefore from an unconscious projection of homosexual self-loathing. "Homosexualism" thus seems to describe a "life-destroying urge"—a desire to kill others—that is the unconscious desire to destroy the self. Igra tells us that the Nazis consider themselves to be a "master class within the master race" because "homosexualists form a group apart and often consider themselves superior to normal people." Yet he feels compelled to move beyond this conventional depiction of a degenerate because effete gay aristocracy in order to explain Hitler's path from homosexuality to "homosexualism" and thus to anti-Semitism. He argues that Hitler was incensed by the accusations of homosexuality made by Magnus Hirschfeld and Maximilian Harden—both Jewish—against Kaiser Wilhelm II's advisers in a series of famous trials that took place between 1906 and 1909. Reading the papers in Vienna, Hitler "felt a personal blow."[50] The trials "awakened Hitler's consciousness of his own sex instincts, which were abnormal," and eventually, like many "morally morbid people when their failings become known—he sought to throw the blame elsewhere":

Hitler displayed at least latent homosexual traits by declaring his solidarity with the German perverts. The natural instincts of human decency, which are in every normal being and react with revulsion at the first mention of sexual perversion, were obviously not a part of Hitler's nature. He could not understand such a feeling in the case of those Jews who, from patriotic motives, exposed the moral obliquity of certain persons occupying the highest positions in Germany. [51]

Hitler, Igra continues, had homosexual connections in the Kaiser's crowd and felt particularly guilty about his own role in the degradation of the monarchy, which he now blamed on Jews. By the time he took power, Hitler's "latent homosexual traits" seem to have become sufficiently conscious that he has Austrian Chancellor Dolfuss assassinated in order to recover documents that proved his connection to the Kaiser's circle.[52]

Another account, Eugen Dollmann's *Roma Nazista*, the memoirs of Himmler's representative (and Hitler's interpreter) in Rome from 1938 to 1945, published in Italian in 1949, makes the same argument. The book was originally written but never printed in German[53] and came out in an expurgated English edition only in 1967 titled *The Interpreter*.[54] Dollmann's is a gossipy and mostly trashy account of his years in Rome. It is full of anecdotes about Himmler, Hitler, and Mussolini and written, it seems, to exculpate its author, who insists on his own disapproval of Nazi policy in a variety of contexts.[55] He spills much ink insinuating that Hitler was homosexual, recounting an evening gathering during which the Bavarian Reichswehr commander Otto von Lossow read aloud papers documenting Hitler's dealings with male prostitutes in Munich; he portrays Hitler as a perverted statesman whose lackeys don't dare call to account, and more generally caricatures Hitler and his henchmen as sappy men who fall far short of their cherished ideal of virility (Hitler is "pale, not at all athletic, slightly hunched [*leggermente curvo*], and his hands are always folded above his waist in an all but martial manner").[56] But, like Igra, Dollmann links this embarrassing effeminacy to which the Nazi leaders themselves are blind to an account of what blinds them:

To understand Hitler's implacable hatred of homosexuals there is no need to invoke Freud: experience over a long period of time teaches us that the religious, political, or sexual renegade, after his "conversion," hates the old intellectual and physical ideal according to which he once lived with a ferocity and a craving for vengeance which are incomprehensible to an outsider. In Hitler's case we have to add that, whether due to his own will or to the caprices of history, he found himself under the blinding light of public life.[57]

Thus Hitler's "persecution mania" derives less from a guilty conscience—Dollmann likens him to Roman emperors who do as they please—than from a convert's zeal, though clearly the convert's zeal derives from the desire to destroy all vestiges of his former self. Dollmann, like Igra, "knows" that Hitler is homosexual. Dollmann is most interested in making money, settling accounts, and exculpating himself, and thus provides the titillating and reassuring information that homosexuality is the open secret of Nazism. But confronted with Hitler's persecution of homosexuals, he insists that the denial of homosexuality is the driving force behind Hitler's feverish persecution of homosexuals and inevitably, though he does not spell this out, of other so-called internal enemies. Hitler is thus logically deduced to be homosexual because of the intensity with which he hates homosexuals.

Such popular accounts name homosexuality or "homosexualism" explicitly as the cause and effect of Hitlerism. Their question now is not whether Hitler is really a homosexual who hides his proclivities, but whether he *knows* that he *is* one. In short, these accounts shift the question away from Hitler's homosexuality to the political ramifications of his latent homosexuality, for now we know who the real Hitler is: in these accounts it is thus not Hitler's homosexuality but his latent homosexuality that figures and explains the murderous anti-Semitism of his reign of power.

Scholarly studies—or at least those written for generally educated audiences—also shift their focus away from the self-consciously perverted, swindling Hitler to the unconscious and therefore latent homosexuality of the Nazi character. In them, however, Hitler is largely part of a psychosocial phenomenon. Study after study emphasized the psychological impact of historical events on the "national character." These studies exemplified an intensified interest, especially by U.S. and exiled German scholars during and after the war, in the anthropological, sociological, and psychological study of German cultural patterns. A focus on the authoritarian character of the German family proved influential.[58] Though their disciplines and methods ranged widely, the majority of these critics generally conceived Nazism as the symptom of economic and political insecurity; of the loss of paternal authority and its compensation, paternal severity; and of sexual repression and its symptoms, namely perversion and homosexuality. Thus in the "Psychology of Hitlerism" published in 1933, the political scientist Harold Lasswell argued: "By projecting blame from the self upon the outside world, inner emotional insecurities are reduced. By directing symbolic and overt attacks against the enemy in our midst, Hitler has alleviated the anxieties of millions of his fellow Germans (at the expense of others)."[59] The great psychohistorian Erik Erikson suggested in his famous portrait of Hitler in *Childhood and Society* (1950) that Nazism was the product of a deficiently integrated, adolescent national psyche whose anxieties were relieved by submission to Hitler.[60] And Erich Fromm, the analyst who sought to join Marxian and Freudian categories in a new synthesis, argued that Nazism was born of the nexus between Protestantism, socioeconomic instability, and cultural and social forms of capitalist domination. He outlined a psychological position of submission and domination—the "sado-masochistic character"—whose origins he traced to a gap between the positive desire for freedom intrinsic in all people and the socioeconomic and political conditions that make that quest for freedom possible. In Germany, people had "lost those ties which gave them security," and that lag thus "makes freedom an unbearable burden."[61] Thus Germans masochistically "longed for submission" as a defense against this terrifying freedom and aloneness, and they projected their aggression against and envy of those more fortunate than they onto helpless others.

In a wide variety of psychodynamically inclined accounts, this collective regression more explicitly expresses latent male homosexuality. Indeed, as both Martin Jay and Elizabeth Young-Bruehl have noted, Fromm's earlier work originally tied sadomasochism to a collective psychological regression from heterosexual genitality to pregenital stages of libidinal development and postulated a homosexual identification between those men bearing marks of this regression and Nazi leaders.[62] Thus the Austrian Marxist psychoanalyst Wilhelm Reich sought to account for what he called the rise of "German fascism" by reference to the sexual repression fundamental to bourgeois social organization: the "authoritative parental home," so pervasive in German society and culture, bred an "acute conflict between sexuality and fear" so that "the youth's sexual drive develops in a homosexual direction. In terms of the drive's energy, passive homosexuality is the most effective counterpart of natural masculine sexuality, for it replaces activity and aggression by passive and masochistic attitudes, that is to say, by precisely those attitudes that determine the mass basis of patriarchal authoritarian mysticism in the human structure."[63] Under fascism, he claimed, "the natural sexual strivings toward the other sex . . . were replaced in the main by distorted and diverted homosexual and sadistic feelings." German cultural patterns thus nurtured homosexuality, which thrives under fascism, which itself exacerbates such patterns.

In a discussion of the psychological profile of Nazi collaborators, the British psychoanalyst Ernest Jones, like Reich, explicitly names the consequences of excessive paternal domination: "Our starting point in any constructive analysis must surely be the fear of the dangerous Father or of one's own dangerous impulses towards him. If one is unable to face this situation then there remain only two alternatives: to submit to him or to ally oneself with the dangerous forces through the mechanisms of acceptance and identification. On the whole the former is more characteristic of the passive homosexual type, the latter of the active one. Both are *exquisitely homosexual solutions.*"[64] Jones thus draws on an explicitly articulated psychoanalytic construction of latent homosexuality to explain the psychology of Nazism. The basic argument goes something like this: after Freud, latent homosexuality designates a passive man who has repressed his childhood desire for intimacy with the father. Although such desire is universal and therefore present in all men (since it is part and parcel of the oedipal conflict), it develops in various ways, so that latent homosexual desire can take the form merely of passive behavior, or it might manifest as homophobia, depending on how the oedipal triangle was played out and resolved (or not). In authoritarian families, the domineering father puts pressure on the normal oedipal conflict. The son's higher level of repressed rage at his domineering, emotionally negligent father usually takes the defensive form of guilt and thus of extremely passive and submissive behavior and idealization of the authority figure, or "identification with the aggressor,"[65] whereby the son identifies with the father's sadistic impulses toward him. The repressed rage is usually displaced, projected onto helpless others. Thus, in a useful formulation, Jones writes that those who "are most subject to the wiles of Nazi propaganda are those who have neither securely established their own manhood and independence of the father nor have been able to combine the instincts of sexuality and love in their attitude towards the mother or other women. This is the psychological position of the homosexual."[66]

This argument is reiterated in a variety of postwar psychoanalytically informed accounts, many of which shifted their emphasis away from the vague entity of "national character" in the light of the active collaboration and compliance of non-Germans in Nazi crimes, and the appearance of "totalitarian" regimes in diverse cultures and traditions. Instead they embedded Nazism in potentially universal psychic patterns that emerge in different times and places depending on historical and cultural variables.[67] In *The Authoritarian Personality* (1951), a book that became one of the most well-known theories of individual prejudice in American social science after the war, the team of Theodor Adorno, Max Horkheimer, and Else Frenkel-Brunswick (alongside American social scientists at the University of California at Berkeley) sought to understand the dissolution of social ties that had facilitated authoritarianism in Germany in order to comprehend the deeper structure of prejudice more generally. They focus on conformity rather than homosexuality in order to construct the dimensions of the "authoritarian personality," and yet latent homosexuality proves to be an essential characteristic of conformity itself. "Insofar," they argue, "as authoritarian submission is a means for overcoming weakness it stands as a kind of defense against the underlying homosexual submission and passivity; it remains to be pointed out that this surface trend offers at the same time gratification for these very same needs."[68]

These psychic patterns become increasingly rooted in what seems to be historical explanation by the mid-1960s and "psychohistory" by the 1970s. Martin Wangh, a psychoanalyst, wrote an influential 1964 essay seeking to understand the universal unconscious dynamics of anti-Semitism as they develop in a specific historical context. The psychohistorian Peter Loewenberg drew on his work to become perhaps the most influential proponent of a psychodynamic approach to the history of Nazism. Both argued that Nazism consisted fundamentally of an ultramasculine identification with a leader that worked as a defense against (and gratification of, through symbolic submission to) homosexual longings. These defenses arise now, however, not as a response to Prussian domination or authoritarian family patterns (though these are contributing factors), but out of a generational experience in which boys were deprived of their fathers, intensifying both homosexual and incestuous longings which are defended against via projection onto other objects, particularly Jews, but also homosexuals. In his essay, Waugh insists that prejudice is a "regressive phenomenon of a defensive nature," and wishes to prove that "the generation in Germany which formed the core of Hitler's stormtroopers was . . . more inclined . . . to resort without restraint to [this] regressive defense."[69] Thus he argues that this particular generation was psychically affected by the events of their early adolescence such that "a fixation of sadomasochistic fantasies and . . . specific defenses directed against them" occurred. The war produced an intense longing for the "absent father," which "led to extraordinarily exacerbated childish, homosexual wishes. Proof that . . . [these wishes] had persisted into adult life was given wide publicity by Hitler himself, in the Röhm episode." Not surprisingly then, the "homosexual component undoubtedly loomed large in the Nazi movement," and some of the "latent homosexual tension was relieved through this submission to a deified, *untouchable* leader."[70]

After Wangh, Loewenberg writes that the most important factor explaining the psychic trauma of the German generation of 1914 and their susceptibility to Hitler was "paternal deprivation in childhood."

[I]t is postulated that a direct relationship existed between the deprivation German children experienced in World War I and the response of these children and adolescents to the anxieties aroused by the Great Depression of the early 1930s. This relationship is psychodynamic: the war generation had weakened egos and superegos, meaning that the members of this generation turned readily to programs based on facile solutions and violence when they met new frustrations during the depression. They then reverted to earlier phase-specific fixations in their child development marked by rage, sadism, and the defensive idealization of their absent parents, especially the father.

Loewenberg too insists that this defense then nurtures a homosexual identification with Hitler that explains the "psychohistorical origins of the Nazi youth cohort."[71]

It turns out then that the link between sadomasochistic character and homosexuality is less interesting (or more predictable) than how it was forged and with what consequences. In all these accounts, writers speak of the "psychological position of the homosexual." That is, these analyses don't necessarily indict homosexuals as such, but refer to a psychic position that could potentially be taken up by anyone raised in a traditional German family, or more generally, in Germany after the Great War. Yet all these accounts either attach latent homosexuality to Nazis or confuse conscious and unconscious homosexuality: that is, they deduce the presence of latent homosexuality tautologically by discovering it in those who are (for the most part high-ranking) Nazis or by verifying that "real" homosexuals join the Nazi Party, thus in the end always reasoning in a rather dizzying fashion back and forth from Nazis to latent homosexuals, from homosexuals to Nazis. Thus Wilhelm Reich, who insisted that German family patterns nurtured latent homosexuality, also thinks that homosexuals somehow cause Nazism: "It comes as no surprise," he says, "when people who are homosexually oriented from the outset seek to exploit such an institution as the SA by attaining leadership positions and then abusing them for their inclinations." Or: "The more clearly developed the natural heterosexual inclinations of a juvenile are, the more open he will be to revolutionary ideas; the stronger the homosexual tendency within him ... the more easily will he be drawn to the right."[72] In other words, while not all Germans are homosexuals, latent or otherwise, Reich implies that most Nazis are.

In his 1950 study of Nazism, which draws on his own contact with the Nazis on trial at Nuremberg where he served as a psychiatrist and interpreter, G. M. Gilbert, who was a German-Jewish refugee, sought to understand the "psychology of dictatorship," and in particular, German indifference to the suffering of Jews around them. In many ways, the book takes over Erich Fromm's conception of a gap between humanity's desire for freedom and the inability of institutions to provide a context within which freedom can be realized: he calls this an "authoritarian lag" persistent in German history and particularly in the German family. The book is organized around a series of biographical and psychological sketches of various groups under Nazism: Hitler, the Party "revolutionists" (Hermann Goering, Rudolf Hess, and Hans Frank), the diplomats, the military, the police, and finally, an overall assessment of the psychodynamics of dictatorship in which the central focus is the German people. Though Gilbert claims that "the importance of homosexuality, both latent and overt . . . need not be overestimated,"[73] he reminds us that many of the Nazis were active homosexuals, especially Ernst Roehm and many of the stormtroopers. Hitler, we learn, was not an overt homosexual, but "it is certain that somewhere in the recesses of [his] libido there lay the smoldering ashes of violent, unresolved Oedipal conflicts: that these rendered his emotional attachments to men stronger than to women . . . and helped to inflame his paranoid hostility toward Jews."[74] And latent homosexuality also "played a part among the revolutionary group":

> The latent-homosexual revolutionists like Hans Frank were driven by passionate devotion to the paternalistic symbol of virility and authority represented by [Hitler]. Above and beyond the prevalent submissiveness to authority, which can be accounted for by the authoritarian cultural lag, Frank and many others like him experienced something akin to "surrender—like a woman . . . a madness—a drunkenness" [he quotes Frank's own words here]—indeed, a symbolic orgasm in submitting to such overpowering strength.[75]

Of course many commentators—famously including Hitler himself—referred to the German people as "womanly" and supple in Hitler's hands. Yet in Gilbert's work, the remarkably ambiguous phrase "others like him" seems to refer not to the German people generally but to "the revolutionary group," though we cannot know for sure. When Gilbert finally turns his attention away from the murderous intent of indubitably committed Nazis to the indifference of Germans to Jewish suffering more generally, all discussion of latent homosexuality disappears, so that Frank's "symbolic orgasm" turns out to be, inexplicably, of a different sort than the "normal social process of group identification" that led so many Germans to worship and follow Hitler. "As a general principle," he writes, "the normal social process of group identification and hostility reaction brings about a *selective* constriction of empathy, which . . . enables normal people to condone or participate in the most sadistic social aggression without feeling it or realizing it."[76] Though Frank's murderous intent is of course substantially different from the general population's propensity to turn a blind eye to the persecution of minorities, there is no articulated reason why latent homosexuality is applicable in one case and not the other, no reason why "others like him" does not include, potentially, all Germans who swooned before Hitler, about whose latent homosexuality Gilbert is oddly "certain."

Finally, both Wangh and Loewenberg talk of latent homosexuality as a general defense against homosexual longings, but the Nazis among them *are* homosexuals, latent or otherwise. Thus Wangh speaks of the "pseudo-phallic identity" taken on by the young German woman as the consequence of the "pronounced homosexuality of her male partner"—in short, men unconsciously or consciously interested in other men force young German women to "abandon all feminine, coquettish resistance," and wear a "Nazi Girl uniform."[77] Loewenberg, who has his share of things to say about the problem of castrating mothers, interprets an episode of a German novel to imply that the "emotional effects of the war" led to "an exacerbation of adolescent homosexuality."[78] At the same time, Wangh cites Hitler's speech after the Roehm purge (which Hitler insisted was a necessary cleansing of immorality in the SA) as "proof" that Nazism involved a powerful "homosexual component."[79] But is homosexuality latent in all German men, as both he and Loewenberg imply, or is it that Nazis, as he suggests here, are all homosexual? One has to assume that "real" or latent homosexual Nazis somehow constitute the empirical proof of the psychoanalytic argument about the unconscious cause of Germans' identification with Hitler.

It should not now be surprising that most essays or studies that focus on Nazis or collaborators rather than on German complicity more generally portray their subjects as latent homosexuals. The British psychiatrists who investigated Rudolf Hess after his capture in Scotland in 1941 (he had flown to England to seek peace with Germany on his own initiative) concluded in 1948 that he had an "unconscious homosexual disposition."[80] Psychiatrist Henry Dicks surmised that most of his Nazi subjects suffered from various degrees of homosexual anxiety.[81] Another Nuremberg psychiatrist, Douglas Kelley, ·found homosexuality too degrading even to be attributed to a Nazi, and he defended Hermann Goering and Baldur von Schirach against such accusations. But he stopped short at Hitler, who "was perhaps even what is called a 'latent homosexual type'—one with a deeply re-pressed homosexuality."[82] And Peter Loewenberg insisted that Hein-rich Himmler suffered from "homosexual panic" (in which an uncon-scious fear of one's homosexual impulses causes loathing of those known or feared to be homosexual).[83]

In accounts from Igra's through Wangh's, a variety of thinkers and writers for different reasons thus developed a "psychological posi-tion" conducive to Nazism that was increasingly identified with ho-mosexuality. Now, in order to understand Hitler's magnetism, we don't necessarily need historical actors to be conscious of what they are doing: we need to understand why they *don't know* what they are doing. Here we are not dealing only with the particular traumatic symptoms of war and political crisis in Germany but also with the general traumatic symptoms of psychosexual repression: The particu-larities of German history—whether Lutheranism, Prussian authori-tarianism, the Eulenburg trials, the Great War, the Depression—un-fold the more central, universal psychological struggle between father and son, or trigger Hitler's and other Nazis' unconscious projections. After all, Dollmann, from whose memoirs we might expect some thicker historical context, simply likens Hitler to a Roman emperor or depicts him in timeless terms as a renegade. In this narrative, latent homosexuality thus emphasizes less the historical particularities of Germany than a potentially universal psychological problem that might flourish as well in other contexts conducive to its formation.

The authors of this seemingly more universal drama also move from the realm of allusions to the realm of declaration, and from de-scription to explanation. Thus the signs of a potential and as yet mostly undeclared homosexuality—effeminacy, sappiness, narcis-sism—now take the form of a potential, undeclared but discussable homosexuality, latent homosexuality: now, to repeat, the question is not whether Hitler or the Nazis are homosexual, but whether they know they are homosexual. Thus in spite of the extraordinary lability of latent homosexuality (since it is a psychic position, not a category of persons), these accounts for the most part identify Nazis as homo-sexuals and *explain* Nazism by reference to homosexuality: they insin-uate that the Nazi Party is quietly hospitable to and nourishes them; that, as Langer noted, "homosexuals frequently regard themselves as a special form of creation whose destiny it is to initiate a new order," and thus found a home in the Nazi Party.[84] Most of these authors, regardless of their audience, depict Hitler and the Nazi elite frankly as latent homosexuals, sometimes using predictable—whether popular or more coded and thus "sophisticated"—stereotypes we have already seen others employ. The homosexual underground forms a "group apart" that helps all its members and doesn't care a whit about the equal rights of anyone else; they are narcissists, passive, and submissive. In short, whether in an overtly sensationalist or more analytical manner, all these accounts conceive Hitler's and other Nazis' homosexuality as an open secret whose truth can be demonstrated via "secret sources" or psychoanalysis, strained accounts of blackmail and speculations about who must have known whom, or the evaluation of psychological patterns. Igra and Dollmann establish Hitler's homosexuality by reference to a psychology of self-hatred that leads the homosexual to persecute other homosexuals, other perceived enemies, and eventually Jews. Other analysts in the end deduce the presence of latent homosexuality by way of clinical observation of Nazis who have maimed and murdered. Now Hitler's gender and sexual deviance no longer signify that his charisma finally escapes meaning: instead, his homosexuality leads the critic to a metaphorically "deeper," repressed place in the psyche of a man and his followers.

These accounts thus resolve the question about whether Hitler was a real "deviant" by reference to an unconscious urge that can only be known by deducing its presence in the form of anti-Semitism, homophobia, and in the worst cases, mass murder—in the form of empathic failure. Homosexuals become identifiable tips of an iceberg. They signal an otherwise unrecognizable potential for destruction and cruelty that must now be everywhere identified and regulated. Though it obviously indicts homosexuality as such, latent homosexuality does not merely insinuate a defense against same-sex desire. As we have seen, it also describes a particular relationship between sexual repression and mass murder that is potentially universal but whose only reference points are homosexuals. In this discourse, the diagnosis of latent homosexuality thus cuts Hitler down to size by making him into potentially everyman who might lurk anywhere, "puny and contemptible."[85] Yet that diagnosis is also so generalized that its dimensions defy the imagination. Or, to put it differently, Hitler no longer seems to escape meaning, and yet the menace he poses is so diffused that it is potentially alive in every man and thus difficult to pin down anywhere. This now ever-present but everywhere denied potential—latent homosexuality—perhaps not surprisingly loses its character as an urgent commentary on events in Germany. Critics begin to focus instead on how homosexuality might signal the emergence of another *potential* Hitler and the rise of *potentially* comparable genocidal forces, mostly in the United States.[86]

In a dramatic 1949 book, *Love and Death,* the progressive social critic Gershon Legman, speaking not even of the Nazi elite or the German population but of Americans, sought to explain how their "sympathy . . . with the inhumanly treated human can be shoved beneath the surface, and [they] are then properly able to enjoy photographs of a Japanese lynched with a *flammenwerfer* or his skull denuded of flesh."[87] Indeed, Legman's work reflected a new consciousness and concern about what one journalist later writing in *Harper's Magazine* in 1960 called the "vicious public consumption of human suffering" in the United States. His work quietly assimilated arguments and images derived from discussions of Nazi Germany.[88] Indeed, diverse texts linked this unempathic, voyeuristic response to suffering to homosexuality. Thus, for example, when in 1954 sociologist Abram Kardiner sought to explain how the purported rise of homosexuality in the United States was linked to a "collapse of the regard that people have for one another's rights . . . and a readiness to hate and to hurt those who oppose or differ," he attributed empathic failure to the psychological position of the (by definition self-loathing) homosexual: "When people with collective self-hatred unite, they usually embark on a concerted policy of denying the self-hatred and electing a scapegoat on whom all the vile attributes they consider themselves to have can be projected, as the Nazis did with the Jews. The general contempt of male homosexuals for females is notorious."[89] Erik Erikson noted that Nazism was only "the German version . . . of a universal contemporary trend"—the identity crisis of man in a secular world—which he attributed to a form of arrested development that impeded the formation of mature, integrated, autonomous, and bounded identity beyond narcissistic defenses manifest overtly in homosexuals and delinquents.[90]

Many commentators now viewed Nazism as a potentially universal phenomenon that might emerge in other contexts, and most of the texts we have discussed at least rhetorically extended the link between authoritarian political forms and homosexuality to the United States. Among others, Martin Wangh, who diagnosed Nazism as the symptom of homosexual identification with Hitler, said that he sought to understand this dynamic in order to examine the problem of "prejudice and discrimination" more generally in the United States. Douglas Kelley, who insisted on Hitler's latent homosexuality, wrote that in seeking to understand Nazi criminals, "I shared the opinion of ethnologists and politicians that Nazism was a socio-cultural disease which, while it had been epidemic only among our enemies, was endemic in all parts of the world. I shared the fear that sometime in the future it might become epidemic in my own nation."[91] The Nuremberg psychiatrist who had diagnosed the Nazi leadership as latent homosexuals, G. M. Gilbert, wrote that the "selective constriction of empathy" characteristic of the psychic structure of Nazism also described race relations in the United States.[92]

Legman himself attributed our indifference to the pain of others—indeed our pleasure at the enemy's painful demise—at first to sexual repression. He extrapolated from the popularity of the murder mystery and comic-book heroes to make this general argument, for it turns out that our voracious consumption of violent material is a sublimated, distorted form of sexual fulfillment in a repressive society. Thus, when we read the murder mystery we identify with the detective conceived as "supralegal avenger" and, in so doing, act out our real contempt for due process of law and thus the right to mercy and justice. In Legman's view, this identification allows us to revel in murder—indeed to commit murder ourselves—under the guise of detached observers: "Make no mistake about it: the murder-mystery reader is a lyncher. A solid citizen by day, by night he rides hooded to watch human beings die. He may, certainly does, think of himself as a mere, harmless literary escapist." But in fact, "he kills for pleasure."[93] This identification with the law, moreover, is itself a form of acting out "guilty terror": "Stunned by our own guilt—as now again with the atom-bomb—we find ourselves desperate either to fasten this guilt upon someone else, or to confuse our fear of punishment with the disproportionate aggression against which we struck. The daily conviction that we are menaced in our innocence, and not by our guilt, must at all costs be maintained."[94]

Legman located this aggressive defense against guilt that invests sadism with righteousness, not in repressed sexuality generally, but in repressed or latent *homo*sexuality. In America, he wrote,

> The Supermen, the Supersleuths, the Supercops . . . align themselves always on the side of law, authority, the father; and accept their power passively from a bearded above. Like Wild Bill Hickok, our own homosexual hero . . . with his long silk stockings and his Lesbian sidekick, Calamity Jane . . . they are too unvirile to throw off fear, and kill as criminals. Instead, unseen and unsuspected in some corner, they put on a black mask, a sheriff's badge and a Superman suit, and do all their killing on the side of the law.[95]

Though Legman bemoaned American atrocities against the Japanese, it is the image of Nazis as latent homosexuals that underlies his argument, indeed makes it possible. In a clear allusion to Nazi state-sponsored murder, Legman personifies homosexuality as a (covertly, unconsciously passive) sheriff or a superhero, thereby linking the psychology of Nazi dictatorship to the psychology of democratic citizens who "righteously" commit atrocities against the Japanese and enjoy watching them but "know not what they do." Reading Legman, we are faced no longer with the singular conundrum posed by mass murder in Nazi Germany, but with yet another specter, this time a culture of potential and potentially unwitting murderers in the United States; we are no longer faced with Nazis who destroy democratic ideals in the name of nation and "race," but democratic citizens who destroy democracy in the name of defending its precepts.

In Legman, homosexuality again points to a palpable, immediate social threat that somehow eludes our grasp, indeed disguises itself as a defender of the law. We now have a specter—the homosexual—with no visible referent. That is, in this third dimension of the narrative associating Nazism and homosexuality we know that fascists are latent or "real" homosexuals, but in democratic societies we can no longer identify the homosexuals for sure. Legman's work thus makes clear that the relationship between murder and homosexuality is not forged by homosexuality per se, but by its dissimulation, its inability to recognize itself as such; by unwitting murderers who don't know that (or why) they are committing or are complicit in horrible crimes. Latent homosexuality describes how empathic failure is inseparable from repressed, guilty pleasure in which the suffering other becomes an object of fascination and eroticized gratification. What looks like moral indifference or habituation to suffering, whatever its form—detachment before horrific images—is really a deep-seated, murderous desire that can never be recognized as such. Now not only Germans but also potentially all human beings "want to commit murder and not know it,"[96] and worse, commit murder all the while believing they are upholding the law.

The unconscious drive that accounted for Hitler's nothingness was finally conceived not as a homosexual one but as a defense against homosexuality,[97] meaning that homosexuality doesn't exist except as the genocidal violence it purportedly causes, as nihilistic self-destruction, even or especially, as homophobia.[98] Hence, as we have seen, Nazism provided the empirical "proof" of a homosexuality otherwise illegible or fundamentally indeterminable. In Legman, and implicitly in other texts such as the sociologist Kardiner's, empathic failure oddly demonstrates the presence of a homosexual drive that is otherwise nowhere in evidence, so that homosexuality is both the cause and effect of Nazism. Homosexuality is thus a tautology for Hitler's magnetism, for Nazism, and for genocide. Like pornography, it also purports to account for the relationship between moral and political perversion, and as an explanatory tool it is tautological and vacuous. But more powerfully than pornography, it designates a group of people who are likely to be Nazis, even as it also designates all men as *potential* Nazis.

The question about Hitler's homosexuality continues to fascinate not because Hitler might be homosexual but because there is no way actually to resolve it one way or the other: the continual query serves to locate, again and again, threats to empathy where they cannot be found, and in so doing offers an untenable solution to the question of how men such as Hitler accomplished what they did. In a variety of works aiming to understand Hitler's psyche in order to identify the danger of potential "Hitlers" more generally, the suspicion of homosexuality or latent homosexuality is not resolved as it had been in works from Igra's to Gilbert's. Rather than claim that these men are homosexual but do not know it themselves, the newer works end with a question mark about whether Hitler or other Nazis were homosexual. Cinematic, literary, and psychoanalytically inflected studies of Nazism casually and often implicitly associate homosexuality and Nazism, so that we "know" that Nazis are (at least latent) homosexuals, but just as often they tell us we cannot know for sure. Thus the homosexuality of Hitler and the Nazi elite is frequently acknowledged or denied, only to leave the question open. In 1971, in the middle of an interview about Vatican complicity in the Holocaust, the British (Vienna-born Hungarian) journalist Gitta Sereny asked Eugen Dollmann if Hitler were *really* homosexual. Dollmann replied, in sharp contrast to his 1949 account, that it was possible but that he couldn't be sure.[99]

In 1973, in a general analysis of "human destructiveness" aimed at discerning the psychic impact of late capitalism, Erich Fromm makes Hitler the emblem of a social pattern of unfeeling narcissism and claims that "there is no evidence" that he was homosexual, but also "no evidence that his sexual relations were normal."[100] And as late as 1983 two psychoanalysts, Norbert Bromberg and Verna Volz Small, tell us that they seek to discern Hitler's "psychopathological structure" less to understand Hitler than to acknowledge the fact that such persons "could again threaten humanity in a new leader who might at first be seen as Hitler was as a savior, or as just another unprepossessing crackpot."[101] In the process of diagnosing Hitler with "borderline personality disorder," they entertain the idea of Hitler's homosexuality, assess the evidence about his homosexual inclinations, and finally dismiss it—or not quite: "*All this* notwithstanding, the prevailing opinion is that Hitler was *probably* not a *practicing* homosexual" (italics added).[102]

Hitler's motives are now located in a murderous impulse that can never be clearly located, in an impetus identified with a group of people who can never be found but about whom there is always suspicion, and it is this diffuse, intangible, quiet, and even unconscious suspicion that continues to inform the way we think about the association between Nazism and homosexuality. Lothar Machtan's 2001 book seeks to prove its case by arguing that Hitler's persecution of homosexuals and his self-loathing dissimulation of homosexuality proves that he was gay. Machtan argues that Hitler's homosexual relations, in particular with Ernst Roehm, explain his rise to power. In his account, just about everyone in proximity to Hitler in his early days was homosexual or latently so, and an extensive underground network nourished and supported him, supplying him with money and connections and thereby smoothing his way to power. Hitler's desire to repress all knowledge of this homosexual past led to the extraordinary persecution of homosexuals for which the Nazis were responsible and, most significantly, explains the so-called "Night of the Long Knives," a massacre in late June and early July 1934 of SA men, their leader Ernst Roehm, and other political rivals. Finally, and perhaps most predictably, in Machtan's portrait Hitler is narcissistic and autoerotic, particularly attached to his mother, and unable to form relations with women even though he seemed to enjoy their company. In the end, Machtan insists that Hitler's homosexuality is not the key to understanding Nazism—after all, there is almost no mention of anti-Semitism in the entire book—but goes a long way to illuminating how one man's "persecution mania," his desperate need "for dissimulation and camouflage" led indirectly to the devastation of Europe and destruction of European Jewry.[103]

Homosexuality does not therefore refer to moral habituation to suffering but to what the German journalist Sebastian Haffner called the desire to "commit murder but not to know it."[104] In the invocation of homosexuality to address the causes of empathic failure, mass murder is finally explained by reference to a sexual pathology that is unspeakably everybody's and thus mostly nobody's. The suspicion that homosexuality and Nazism belong together but that we can't ever know for sure serves the particular cultural aim of diffusing suspicion so widely that it exonerates the "not-knowing" bystander, the good citizen whose mysterious attraction to a murderous and barbarous leader has been perhaps the central moral dilemma of discussions about Nazi genocide.[105] Or to put it differently, the continued fascination with the question of whether or not Hitler or the Nazis were homosexuals has become a way of "explaining" mass murder while at the same time pointing to the failure of this explanation. That is, homosexuality holds out the promise of an explanation for why some people commit or are complicit in terrible crimes but then can't finally generate satisfactory answers. It figures a moral responsibility that cannot be assumed, that is always located somewhere—with someone else—that is, in effect, nobody's.

The association between homosexuality and Nazism may seem easily discredited—as we have seen in most reviews of Machtan—mostly because it is mistaken for a wholesale identification of Nazism and homosexuality that has now become untenable if not unthinkable.

After all, when historian Richard Bessel praises Machtan's book, it is only after a long, implicit apology for taking it seriously. But as Andrew Hewitt first argued systematically and persuasively in the context of modernist texts, it is the indirect relation between homosexuality and Nazism, one that does not seem to indict homosexuality proper but some potentially repressed desire in all men, that most perniciously and forcefully forges that relation: most perniciously, because it tantalizes the inquirer sufficiently to ensure that any questions about that relation are never resolved but destined to be asked again and again. As we have seen, it is the intrinsically, necessarily tautological nature of this explanation of a relationship between homosexuality and Nazism that explains pathological politics. From Samuel Igra to Theodor Adorno, and from Eugen Dollmann to Erik Erikson, Peter Loewenberg, and Michel Foucault, sexual (in this case homosexual) "pathology" figures pathological politics.[106] That figuration constitutes a systematic, complex, pervasive, and yet not always obvious or explicit mode of making an argument about phenomena that seem to overwhelm explanatory categories. It should be exposed as a form of broad cultural displacement. Homosexuality keeps pointing to something that dazzles but will always turn out to be a false lead, and in this way also looks like a reasonable inquiry into the causes of empathic failure but will finally go nowhere. Homosexual as well as heterosexual desires, repressed or self-conscious, are necessarily mobilized in various forms of social and political organization. But, as the relatively short history of the ever unfolding and increasingly diffuse narrative linking male homosexuality and Nazism should demonstrate, when homosexuality explains political failure, political catastrophe, and at worst, genocide, it ceases to be a component of a rich and complex analysis. It becomes a false alibi for bystanders and thus a way to avoid asking why and how empathy so often fails.

Epilogue

The narrative that cuts through these different essays suggests that collective responsibility to stop suffering requires us to be ever vigilant. Yet we must anticipate and prevent injury at the same time as the fragility of empathy as it has manifested itself over and over since the Second World War suggests that we are all potential victims and perpetrators, and makes our goal that much more difficult to attain. This narrative is finally about how we express, explain, and defend against this construction of "ourselves" and our neighbors as people who might one day turn out to be monsters. If these four essays have told a coherent story about how we conceive the fragility of empathy, it is that "we" have displaced and deferred hard questions about our perceived failure to live up to our ideals: that we confront "our" own fragility in ways that are not always honest and perhaps cannot be honest.

In an interesting analysis of Robert Jay Lifton's effort to explain in psychological terms how Nazi doctors in Auschwitz lived with themselves, Lawrence Langer rejects his effort to conceive them as having "double" selves that compartmentalized and thus protected them from the inhumanity with which they treated others day after day. Langer wonders instead whether or not these doctors' "experimentation on helpless victims [w]as an expression of their values, and hence of their 'normal' selves because they believed that a chief aim of their duty was to support the goals of Nazi racial ideology."[1] It is this probability that moves him, if not to despair, then to a weighty pessimism balanced in his work by a gentle and profound humanity. The possibility that there is a continuity between a "normal" person and a monstrous one and that indeed that person may be lurking anywhere and may even be "us" was first rendered thinkable and discussable after the Holocaust.

In these essays I have sought to demonstrate how accusations of pornography, celebrity, assertions of "natural" indifference, and the increasingly tenuous link between male homosexuality and Nazism are culturally significant but barely recognized defenses against this possibility, even as they articulate it over and over in different ways. This rhetoric constantly raises the question about the precariousness of our empathy: the invocation of the word pornography is perhaps the most dramatic evocation of a perceived empathic failure that cannot at the same time say what it refers to, so that we have to know it when we see it. What better example of how we collectively point to essential and troubling cultural questions about the fragility of empathy and yet just as quickly look away? References to pornography and the relationship between homosexuality and Nazism in different ways perform this task by permitting us to look at ourselves but also to quietly assign responsibility for what we see elsewhere, onto people or behaviors real or imagined who are not really embraced by "us." Recourse to "indifference" as an explanatory tool also forces us to look at ourselves. At the same time, it naturalizes our behavior so that we don't really have to take indifference into account (except as hand-wringing about the past and future) and identifies "us" with an ever-expansive "community of humanity" whose real membership list is constricted to an "us," which necessarily implies a "them." We bask in the comfort of our convictions by having it both ways: we are naturally indifferent to others, but then the category "we" comprises us all. These essays have sought to expose the new narrative about "numbness" in its myriad forms as a profound cultural investment in not fully confronting the failure of empathy that we seek to come to terms with, discuss, and feel despair about every day.

NOTES

INTRODUCTION

1. Brent Staples, Editorial, *New York Times*, April 9, 2000, sec. 4, p. 16. See also Leon Litwack's discussion of the potentially numbing effects of these images in his introduction to the exhibition catalogue, *Without Sanctuary: Lynching Photography in America* (Santa Fe: Twin Palms, 2000), 33–34.

2. George Steiner, *Portage to San Cristóbal of A. H.* (Chicago: University of Chicago Press, 1999), 173–74.

3. For example, Susan Moeller, *Compassion Fatigue* (New York: Routledge, 1999). Terms such as "compassion fatigue," "psychic numbing," and "states of denial" presume that an older humanitarian belief in the power of words and images to provoke compassion has eroded. For other pertinent examples: in her book on Albert Speer, the famous Austrian-born journalist Gitta Sereny notes that the now voluminous literature on "the Final Solution has created a kind of resistance. But it would be perilous if we allowed this 'compassion fatigue' to make us forget the singularity of this horror." Gitta Sereny, *Albert Speer: His Battle with Truth* (New York: Vintage, 1996), 344. As the sociologist Stanley Cohen and the psychologist Bruna Seu have written, "it is fashionable to claim that our emotions have been seized by 'compassion fatigue,' that we are too desensitized, numbed, or brutalized to feel." Stanley Cohen and Bruna Seu, "Knowing Enough Not to Feel Too Much: Emotional Thinking about Human Rights Appeals," in *Truth Claims: Representation and Human Rights*, ed. Mark Philip Bradley and Patrice Petro (New Brunswick, N.J.: Rutgers University Press, 2002), 193.

4. This is particularly true of recent critics of humanitarian efforts to rouse audiences to donate money and support in France. See, for example, Bernard Kouchner, "Le mouvement humanitaire: Questions à Bernard Kouchner," *Le Débat* 67 (1991): 30–39; and Georges Sebbag, "De la purification éthique," *Le Débat* 75 (1993): 24–35. For a general discussion of the

media, see Robert I. Rotberg and Thomas G. Weiss, eds., *From Massacres to Genocide: The Media, Public Policy, and Humanitarian Crises* (Washington, D.C.: Brookings Institution, 1996). For a general discussion of fund-raising strategies, see Stanley Cohen, *States of Denial: Knowing about Atrocities and Suffering* (Oxford: Polity Press in association with Blackwell Publishers, 2001), 168–221. Of course, empathic identification is hardly the only concern of human rights organizations. Also see the chapter by Robert Jay Lifton, "American Numbing," in *Hiroshima in America: Fifty Years of Denial,* ed. Robert Jay Lifton and Greg Mitchell (New York: Putnam, 1995), 337–40.

5. On the question of "we," one might point, as has Susan Sontag most recently, to Virginia Woolf's invocation of our visceral empathy: "But the human figure even in a photograph . . . suggests that we cannot dissociate ourselves from that figure but are ourselves that figure." She draws the conclusion that such photographs make us want to alter the conditions that made the atrocity possible. Sontag rightly notes that this usage of the atrocity photograph—its status as evidence for the existence of a universal "we"— now appears almost quaint if not naïve. Virginia Woolf, *Three Guineas* (New York: Harcourt Brace Jovanovich, 1938), 142; Susan Sontag, *Regarding the Pain of Others* (New York: Farrar, Straus and Giroux, 2003), 3–12.

6. For criticism of the ethnocentrism of this view, see Scott L. Montgomery, "What Kind of Memory? Reflections on Images of the Holocaust," *Contention* 5 (Fall 1995): 79–103, and Steven E. Aschheim, "Nazism, Culture and the Origins of Totalitarianism: Hannah Arendt and the Discourse of Evil," *New German Critique* 70 (Winter 1997): 117–39. For an interesting and slightly different approach to this question, see Anson Rabinbach, "'The Abyss that opened before us': Thinking about Auschwitz and Modernity," in *Catastrophe and Meaning: The Holocaust and the Twentieth Century,* ed. Moishe Postone and Eric Santner. (Chicago: University of Chicago Press, 2003), 51–66.

7. One of the aims of the book edited by Bradley and Petro on the cultural politics of human rights is to move away from now clichéd invocations of "information overload" or "compassion fatigue" "that often accompany analysis of human rights representations." Instead, they seek to "locate the problem [of how human rights are represented] not in the proliferation of images and information but in a prevailing decontextualization of their history." Bradley and Petro, *Truth Claims,* 4.

8. Diderot, quoted in Carlo Ginzburg, "Killing a Chinese Mandarin: The Moral Implications of Distance," in *Historical Change and Human Rights: The Oxford Amnesty Lectures,* ed. Olwen Hufton (New York: Basic Books, 1995), 62.

9. Quoted in Luc Boltanski, *Distant Suffering: Morality, Media and Politics* (Cambridge: Cambridge University Press, 1999), 101.

10. Karl Marx, *The Civil War in France* (New York: International Publishers, 1940), 52. Most of these narratives about public executions were relegated to secondary cultural status because they were overtly sensationalist. The morbid excitement tended to be represented as literally or symbolically feminine, as in Marx's account, which is, of course, satirical.

11. See Karen Haltunnen, "Humanitarianism and the Pornography of Pain in Anglo-American Culture," *American Historical Review* 100, no. 2 (1995): 303–34.

12. A famous discussion of sympathy occurs in Adam Smith, *Theory of Moral Sentiments*, ed. D. D. Raphael and A. L. Macfie (Oxford: Clarendon Press, 1982), 76–77.

13. Jean-Jacques Rousseau, "Discourse on Political Economy," in *On the Social Contract with Geneva Manuscripts and Political Economy*, ed. Roger D. Masters, trans. Judith D. Masters (New York: St. Martin's Press, 1978), 219.

14. It has often been noted that the Nuremberg trials focused on war crimes specifically (on the Germans' responsibility for conducting a "war of aggression" rather than on crimes against humanity and thus on genocide more generally). See the essays by David Cohen, "Beyond Nuremberg: Individual Responsibility for War Crimes," and Michael Ignatieff, "Human Rights," both in *Human Rights in Political Transitions: Gettysburg to Bosnia*, ed. Carla Hesse and Robert Post (New York: Zone Books, 1999), 53–92, 313–24. Adam Hochschild claims that the term "crimes against humanity" was actually first coined by George Washington Williams, an American shocked by the Europeans' treatment of Africans in the Congo. Adam Hochschild, *King Leopold's Ghost: A Story of Greed, Terror, and Heroism in Colonial Africa* (Boston: Houghton Mifflin, 1998), 112. As the historian Tony Kushner writes about attention to the Holocaust, "before the 1960s at the earliest, the Holocaust as a self-enclosed entity had not yet entered into the general consciousness or memory of the Western world." Tony Kushner, *The Holocaust and the Liberal Imagination: A Social and Cultural History* (Oxford: Blackwell, 1994), 2–3.

15. Isaiah Berlin, quoted in Michael Ignatieff, "Human Rights as Idolatry," in *Michael Ignatieff: Human Rights as Politics and Idolatry*, ed. Amy Gutmann (Princeton: Princeton University Press, 2001), 80–81. Ignatieff insists that "the Holocaust demonstrates both the prudential necessity of human rights and their ultimate fragility" (81).

16. In particular, revelations about the failure to bomb Auschwitz and indirect British negotiations over Hungarian Jews (the "Jews for trucks" deal) damaged idealized views of Allied policy. Discussions about the Allied responses to the Nazi persecution of Jews are voluminous. I will address these in greater depth in Chapter 3.

17. There is of course an enormous scholarship on the "Americanization" of the Holocaust, which I use implicitly but do not address centrally. And

though such representations are always inflected by the national culture in which they emerge, my project is to describe this narrative of empathic failure in the most general terms possible. See Alan Mintz, *Popular Culture and the Shaping of Holocaust Memory in America* (Seattle: University of Washington Press, 2001), 167–78.

18. William Reddy has recently sought to define a project on the history of emotion between 1650 and 1850 that seeks to account for the rise and fall of a model of high-pitched emotionalism that was "forgotten" once Napoleon came to power. Reddy looks to the self-altering work emotions permit to design a model of agency that demonstrates how change in "emotional regimes" can occur. In so doing, he relies on a cognitive model of emotions borrowed from recent comparative and cross-cultural discussions of emotions in anthropology as well as from cognitive psychology. William Reddy, *The Navigation of Feeling: A Framework for the History of Emotions* (Cambridge: Cambridge University Press, 2001).

19. Samantha Power persuasively documents the disjunction between American rhetoric about the horrors of genocide and the reality of American policy in *"A Problem from Hell": America in the Age of Genocide* (New York: Basic Books, 2002). And Martha Minow urges us to be aware that in spite of the promise of international human rights law established at the Nuremberg trials, no "comparable effort to prosecute war crimes in international settings" emerged for another forty years. Martha Minow, *Between Vengeance and Forgiveness* (Boston: Beacon, 1998), 27. For a more positive view of the Nuremberg trials, see Lawrence Douglas, *The Memory of Judgment: Making Law and History in the Trials of the Holocaust* (New Haven: Yale University Press, 2001), 4–5, 46–47, 90.

20. Thomas Haskell notes that the "principal novelty [of humanitarianism in its early incarnation in antislavery campaigns] was an expansion of the conventional limits of moral responsibility that prompted people . . . to behave in ways that were unprecedented and not necessarily well suited to their material interests." Thomas Haskell, *Objectivity Is Not Neutrality* (Baltimore: Johns Hopkins University Press, 1998), 256.

21. By emphasizing numbness, I am not trying to assert that all individuals are constrained by it—after all, humanitarian organizations are far more numerous now than they were fifty years ago. Clearly no discourse dictates what individuals do, but I wish to suggest that numbness may be becoming a conventional framework within which we think about our connections to others. Moreover, although the view that we should stop suffering, that we suffer from others' suffering but are pragmatic enough to know better given the complexity of conflict and *realpolitik*—the diplomat's view—still can't account for what Elazar Barkan, for example, claims is our desire to stop suffering but our refusal to commit resources to do it. Though the public's

pragmatism is certainly part of the answer to the question of why more is not done, it doesn't begin to explain the complexity of the narrative on numbness. See Elazar Barkan, *The Guilt of Nations: Restitution and Negotiating Historical Injustices* (Baltimore: Johns Hopkins University Press, 2000), xxxix–xl.

22. For a probing essay on recent French liberal responses to implicit poststructuralist criticism of foundationalist concepts of human rights, see Martin Jay, "Lafayette's Children: The American Reception of French Liberalism," *Substance* 1 (2002): 9–26.

23. In a recent repudiation of her own earlier argument that photographs had inevitably numbing effects, Susan Sontag writes: "It has become a cliché of the cosmopolitan discussion of images of atrocity to assume that they have little effect, and that there is something innately cynical about their diffusion." She claims that photos don't necessarily numb because so much depends on who the audience is and how the image is framed. If you believe that a particular war is unjust, the images of atrocities never stop making you weep, or numbness—as implied in the notion of "compassion fatigue"—may be a form of repression of one's powerlessness, fear, or rage before images of inhumanity. These assertions are all certainly valid. The significant question remains that if all of this is true, if we know and even have a diagnosis for the way our overwhelming emotion about what we see manifests itself as numbness, if we know that context determines how photographs are received and certainly determines who ultimately gets to be an "official" victim, why does numbness remain such a powerful cultural trope? Sontag, *Regarding the Pain of Others*, 111, 82–94.

24. The apt phrase comes from Arthur and Joan Kleinman, "The Appeal of Experience: The Dismay of Images: Cultural Appropriations of Suffering in Our Times," *Daedalus* 1 (Winter 1996): 9.

25. For a discussion of empathy's adventures from which some of this account is drawn, see Gail Reed, "The Antithetical Meaning of the Term 'Empathy' in Psychoanalytic Discourse," in *Empathy I*, ed. Joseph Lichtenberg, Melvin Borstein, and Donald Silver (New Jersey: Analytic Press, 1984), 7. In 1908 Wilhelm Worringer articulated a modernist construction of empathy by contrasting it with abstraction, which he claimed expressed man's desire to transcend rather than connect empathically with his environment. See Wilhelm Worringer, *Abstraction and Empathy: A Contribution to the Psychology of Style* [*Abtraktion und Einfühlung*], trans. Michael Bullock (New York: International Universities Press, 1953). For a discussion of the diffusion of Worringer's concept, see Marcia Brennan, *Painting Gender, Constructing Theory: The Alfred Stieglitz Circle and American Formalist Aesthetics* (Cambridge: MIT Press, 2001), 12, 253, and 344 n. 74.

26. Wilhelm Dilthey, *Introduction to the Human Sciences,* ed. Rudolf A. Makkreel and Frithjof Rodi (Princeton: Princeton University Press, 1989).

27. The fairly technical usage of *Einfühlung* and the English "empathy" gave way after the 1960s, as cultural critics more generally sought to understand genocide, to a far more diverse and cross-disciplinary discourse about "our" inability to empathize with suffering. Boltanski notes in passing that empathy signifies not the attenuated experience of another's suffering, but emotional "contagion" (a word in fact used by the Scottish moral philosopher Francis Hutcheson in 1753 to describe sympathy), reflecting the "feeling-in" quality that emphasizes a psychic occupation of the other rather than the symbolic likeness implicit in renderings of sympathy. For a brief summary of the aesthetic and psychological meaning of *Einfühlung*, see Jadwiga Dorosz, "Le problème de l'einfuelung," *Archives de Psychologie* 26 (1937): 198–203. For a discussion of empathic identification as the "psychological foundation of democracy and human rights," see Lynn Hunt, "The Origins of Human Rights in France," *Proceedings of the Annual Meeting of the Western Society for French History* 24 (1997): 9–24. For Hutcheson's remarks, see Francis Hutcheson, *Short Introduction to Moral Philosophy in Three Books containing the Elements of Ethiks and the Law of Nature*, 2d ed., (Glasgow: Robert Andrew Foulis, 1753), bk. 1, chap. 1, 14.

28. See, for example, Martin Davies and Tony Stone, eds., *Mental Simulation: Evaluations and Applications* (Oxford: Blackwell, 1995).

29. George Steiner, *In Bluebeard's Castle: Some Notes toward the Redefinition of Culture* (New Haven: Yale University Press, 1971), 79 (from which comes the term "post-culture"). See, among others, Karl F. Morrison, *"I Am You": The Hermeneutics of Empathy in Western Literature, Theology, and Art* (Princeton University Press, 1988), xiii.

30. Žižek refers to the condition of the "Muslim" in concentration camps (a word used by camp inmates to designate those of their brethren who had lost all recognizable qualities of being human and yet were still alive) as the referent of a new way of thinking about humanity. Agamben too calls humanist concepts of dignity into question by reference to this figure. On the "post-tragic," see Slavoj Žižek, *Did Somebody Say Totalitarianism? Five Interventions in the (Mis)Use of a Notion* (London: Verso, 2001), 61–88, esp. 73–78; Giorgio Agamben, *Remnants of Auschwitz: The Witness and the Archive* (New York: Zone Books, 1999), esp. 68–72, 80–82.

31. David Morris, "About Suffering: Voice, Genre, and Moral Community," *Daedalus* 1 (Winter 1996): 28. Also Susan Moeller, in *Compassion Fatigue*, suggests that the predominance of images over texts and competition among news media saturates audiences with so much information and by such superficially rendered and sensational accounts of atrocities that they no longer really take it in. In a more sophisticated account, John Taylor seeks to account for how the media construct and interpret horror ideologically—war atrocities, murder, and so forth—and thus control our concerns and de-

termine our objects of empathy in particular ways. They present suffering as entertainment but also self-consciously restrict voyeurism in the name of respectability. See John Taylor, *Body Horror: Photojournalism, Catastrophe, and War* (New York: New York University Press, 1998).

32. Barbie Zelizer, *Remembering to Forget: Holocaust Memory through the Camera's Eye* (Chicago: University of Chicago Press, 1998), 209, 214.

33. Arthur and Joan Kleinman, "Appeal of Experience," 19.

34. Jean Baudrillard, "Requiem for the Media," in *Video Culture: A Critical Investigation*, ed. John G. Hanhardt (Rochester, N.Y.: Video Studies Workshop Press, 198), 131. See also Mark Poster, ed., *Jean Baudrillard: Selected Writings* (Stanford: Stanford University Press, 1988). See also, among others, Anton Kaes, "History and Film: Public Memory in the Age of Electronic Dissemination," *History and Memory* 2, no. 1 (1990): 111–29; Hans Magnus Enzenberger, "Constituents of a Theory of the Media," in *Video Culture*, ed. Hanhardt, 96–123.

35. Jean Baudrillard, *The Evil Demon of Images* (Sydney: Power Institute of Fine Arts, University of Sydney, 1987), 24. In an even more extravagant comment in the same text, Baudrillard also says that the television movie *Holocaust* is "an attempt to reheat a *cold* historical event—tragic but cold, the first great event of cold systems, those cooling systems of dissuasion and extermination which were subsequently deployed in other forms . . . and in relation to the cold masses (the Jews no longer even concerned by their own death, eventually self-managing it, no longer even masses in revolt: dissuaded unto death, dissuaded even of their own death)" (24–25).

36. Zelizer, *Remembering to Forget*, 209. The French sociologist Luc Boltanski claims that what he calls a "politics of pity" is central to humanitarian thought and by definition presumes distance from the suffering of others. To define a normative response like pity or sympathy to suffering, he writes, it is essential to establish "equivalence between spatially and temporally local situations": in other words, to abstract from particular mores governing behavior in order to create universally appropriate and thus normative emotional responses to pain. Boltanski, *Distant Suffering*, 7.

37. See Lindsay French, "Exhibiting Terror," in *Truth Claims*, ed. Bradley and Petro, 151. The question of whether images of the Holocaust can be aestheticized and with what consequences is taken up in Chapter 1.

38. James E. Young, *The Texture of Memory: Holocaust Memorials and Meaning* (New Haven: Yale University Press, 1993), 342–45; Andrea Liss, *Trespassing through Shadows: Memory, Photography, and the Holocaust* (Minneapolis: University of Minnesota Press, 1998), 22–23. Young and Liss do not share the same conceptual framework for understanding Holocaust memory, since she reiterates a fairly standard poststructuralist emphasis on historical memory as fundamentally unknowable, and he seeks to understand the

social effects of particular representations of historical memory. For a discussion of how the U.S. Holocaust Memorial Museum's board aimed at empathic identification, see Edward T. Linenthal, *Preserving Memory: The Struggle to Create American's Holocaust Museum* (New York: Viking, 1995), 163–64. For a positive valuation of empathic identification as the Museum stages it, see Alison Landsberg, "America, the Holocaust, and the Mass Culture of Memory: Toward a Radical Politics of Empathy," *New German Critique* 71 (1997): 63–86.

39. Ruth Klüger, *Von hoher und niedriger Literatur* (Göttingen: Wallstein Verlag, 1996), 32–33.

40. Jonathan Boyarin, *Storm from Paradise: The Politics of Jewish Memory* (Minneapolis: University of Minnesota Press, 1992), 86–88. In another context (that of slavery), Saidiya V. Hartman far more explicitly criticizes sentimentality in this vein: *Scenes of Subjection: Terror, Slavery, and Self-Making in Nineteenth-Century America* (Oxford: Oxford University Press, 1998), esp. 17–23.

41. In the United States an emphasis on competing claims of victims is often associated with the State's refusal to recognize officially the horrors of slavery but its willingness to acknowledge the Holocaust of European Jewry. The literature on this topic is voluminous. See also the more general discussions in Joseph Amato, *Victims and Values* (New York: Praeger, 1990); and Haskell, *Objectivity Is Not Neutrality*, 235–306. For a facile but suggestive contribution from the Left, which aligns the American "therapeutic idiom" rather reductively with American identity politics (and thus with a politics of victimization), see Michel Feher, "Empowerment Hazards: Affirmative Action, Recovery Psychology, and Identity Politics," *Representations* 55 (Summer 1996): 84–91. In Europe, a new discourse has also developed regarding the "competition of victims," particularly in reference to a discussion of totalitarianism in which the experience of suffering under Nazism and Stalinism has been compared anew. This discourse is particularly pervasive in both eastern Europe and France. For an updated account that covers the spectrum, see Henry Rousso, ed., *Stalinisme et nazisme: Histoire et mémoire comparées* (Paris: Editions Complexes, 1999), and Jean-Michel Chaumont, *La concurrence des victimes: Genocide, identité, reconnaissance* (Paris: Editions de la Découverte, 1997). Chaumont's study focuses on the after-effects of the immediate postwar refusal to acknowledge Jewish suffering and claims that Jews' so-called insistence on the primacy of their own suffering derives from this initial refusal of recognition (see esp. 40–45). In Germany, this discussion now most often revolves around the demand for recognition of German suffering under Allied carpet-bombing during the Second World War. See the best-selling work by Jörg Friedrich, *Der Brand: Deutschland im Bombenkrieg 1940–45* (Berlin: Propyläen, 2002).

42. Peter Novick, *The Holocaust in American Life* (New York: Mariner Books, 2000), 121, 189.

43. Barkan, *Guilt of Nations,* ix. Since he is particularly interested in restitution as conflict resolution, Barkan moves quickly beyond such rhetoric (the idea that victims are "autistic" and "self-indulgent"—xviii) to discuss the potential of a new, pragmatic dialogue between perpetrators and victims' groups.

44. Tzvetan Todorov, "In Search of Lost Crime," *New Republic* 489 (January 29, 2001): 25.

45. Ibid., 33.

46. Jane Caplan, "Reflections on the Reception of Goldhagen in the United States," in *The "Goldhagen Effect": History, Memory, Nazism—Facing the German Past,* ed. Geoff Eley (Ann Arbor: University of Michigan Press, 2000), 161.

47. István Deák, "The Crime of the Century," *New York Review of Books* 14 (September 26, 2002): 49.

48. Jack Kugelmass, " 'Missions to the Past': Poland in Contemporary Thought and Deed," in *Tense Past: Cultural Essays in Trauma and Memory,* ed. Paul Antze and Michael Lambek (New York: Routledge, 1996), 202, 205.

49. Philip Gourevitch, "Behold Now Behemoth: The Holocaust Memorial Museum: One More American Theme Park," *Harper's* 287 (1993): 62. Charles Maier has written that "modern American politics, it might be argued, has become a competition for enshrining grievances." A recent review of a new work on *Selling the Holocaust* notes as an aside that the so-called Holocaust industry is successful in the United States, where " 'victim culture' is famous for appropriating the pain of others and turning it into a national heritage." See Charles Maier, "A Surfeit of Memory? Reflections on History, Melancholy, and Denial," *History and Memory* 5 (1993): 147; and Adam Frost, review of Tim Cole, *Images of the Holocaust: The Myth of the Shoah Business* (London: Duckworth, 1999), in *Contemporary Review* 275 (December 1999): 324. In the United States, Cole's book was published with a different title (or the title was revised upon publication): *Selling the Holocaust: From Auschwitz to Schindler, How History Is Bought, Packaged, and Sold* (New York: Routledge, 1999).

50. Alvin H. Rosenfeld, "The Americanization of the Holocaust," in *Thinking About the Holocaust: After Half a Century,* ed. Alvin H. Rosenfeld (Bloomington: Indiana University Press, 1997), 131.

51. Efraim Sicher, "The Future of the Past: Countermemory and Postmemory in Contemporary American Post-Holocaust Narratives," *History and Memory* 12, no. 2 (2001): 61–63. See also Alain Finkielkraut's discussion of Jewish identity and victimization in *The Imaginary Jew* (Lincoln: University of Nebraska Press, 1994).

52. Detailed histories of how various groups identify themselves as victims would be necessary to analyze how "being a victim" operates as a form of identity, but such studies would still not explain why cultural critics perceive that identity to be such a powerful one, even trumping heroism. For critical analyses both of "wounded attachment" to victim identity and of the "will to power" often implicit in victims' longings that begin to explore such questions, see Wendy Brown, *States of Injury: Power and Freedom in Late Modernity* (Princeton: Princeton University Press, 1995); and Wendy Brown and Janet Halley, eds., *Left Legalism/Left Critique* (Durham: Duke University Press, 2002).

53. Todorov, "In Search of Lost Crime," 25.

54. I am referring to President Reagan's infamous visit to the cemetery in Bitburg in 1985, in which he was to honor slain German soldiers. A controversy erupted when it was revealed that members of the SS were also buried there. Reagan nevertheless insisted on going. The writer and Jewish Auschwitz survivor Elie Wiesel took the President to task publicly for making the decision to go, urging him to change his mind. "Mr. Wiesel spoke before learning of remarks today in which the President contended that both the Jews slain in the Holocaust, and some of the soldiers, many of them draftees, who are buried in the German cemetery that he intends to visit, were victims of Nazism." Francis X. Clines, *New York Times*, April 19, 1985, sec. A, p. 1. For scholarly analysis of this event, see Geoffrey Hartman, ed., *Bitburg in Moral and Political Perspective* (Indianapolis: Indiana University Press, 1986).

55. Lawrence L. Langer, *Preempting the Holocaust* (New Haven: Yale University Press, 1998), 66.

56. Though works on Holocaust representation are infinite, for more specific discussions about how Holocaust survivors can and cannot "speak" that indirectly take up Langer's claims, see among others Thomas Trezise, "Unspeakable," and Jared Stark, "Suicide after Auschwitz," both in *Yale Journal of Criticism* 14, no. 1 (2001): 39–66 and 93–114. The entire issue is devoted to interpretations of Holocaust testimony and memory. See also Trezise, "The Question of Community in Charlotte Delbo's *Auschwitz and After*," *MLN* 117, no. 4 (2002): 858–86.

57. For the view that historical trauma requires a radical rethinking of intersubjective relations as they have been conventionally defined, see William Haver, *The Body of This Death: Historicity and Sociality in the Time of AIDS* (Stanford: Stanford University Press, 1996).

58. That is, as he puts it, "modern universal human rights culture" and the idea of "crimes against humanity" were born of our "awakening to the shame of having done so little to help the millions of strangers who died in this century's experiments in terror and exterminations. . . . It is the 'thing it-

self' [the suffering body shorn of reason and dignity] that has become the subject—and the rationale—for the modern universal human rights culture." Michael Ignatieff, *The Needs of Strangers* (London: Hogarth Press, 1984), 28–30, 51–52.

59. Michael Geyer, foreword to *The German Army and Genocide: Crimes Against War Prisoners, Jews, and other Civilians, 1939–1944*, Hamburg Institute for Social Research (New York: New Press, 1999), 8.

1. EMPATHY, SUFFERING, AND HOLOCAUST "PORNOGRAPHY"

1. Quoted in Norman L. Kleeblatt, "Roee Rosen Live and Die as Eva Braun, 1995. Male Fantasies of Hitler: Confusing Gender and Identity," in *Mirroring Evil: Nazi Imagery/Recent Art*, ed. Norman L. Kleeblatt (New Brunswick, N.J.: Rutgers University Press, 2001), 103. Unfortunately, Kleeblatt cites no specific references, but he is referring to the exhibit of Roee Rosen's piece "Live and Die as Eva Braun" at the Israel Museum (Jerusalem) in 1997.

2. Omer Bartov has discussed the brutalizing effects of representing atrocity in Israel via a discussion of the concentration camp pornography authored by the Polish survivor become Israeli Ka-Tzetnik (pseudonym for Yehiel Dinur). As Bartov notes, their "obsession with violence and perversity" rendered Ka-Tzetnik's works fascinating (if also troubling) to Israeli youths born between the 1940s and the early 1960s. My point is that whatever the Israeli media had to say about this exhibit, the questions it poses have clearly been discussed extensively in Israel for a long while. Omer Bartov, *Mirrors of Destruction: War, Genocide, and Modern Identity* (Oxford: Oxford University Press, 2000), 183.

3. The Museum is particularly important, because it has been enormously successful. In the first year after it opened in 1993, CNN reported that four thousand people a day sought entry, and a Museum spokeswoman claimed that they were probably turning away at least a thousand people a day. The Museum continues to draw enormous crowds a decade later. See transcripts of *CNN*; New York, November 20, 1993, 8:00 P.M. ET.

4. By the mid-nineteenth century, western European nations began to regulate moral order in the interest of assuring healthy, "normal" populations, fit for combat, reproduction, and productive labor. In France, England, Germany, and the United States, the modern concept of the "pornographic" was invented by the 1880s, as elites determined to control the publication and distribution of literature that provoked antisocial sexual sensations and acts in those they deemed morally weak or unformed—women, children, and working-class men. After the Great War, pornography began to lose its

reference to a specific genre of material. For an account of these developments, see Carolyn J. Dean, *The Frail Social Body: Pornography, Homosexuality, and Other Fantasies in Interwar France* (Berkeley: University of California Press, 2000), 25–129.

5. For one of the most important efforts to define a genre of "pornography," see Linda Williams, *Hard Core: Power, Pleasure, and the Frenzy of the Visible* (Berkeley: University of California Press, 1989). For a history of the regulation of pornography that concludes it has no intrinsic meaning (because pornography is in the eye of the beholder), see Walter Kendrick, *The Secret Museum: Pornography in Modern Culture* (New York: Penguin, 1987).

6. Catharine MacKinnon, *Feminism Unmodified: Discourses on Life and Law* (Cambridge: Harvard University Press, 1989); *Toward a Feminist Theory of the State* (Cambridge: Harvard University Press, 1989); *Only Words* (Cambridge: Harvard University Press, 1993).

7. There is now a voluminous literature on post-Holocaust art and literature, most of which seeks to go beyond debates about "can the Holocaust be represented?" to how it *is* being represented in art, architecture, photography, and memorials. See James E. Young, *At Memory's Edge: After-Images of the Holocaust in Contemporary Art and Architecture* (New Haven: Yale University Press, 2000); Vivian M. Patraka, *Spectacular Suffering: Theatre, Fascism, and the Holocaust* (Bloomington: Indiana University Press, 1999), esp. 87, 109–10. Important also are essays in Shelley Hornstein and Florence Jacobowitz, eds., *Image and Remembrance: Representation and the Holocaust* (Bloomington: Indiana University Press, 2003), esp. those by Marianne Hirsch and Susan Rubin Suleiman, "Material Memory: Holocaust Testimony in Post-Holocaust Art," 89; Ernst van Alphen, "Caught by Images: Visual Imprints in the Holocaust," 98–99; Janet Woolf, "The Iconic and the Allusive: The Case for Beauty in Post-Holocaust Art," 154–57; Carol Zemel, "Emblems of Atrocity: Holocaust Liberation Photographs," 205. See also Dora Apel, *Memory Effects: The Holocaust and the Art of Secondary Witnessing* (New Brunswick, N.J.: Rutgers University Press, 2002), esp. 58, 78–79, 112, 127, 139, 190, for an overview of recent art from Shimon Attie to Susan Silas's work, and Gertrud Koch, "The Aesthetic Transformation of the Unimaginable: Notes on Claude Lanzmann's *Shoah*," in *October* 48 (1989): 15–24. Essays in Julia Epstein and Lori Hope Lefkovitz, eds., *Shaping Losses: Cultural Memory and the Holocaust* (Urbana: University of Illinois Press, 2001) offer testimonials by the second and third generation of Jews (children of survivors or more distant relatives whose families had for the most part perished).

8. Fredric Jameson, *Signatures of the Visible* (New York: Routledge, 1990), 1 and 87.

9. Jorgen Lissner, quoted in Stanley Cohen, *States of Denial: Knowing*

about Atrocities and Suffering (Oxford: Polity Press in association with Black-well Publishers, 2001), 178.

10. This use of the camera was given perhaps one of its earliest and most powerful (and problematically enthusiastic) expressions by Ernst Jünger. As he put it, "The photograph stands outside the realm of sensibility. It has something of a telescopic quality: one can tell that the object photographed was seen by an insensitive and invulnerable eye." Jünger's comments expressed excitement about the new technology as a potential instrument of domination and are not coincidentally written in 1934, when "pornography" was first associated as much with images of war dead and violence more generally. Ernst Jünger, "Photography and the 'Second Consciousness,'" in *Photography in the Modern Era: European Documents and Critical Writings, 1913–1940*, ed. Christopher Phillips (New York: Museum of Modern Art, 1989), 19. Jünger's comments on the camera were part of a broader discourse on both the Left and Right about the dangers of mass media and its capacity to objectify. In an interesting article on Jünger, Anton Kaes argues that for him the camera allowed viewers to "adopt a cool and detached attitude vis-à-vis the horror picture of warlike casualties." More pertinently, he suggests that Jünger's conception of the photograph "changes our ability to experience pain," so that we can watch violence with increasing detachment. Anton Kaes, "The Cold Gaze: Notes on Mobilization and Modernity," *New German Critique* 0, no. 59 (Spring–Summer 1993): 108, 110.

11. Ruth Klüger, *Von hoher und niedriger Literatur* (Göttingen: Wallstein Verlag, 1996), 35.

12. Lynn Hunt, *The Family Romance of the French Revolution* (Berkeley: University of California Press, 1994); Sarah Maza, *Public Lives and Private Affairs: The Causes Célèbres of Prerevolutionary France* (Berkeley: University of California Press, 1993). More generally, historians have pointed to the ways in which so-called deviant sexual groups such as prostitutes and homosexuals became complicated symbols of social and moral disorder and of challenges to normative class divisions and gender roles more specifically: male homosexuality, for example, symbolizes the emasculation of the virile nation-state, and prostitution represents the traversal of class boundaries. Of course, sexual deviance symbolizes such transgressions in a wide variety of ways. I discuss the fantasmic connection between fascism and male homosexuality in detail in Chapter 4.

13. See Carolyn J. Dean, *The Frail Social Body: Pornography, Homosexuality, and Other Fantasies in Interwar France* (Berkeley: University of California Press, 2000), 25–129; and "History, Pornography, and the Social Body," in *Surrealism: Desire Unbound*, Exhibition Catalogue (London: Tate Publishing, 2001), 227–44.

14. James Agee, "Films," *Nation*, March 24, 1945, 342.

15. Geoffrey Gorer, "The Pornography of Death," *Encounter* 5, no. 4 (1955): 49–52.

16. Lionel Rubinoff, *The Pornography of Power* (Chicago: Quadrangle Books, 1967).

17. George Steiner, "Night Words," *Encounter* 25, no. 4 (1965): 18, 17. See also Steiner, "Pornography and Its Consequences," *Encounter* 36, no. 3 (1966): 46–47; and Steiner's letter to the *Times Literary Supplement,* May 26, 1966, 475.

18. Donald M. Gillmor, "The Puzzle of Pornography," *Journalism Quarterly* 42 (Summer 1965): 372.

19. For a synthesis of recent work on the "Americanization of the Holocaust," see Alan Mintz, *Popular Culture and the Shaping of Holocaust Memory in America* (Seattle: University of Washington Press, 2001), 3–35. On Holocaust representations on American television (and for a useful discussion of the Eichmann trial and its impact), see Jeffrey Shandler, *While America Watches: Televising the Holocaust* (New York: Oxford University Press, 1999).

20. Saul Friedländer, *Memory, History, and the Extermination of the Jews* (Indianapolis: Indiana University Press, 1993), 97.

21. John J. O'Connor, "TV: NBC 'Holocaust,' Art Versus Mammon," *New York Times,* April 20, 1978, sec. C, p. 22.

22. Alvin H. Rosenfeld, *Imagining Hitler* (Bloomington: Indiana University Press, 1985), 60.

23. Armond White, "Toward a Theory of Spielberg History," *Film Comment* 30, no. 2 (1994): 55. Indeed, to the dismay of countless cultural critics, Steven Spielberg's *Schindler's List* generated much hand-wringing over its populist appeal from France to the United States. See the essays in Yosefa Loshitzky, ed., *Spielberg's Holocaust: Critical Perspectives on Schindler's List* (Bloomington: Indiana University Press, 1997). In the introduction, Loshitzky notes that the journalist Frank Rich declared a "Holocaust boom" in 1994 to express the coincidence of the opening of the U.S. Holocaust Memorial Museum, the release of *Schindler's List,* Pope John Paul II's invitation to the Chief Rabbi of Rome to visit him in the Vatican, and a bill signed by then New Jersey Governor Christine Todd Whitman requiring schoolchildren in that state to be taught about the Holocaust and other genocides (5).

24. Paula E. Hyman, "New Debate on the Holocaust: Has the Popularization of This Tragedy Diluted Its Meaning and Diminished Other Aspects of Judaism?" *New York Times Magazine,* September 14, 1980, 67, 109.

25. Lucy Dawidowicz, *The Jewish Presence: Essays on Identity and History* (New York: Holt, Rinehart and Winston, 1977), 217, 224.

26. Elie Wiesel, "Trivializing Memory," *New York Times,* June 11, 1989, sec. 2, p. 1.

27. Sybil Milton, "The Camera as Weapon: Documentary Photography and the Holocaust," in *The Simon Wiesenthal Center Annal Volume 1*, ed. Alex Grobman (Chappaqua, N.Y.: Rossel Books, 1984), 60; Geoffrey Hartman, "Public Memory and Its Discontents," *Raritan* 13, no. 4 (1994): 25; Daphne Merkin, "Meditations on the Unthinkable," *New York Times Book Review*, April 11, 1999, 17; Andrew R. Carlson, review of Inga Clendinnen, *Reading the Holocaust*, in *Germanic Studies Review* 22 (2000): 379.

28. Quoted in Norman Finkelstein, *The Holocaust Industry: Reflections on the Exploitation of Jewish Suffering* (London: Verso, 2000), 55.

29. Thomas Laqueur, "The Sound of Voices Intoning Names," *London Review of Books*, June 5, 1997, 3–6.

30. Stefan Maechler, *The Wilkomirski Affair: A Study in Biographical Truth*, trans. John E. Woods (New York: Schocken Books, 2001), 277.

31. Michael Rothberg, *Traumatic Realism: The Demands of Holocaust Representation* (Minneapolis: University of Minnesota Press, 2000), 187–88.

32. Jacquelyn Dowd Hall, quoted in Leon Litwack's introduction to *Without Sanctuary: Lynching Photography in America* (Santa Fe, N.M.: Twin Palms Press, 2000), 22.

33. Tim Cole, *Selling the Holocaust: From Auschwitz to Schindler, How History Is Bought, Packaged, and Sold* (New York: Routledge, 1999), 97.

34. Ibid., 114.

35. Gourevitch, quoted in Cole, *Selling the Holocaust*, 156.

36. Victoria Barnett, "Bearing Witness," *Christian Century*, May 12, 1993, 509.

37. Michael Sorkin, "The Holocaust Museum: Between Beauty and Horror," *Progressive Architecture* 74 (1993): 74.

38. Alvin Rosenfeld, "Another Revisionism: Popular Culture and the Changing Image of the Holocaust," in *Bitburg in Moral and Political Perspective*, ed. Geoffrey H. Hartman (Indianapolis: Indiana University Press, 1986), 90–91.

39. Barnett, "Bearing Witness," 509.

40. Sorkin, "Holocaust Museum," 74.

41. Cole, *Selling the Holocaust*, 76.

42. The catalogue, which I discuss below, presents the positive view (as do other critics in various art journals and newspaper articles). For a hostile but thoughtful effort to set her objections in the context of "culture wars" and their meaning(s), see Michelle Goldberg, "No Business like Shoah Business," *Salon.com*, April 3, 2002.

43. For illustrations and commentary by specialists, see the catalogue, *Mirroring Evil*, ed. Kleeblatt. The catalogue came out in December, well in advance of the exhibition's opening in March, creating tremendous controversy based on the illustrations therein.

44. Rosensaft, quoted in Alan Cooperman, "Art of Insult: A Dialogue Shaped by the Holocaust," *Washington Post*, February 24, 2002, B02. Rosensaft also claimed that the Museum's offer to put up warning signs for survivors who might be pained by various installations was "moving anthrax from one part of a building to another," in an odd analogy with terrorist threats to democracy. See Rosensaft's comments to journalist Barbara Stewart, in "Jewish Museum to Add Warning Label on Its Show," *New York Times*, March 2, 2002, 1.

45. Elie Wiesel, "Holocaust Exhibit Betrays History," *Newsday*, February 1, 2002, A41.

46. Geoffrey Wheatcroft, "Diary," *Spectator*, April 13, 2002, 8.

47. In order of citation, see Alexander Rose, "In Defense of 'Mirroring Evil,'" *Providence-Journal Bulletin*, March 2, 2002; Richard Goldstein, "Managing the Unmanageable," *Village Voice*, March 12, 2002, 45; Liz Trotta, "Jewish Museum Creates a Stir; Exhibit Takes Unusual Tack in Explaining the Holocaust," *Washington Times*, March 14, 2002, A07; Dan Bischoff, "Protests Rage over Display of Modern Holocaust Art," *Newhouse News Service*, March 11, 2002.

48. Ellen Handler Spitz, quoted in Steven Edwards, "Artists under Attack for Modern Take on Holocaust," *National Post*, February 7, 2002, A17.

49. Linda Nochlin, "Mirroring Evil: Nazi Imagery/Recent Art," *Art Forum International* 40, no. 10 (Summer 2002): 167.

50. The phrase is from Michael Kimmelman, "A Show about the Holocaust Raises Hackles," *International Herald Tribune*, February 2–3, 2002, 18.

51. James E. Young, foreword to *Mirroring Evil*, ed. Kleeblatt, xvii. Young's foreword is more or less a synopsis of his argument about Holocaust postmemory and its representation in Young, *At Memory's Edge: After-Images of the Holocaust in Contemporary Art and Architecture* (New Haven: Yale University Press, 2000), 3. His extensive discussion of David Levinthal's work (54–61) is particularly important (Levinthal uses toy Nazi figurines and has been criticized for, among other things, sexualizing female victims represented in crematoria). Young suggests that this kind of "pornography" may not only call attention, as the artist himself claims, to the fact that both victims and killers knew that sexual degradation was part of victims' humiliation, but is also a way of acknowledging that contemporary cultural representations of the Holocaust have thrived on the link between sex and death. Young claims that Levinthal thus confronts "the possibility of their visitors' pornographic gaze" (57). In the book, however, Young seems a bit more ambivalent about such representations than he does in the catalogue. Most importantly, he defends the intellectual grounds of the project more generally, if not each individual work of art.

52. Kimmelman, "A Show about the Holocaust," 18.

53. Michael Frank, "Springtime for Hitler," *Los Angeles Times Book Review,* March 31, 2002, 65.

54. James E. Young, cited in "The Limits of Taste," *Chronicle of Higher Education,* March 29, 2002, B19. The author, whoever he or she is, does not credit Young with the quotation, which comes from the foreword of the catalogue, *Mirroring Evil,* xvi.

55. Norman L. Kleeblatt, "The Nazi Occupation of the White Cube: Transgressive Images/Moral Ambiguity/Contemporary Art," in *Mirroring Evil,* 9.

56. Joan Rosenbaum, "Director's Preface," in *Mirroring Evil,* vii.

57. Nochlin, "Mirroring Evil," 168, 207.

58. Lisa Saltzman, " 'Avant-garde and Kitsch' Revisited: On the Ethics of Representation," in *Mirroring Evil,* 47–48. The analogy she makes between the Nazis' victims and "we" who have been seduced and rendered powerless by the imagery is clearly problematic. It is not at all clear how being seduced by these images "doubles" the powerlessness of victims.

59. Ellen Handler Spitz, "Exhibition Challenges Our Ideas about Evil," *Baltimore Sun,* February 15, 2002, 23A. For the second quotation, "The Limits of Taste and Irony," *Chronicle of Higher Education,* March 29, 2002, B19.

60. Ernst van Alphen, "Playing the Holocaust," in *Mirroring Evil,* 75.

61. Judith Doneson, *The Holocaust in American Film* (Philadelphia: Jewish Publication Society, 1987), 185.

62. This critique was present in myriad discussions of documentary photography during the 1970s and 1980s. Quoted here is Martha Rosler, arguing that the reform impulse of documentary "has shaded over into . . . tourism, voyeurism, and trophy hunting" and urging artists to frame this shift critically. Martha Rosler, *Three Works* (Halifax: Press of the Nova Scotia College of Art and Design, 1981), 72. Susan Sontag's oft-quoted *On Photography* (New York: Delta, 1973) is perhaps still the most important essay in which these criticisms are articulated. In spite of a spate of recent work that seeks to complicate the meaning of the camera as metaphor of domination, this view remains fairly mainstream, especially in relation to images of the Holocaust, which, as Marianne Hirsch persuasively argues, "overwhelm all viewing relations." Much recent analysis (as well as avant-garde work) suggests that documentary should formally incorporate the limits of its realism, in some manner staging the failure of its ability to represent (in this case) the Holocaust truthfully. See (also for a fascinating challenge to the notion of the saturation-effect created by so many atrocity photos) Marianne Hirsch, "Surviving Images: Holocaust Photographs and the Work of Postmemory," in *Visual Culture and the Holocaust,* ed. Barbie Zelizer (New Brunswick, N.J.: Rutgers University Press, 2001), 233. For other discussions, see also Andrea Liss, *Trespassing through Shadows: Memory, Photography, and the Holocaust*

(Minneapolis: University of Minnesota Press, 1998), xiii–xvii; and for a general discussion, Abigail Solomon-Godeau, "Who Is Speaking Thus? Some Questions about Documentary Photography," in *The Event Horizon: Essays on Hope, Sexuality, Social Space and Media(tion) in Art,* ed. Lorna Falke and Barbara Fischer (Toronto: Coach House Press, 1987), 193–214; Woolf, "The Iconic and the Allusive," 154–57, where she claims that too-literal representations collude with a "pornography of violence" (154).

63. Berenbaum, quoted in Liss, *Trespassing through Shadows,* xiv.

64. Philip Gourevitch, "Behold Now Behemoth: The Holocaust Memorial Museum: One More American Theme Park," *Harper's,* no. 287 (July, 1993), 60.

65. In contrast, Marianne Hirsch has argued that identification is not necessarily generated by the reality but by the photograph's representation and interpretation of reality. She calls for a "postmemorial aesthetic based on a mediated, non-appropriative, indirect form of identification that would clarify the *limits* of retrospective understanding, rather than make the past too easily available." Marianne Hirsch, "Nazi Photographs in Post-Holocaust Art: Gender as an Idiom of Memorialization," in *Crimes of War: Guilt and Denial in the Twentieth Century,* ed. Omer Bartov, Atina Grossmann, and Mary Nolan (New York: New Press, 2002), 110. See also Silke Wenk, "Rhetoriken der Pornografisierung: Rahmungen des Blicks aus die NS Verbrechen," in *Gedächtnis und Geschlecht: Deutungsmuster in Darstellungen des nationalsozialistischen Genozids,* ed. Insa Escehbach, Sigrid Jacobeit, and Silke Wenk (Frankfurt: Campus Verlag, 2002), 269–94, especially the discussion of Goldhagen.

66. Berel Lang uses the specialized genre of concentration camp pornography as the ground zero of unacceptable Holocaust representations in his effort to define appropriate limits to how the genocide can be depicted. Since he refers literally rather than metaphorically to pornographic literature, his comments do not quite fit here; at the same time, his use of literal pornography as the one self-evident limit of Holocaust representation is worth noting. See Berel Lang, *Holocaust Representation: Art within the Limits of History and Ethics* (Baltimore: Johns Hopkins University Press, 2000), 7, 19, 48.

67. Daniel Jonah Goldhagen, *Hitler's Willing Executioners: Ordinary Germans and the Holocaust* (New York: Vintage, 1996). It is nevertheless important to recognize that Goldhagen's work forced two generations of functionalist German historians to acknowledge their tendency to neglect Jewish victims of genocide. I address this in far more detail in Chapter 2. See Ulrich Herbert, ed., *National Socialist Extermination Policies: Contemporary German Perspectives and Controversies* (New York: Berghahn Books, 2000), esp. 17.

68. See the exchange between Josef Joffe and Michael Bodeman in the

New York Review of Books, April 10, 1997. I discuss this critique of Goldhagen in detail in Chapter 2.

69. Atina Grossmann, " 'The Goldhagen Effect': Memory, Repetition, and Responsibility in the New Germany," in *The "Goldhagen Effect": History, Memory, Nazism—Facing the German Past,* ed. Geoff Eley (Ann Arbor: University of Michigan Press, 2000), 117. See the list of references in Chapter 2.

In a probing essay, Dominick LaCapra accuses the author of bad or false empathy, arguing that in the course of his text Goldhagen so identifies with the Jewish victims that he loses any empathic perspective and transforms the book into polemic, failing to empathize with the Jews as historical others and putting himself scandalously in their place. LaCapra is right to interpret Goldhagen's narrative in terms of narcissistic merging with victims; yet we are interested in understanding how the accusation of "pornography" describes and condemns this narcissism. LaCapra conceives empathy as the ability to feel for the other as other rather than as a projection of the self. Dominick LaCapra, *Writing History, Writing Trauma* (Baltimore: Johns Hopkins University Press, 2000), 114–40.

70. I should note that in the insightful essays in Barbie Zelizer, ed., *Visual Culture and the Holocaust,* pornography—literally or metaphorically—is oddly not discussed at all.

71. Chapter 2 addresses this question in detail.

72. Dawidowicz, *Jewish Presence,* 224.

73. The first reference is to Steiner, "Pornography and Its Consequences," 47; the second to his letter to the *TLS,* 475.

74. This meaning attributed to pornography was made in another context: the writings of advocates of sexual reform in the 1960s, who believed that pornography and homosexuality were both symptoms of a narcissistic inability to connect to an autonomous other and were both products of sexual repression, which led to a regressive, "immature" sexuality. Of course, the usage I discuss is not in any way consciously connected to that argument but arguably partakes of it nonetheless. This logic also accounts for one of the fantasmic associations made between homosexuality and pornography and, as we will see, between homosexuality and fascism.

75. Another way of expressing this concept might be to note that critics once perceived as pornography what is now considered canonical art and literature. That this could happen has become a battle cry against censorship, because pornography's definition is so unstable that we never know if it might actually refer to great art or literature (so that my pornography is your great literature). The threat articulated by pornography as I've argued it here—the potentially narcissistic relationship to suffering and thereby to self-implosion—thus only ever appears as the recognition that everything from great art to the Holocaust is *potentially* pornographic. Our narcissistic

relationship to suffering can only be represented as a potential threat to the transmission of historical memory and the dignified self and is thus asserted by some only to be denied by others and eventually to be defined merely as a "point of view."

76. Walter Laqueur, *Fascism: Past, Present, Future* (Oxford: Oxford University Press, 1996), 6.

77. For efforts to address the current construction of Nazism in various (and popular) cultural forms, see Susan Sontag, "Fascinating Fascism," in *Under the Sign of Saturn* (New York: Farrar, Straus & Giroux, 1980), 73–105, and Saul Friedländer's oft-cited *Reflections on Nazism: An Essay on Kitsch and Death*, trans. Thomas Weyr (New York: Harper & Row, 1984). Friedländer's book is one of the few essays (since Sontag's) to analyze systematically the social and ideological meaning of recent representations of Nazism. The most recent books to address the relationship between sexual deviance and fantasies of fascism are Andrea Slane, *A Not So Foreign Affair: Fascism, Sexuality, and the Cultural Rhetoric of American Democracy* (Durham, N.C.: Duke University Press, 2001); and Laura Frost, *Sex Drives: Fantasies of Fascism in Literary Modernism* (Ithaca: Cornell University Press, 2002). See also Andrew Hewitt, *Political Inversions: Homosexuality, Fascism, and the Modernist Imaginary* (Stanford: Stanford University Press, 1996); and Kriss Ravetto, *The Unmaking of Fascist Aesthetics* (Minneapolis: University of Minnesota Press, 2001).

78. Robert Cover, "Violence and the Word," in *Narrative, Violence, and the Law: The Essays of Robert Cover*, ed. Martha Minow, Michael Ryan, and Austin Sarat (Ann Arbor: University of Michigan Press, 1992), 218–19.

79. Cover, "Violence and the Word," 218.

80. Michel Foucault, *The History of Sexuality, Volume 1: An Introduction* (New York: Random House-Vintage Books, 1980), 45. In this vision, bodily weakness does not give way to the strength of the martyr redeemed by a higher truth, but generates its own epistemology: the compulsion to erotic pleasures is not the tragic denouement of a person broken, who has lost possession of him- or herself, but represents another way of knowing that cannot be rationally assessed.

2. GOLDHAGEN'S CELEBRITY, NUMBNESS, AND WRITING HISTORY

1. This redemptive mission is embedded in history's originally ambiguous status, made explicit by Hegel, as knowledge whose meaning can only be revealed in narrative form, uniting facts (things that happened) and interpretation (the meaning conferred on them). It has been muted in histori-

ography that rejects the traditional narrative form (and the focus on events and individuals) most conducive to generating sympathetic identification with historical actors—for example, French history in line with the *Annales* school. That mission has been particularly absent in structural-functionalist German scholarship of the Nazi period not only because of its theoretical approach but also because of an intense desire to repress an engagement with Jewish victims' suffering. That is, the majority of German historians, until a new generation began to focus more on ideology and the personalities of perpetrators, do not deny the victims' suffering; they just don't engage it actively. The structural-functionalist paradigm may be seen as cause and symptom of this tendency. See, for an introduction to and collection of recent work, Ulrich Herbert, ed., *National Socialist Extermination Policies: Contemporary German Perspectives and Controversies* (New York: Berghahn Books, 2000). Until recently, Jewish suffering in the Holocaust was not at the center of historical consciousness in Anglo-American historiography either. See, in particular, Gerd Korman, "The Holocaust in American Historical Writing," *Societas—A Review of Social History* 2 (Winter 1972): 262–63. Certainly not all historians who feel that the generation of sympathetic identification with victims is important seek to perform the task in their own work. My point is simply that, in historiography of the Holocaust, this redemptive desire, particularly in relation to Jewish suffering, seems most characteristic of recent English-language scholarship that employs traditional narrative form but is hardly confined to such scholarship, particularly when the objects of sympathetic identification are not Jews but, for example, German soldiers on the Eastern Front or French resistance fighters. Moreover, since my project involves understanding the construction and analysis of empathy's decline as it is worked through Anglo-American scholarship and culture (indeed, the problem defined as such exists in radically different forms in Germany and France), I address non-English language scholarship only when it is particularly relevant or significant.

2. Jane Caplan, "Postmodernism, Poststructuralism, and Deconstruction: Notes for Historians," *Central European History* 22 (1989): 278.

3. Omer Bartov, *Murder in Our Midst: The Holocaust, Industrial Killing, and Representation* (New York: Oxford University Press, 1996), 11.

4. Omer Bartov, "The Path Away from Hell," *Times Literary Supplement*, March 5, 1999, 5. In this book review, historian Omer Bartov asserts that Dominick LaCapra's psychoanalytically inflected *Representing the Holocaust* combines "penetrating analysis and emotional detachment vis-à-vis the real object of inquiry, namely mass murder." Bartov is concerned that LaCapra's book as well as some of the texts that book addresses are "distinguished by a powerful reluctance to engage with the blood and gore of the event as such."

5. The term is from Dominick LaCapra, "History, Language, and Reading: Waiting for Crillon," *American Historical Review* 100, no. 3 (1995): 819–24; see also his *Representing the Holocaust: History, Theory, Trauma* (Ithaca: Cornell University Press, 1995), 178–92. LaCapra terms this strain of historical analysis a "totalizing neo-Hegelian vision of humanity triumphal." For these discourses about dignity see references to Giorgio Agamben in the Introduction and later in this chapter.

6. The phrase comes from Christopher Browning, glossing G. M. Trevelyan in *Nazi Policy, Jewish Workers, German Killers* (Cambridge: Cambridge University Press, 2000), ix.

7. Saul Friedländer notes that for many years in Holocaust historiography the "mythic memory of victims" was set against "rational understanding." This dichotomy, he notes, is problematic, since no historian can "avoid a measure of transference" in relation to his or her background. My point in what follows is thus not to reinforce this dichotomy, but to explore the complexities of historical works that address the moral dimension of the Holocaust, in particular the suffering of Jewish victims. See Saul Friedländer, "History, Memory, and the Historian: Facing the Shoah," in *Disturbing Remains: Memory, History, and Crisis in the Twentieth Century,* ed. Michael S. Roth and Charles Salas (Los Angeles: Getty Research Institute, 2001), 277. Friedländer makes allusions to Martin Broszat's problematic contrast between "mythical memory" and rational understanding in their exchange in "A Controversy about the Historicization of National Socialism," in *Reworking the Past: Hitler, the Holocaust, and the Historians' Debate,* ed. Peter Baldwin (Boston: Beacon Press, 1990), 106.

8. But see Michael Geyer's insistence that historians might well confront moral questions rather than evading them, as difficult and conceptually challenging as that may be. He notes that such confrontation is crucial when we address events such as the Holocaust or—in his example—German resistance to it. Michael Geyer, "Introduction: Resistance against the Third Reich as Intercultural Knowledge," in *Resistance against the Third Reich,* ed. Michael Geyer and John W. Boyer (Chicago: University of Chicago Press, 1994), 8.

9. For an interesting discussion of narrative style in Goldhagen, see Nancy Wood, *Vectors of Memory: Legacies of Trauma in Postwar Europe* (New York: Berg, 1999), 79–111.

10. Perhaps the most significant proponent of this "structuralist" or "functionalist" point of view, who developed many of its premises, is Hans Mommsen. See, for example, in English, Hans Mommsen, *From Weimar to Auschwitz,* trans. Philip O'Connor (Cambridge: Polity Press, 1991), 224–53, and his essay, "Cumulative Radicalization of Progressive Self-destruction as Structural Determinants of the Nazi Dictatorship," in *Stalinism and Nazism: Dictatorships in Comparison,* ed. Ian Kershaw and Moshe Lewin (Cambridge:

Cambridge University Press, 1997), 75–86; and "National Socialism: Continuity and Change," in *Fascism: A Reader's Guide*, ed. Walter Laqueur (New York: Penguin, 1979), 151–92. See also Götz Aly's later but pathbreaking *"Final Solution": Nazi Population Policy and the Murder of the European Jews*, trans. Belinda Cooper and Allison Bron (London: Arnold, 1999).

11. Christoph Dieckmann, "The War and the Killing of the Lithuanian Jews," in *National Socialist Extermination Policies*, ed. Ulrich Herbert, 265–66. This younger generation of modified functionalist historians, Ulrich Herbert in particular, seeks to integrate anti-Semitic ideology in their work, but many of them still tend to relate anti-Semitism "functionally" to extermination and population policies.

12. Daniel Jonah Goldhagen, *Hitler's Willing Executioners: Ordinary Germans and the Holocaust* (New York: Vintage, 1996), 9, 369, 493 n. 43.

13. Goldhagen, *Willing Executioners*, 357. This point about Goldhagen's important focus on victims is emphasized in most efforts to explain the significance of his work as well as its popular appeal. For two excellent overviews of the accomplishments and limitations of the structural-functionalist conception of the Nazi dictatorship, see Geoff Eley, "Ordinary Germans, Nazism, and Judeocide," the introduction to *The "Goldhagen Effect": History, Memory, Nazism—Facing the German Past*, ed. Geoff Eley (Ann Arbor: University of Michigan Press, 2000), 1–31; and Omer Bartov, "Reception and Perception: Goldhagen's Holocaust and the World," in *The "Goldhagen Effect,"* esp. 43–56. Bartov also discusses the necessary historical distortion that occurs when victims and perpetrators are not analyzed together in "German Soldiers and the Holocaust: Historiography, Research, and Implications," in *The Holocaust: Origins, Implementation, Aftermath*, ed. Omer Bartov (New York: Routledge, 2000), 174–79. See also Yehuda Bauer, *Rethinking the Holocaust* (New Haven: Yale University Press, 2001), who says, "however erroneous [Goldhagen's position is], the renewed emphasis he puts on the ideological, antisemitic factor is useful," and that "Goldhagen's redirection of attention to antisemitism has to be valued positively" (96). Enzo Traverso notes that "the functionalism that has dominated 'Holocaust Studies' in both Europe and the US for several years seems to have obscured a basic truth recalled by Goldhagen, despite his bad arguments: that Nazism would never have been able to conceive or carry out the destruction of 6 million Jews without several prior centuries of anti-Semitism." Enzo Traverso, *Understanding the Nazi Genocide: Marxism after Auschwitz*, trans. Peter Drucker (London: Pluto Press, 1999), 102–3. Ulrich Herbert too acknowledges that "public discussion of National Socialist extermination policy has changed significantly" due to all the debate surrounding Goldhagen's book, in particular because of its focus on victims. Ulrich Herbert, "Extermination Policy," in Herbert, ed., *National Socialist Extermination Policies*, 1.

14. For critiques of the book's conceptual and empirical claims see, among others, Omer Bartov, "Ordinary Monsters," *New Republic*, April 29, 1996: 32–38; István Deák, *Essays on Hitler's Europe* (Lincoln: University of Nebraska Press, 2001), 100–110 (this piece was originally published in 1997 and already sees itself as a retrospective, but nevertheless repeats most of the criticisms I have already noted here); Norman G. Finkelstein and Ruth Bettina Birn, *A Nation on Trial: The Goldhagen Thesis and Historical Truth* (New York, 1998); Fritz Stern, "The Goldhagen Controversy," *Foreign Affairs* 75 (November/December 1996): 128–38; Hans Ulrich-Wehler, "The Goldhagen Controversy: Agonizing Problems, Scholarly Failure, and the Political Dimension," *German History* 15 (1997): 80–91. Some of the most important German commentary (much of it from *Die Zeit*, especially Summer and Fall 1996, but also from other newspapers, including the *Frankfurter Allgemeine Zeitung* and the *Süddeutsche Zeitung*) is in Julius H. Schoeps, ed., *Ein Volk von Mördern? Die Dokumentation zur Goldhagen-Kontroverse um die Rolle der Deutschen im Holocaust* (Hamburg: Hoffman und Campe, 1996). Excerpts have also been translated in Robert R. Shandley, ed., *Unwilling Germans? The Goldhagen Debate* (Minneapolis: University of Minnesota Press, 1998). For two sociological perspectives on Goldhagen's text, see James Mahoney and Michael Ellsberg, "Goldhagen's Hitler's Willing Executioners: A Clarification and a Methodological Critique," *Journal of Historical Sociology* 12 (1999): 422–36; Michael Brennan, "Some Sociological Contemplations on Daniel Goldhagen's *Hitler's Willing Executioners*," *Theory, Culture & Society*, 18 (2001): 83–109. In contrast to historians, Mahoney and Ellsberg's essay argues that Goldhagen's evidence cannot substantiate his model, but their criticisms of his substantive claims are similar to those of historians. Brennan instead thoughtfully criticizes historians' lack of self-reflexiveness about their own relationship to Goldhagen's text, but in a very different vein from my emphasis on accusations of pornography. Thanks to Calvin Goldscheider for these references.

15. Bauer, *Rethinking*, 110, and also 104, 107.

16. Hans Ulrich-Wehler, "The Goldhagen Controversy," 85.

17. The work of Berel Lang, an eminent nonhistorian, is exemplary of all these arguments. It's also possible that professional envy of Goldhagen's crossover status may account for some of the intensity of the invective directed against him. Berel Lang, *Holocaust Representation: Art within the Limits of History and Ethics* (Baltimore: John Hopkins University Press, 2000), 112–15. In reference to Goldhagen's reception in Germany, Jan Phillip Reemtsma, director of the *Institut für Sozialforschung*, explained the level of historians' hostility manifested toward him there by referring to the book as the "abandonment of any wish for denial." Jan Phillip Reemtsma, "Turning Away from Denial: Hitler's Willing Executioners as a Counterforce to 'Historical Explanation,' in *Unwilling Germans?*, ed. Shandley, 257. That is, in the

German context, *Hitler's Willing Executioners* could be lauded for insisting on the responsibility of Germans who had by and large—and with the complicity of the state—avoided a full moral reckoning with the past, in particular by viewing themselves as Hitler's victims rather than acknowledging their role as perpetrators or bystanders. In a far more polemical attack on historians Hans Mommsen, Eberhard Jäckel, Hans-Ulrich Wehler, and Canadian archivist Ruth Bettina Birn, Fred Kautz seeks to make the same point about the German historical profession. Fred Kautz, *The German Historians: Hitler's Willing Executioners and Daniel Goldhagen* (Montréal: Black Rose Books, 2003). In the United States, where Holocaust Studies flourish, other factors—in particular, the interest in the Holocaust manifest by American Jews seeking a more powerful identification with their own past—account for Goldhagen's popularity.

18. Hans Mommsen, "The Thin Patina of Civilization: Anti-Semitism Was a Necessary, but by No Means a Sufficient, Condition for the Holocaust," in *Unwilling Germans?*, ed. Shandley, 194 (originally published in *Die Zeit* on August 31, 1996).

19. Norman Finkelstein, quoted in Brennan, "Some Sociological Contemplations," 88.

20. Eley, "Ordinary Germans, Nazism, and Judeocide," 7.

21. Atina Grossmann, "The 'Goldhagen Effect': Memory, Repetition, and Responsibility in the New Germany" in *The "Goldhagen Effect,"* ed. Eley, 117

22. Silke Wenk, "Rhetoriken der Pornografisierung: Rahmungen des Blicks auf 286-91 die NS-Verbrechen," in *Gedächtnis und Geschlecht: Deutungsmuster in Darstellung des nationalsozialistischen Genozids*, ed. Insa Eschebach, Sigrid Jacobeit, and Silke Wenk (Frankfurt: Campus Verlag, 2002), 286–91; Ruth Bettina Birn and Volker Riess, "Das Goldhagen-Phänomen oder: fünfzig Jahre danach," *Geschichte in Wissenschaft und Unterricht* 49 (1998): 91. They refer to a 1996 article by journalist Jacob Heilbrunn in *Der Tagesspiegel* (91 n. 54).

23. Jane Caplan, "Reflections on the Reception of Goldhagen in the United States," in *The "Goldhagen Effect,"* ed. Eley, 162.

24. Ibid., 161.

25. In an article about how the sexual revolution proved to be a displaced way of working through the German New Left's relationship to the Holocaust, Dagmar Herzog notes as an aside (in a footnote) that "the undecidability of the relationship between pleasure and evil—or to put it another way, the problem of sadism—was one of the almost everywhere undertheorized but also ubiquitously present elements of the frenetic debates about Daniel Goldhagen, *Hitler's Willing Executioners*." There is still an essay to be written about the reception of Goldhagen's work among the younger German generation from this point of view. For both generations of historians, as I hope this discussion has made clear, the problem of "sadism" is indeed

undertheorized and yet extremely important in evaluating both American and German scholarly responses to the sort of methodological challenges Goldhagen's book represents. Here I limit the discussion to historians' projection of their own anxieties onto Goldhagen's young audiences. See Dagmar Herzog, " 'Pleasure, Sex, and Politics Belong Together': Post-Holocaust Memory and the Sexual Revolution in West Germany," *Critical Inquiry* 24 (Winter 1998): 443 n. 115.

26. I draw here from Jacqueline Rose's discussion of the politics surrounding Lady Diana's death, "The Cult of Celebrity," *Law Formations* 36 (1999): 9–20. The way she analyzes responses to Diana's death to gauge normative relations between emotion and politics is extremely useful in dissecting the debate about Goldhagen.

27. Josef Joffe, " 'The Killers Were Ordinary Germans, ergo the Ordinary Germans Were Killers': The Logic, the Language, and the Meaning of a Book That Conquered Germany," in *Unwilling Germans?*, 221.

28. Ibid., 225.

29. For a different take on Goldhagen's "overidentification" with the victim that is particularly sensitive to the complexity of Goldhagen's relationship to his subject, see Dominick LaCapra, *Writing History, Writing Trauma* (Baltimore: Johns Hopkins University Press, 2001), 114–40.

30. Elizabeth D. Heineman, "Sexuality and Nazism: The Doubly Unspeakable?" *Journal of the History of Sexuality* 11 (January/April 2002): 55, 65. For a most dramatic assertion of this position in other terms, see historian Peter Hayes's condemnation of the "scholasticism now rampant in the academy . . . in which how we learn and relate what we know becomes as intellectually significant and preoccupying as the knowledge itself." Hayes refers here to James E. Young and Saul Friedländer and clearly believes that attention to questions of how we represent the Holocaust "displaces the participants themselves." Hayes quoted in James E. Young, *At Memory's Edge: After-Images of the Holocaust in Contemporary Art and Architecture* (New Haven: Yale University Press, 2000), 224 n. 3.

31. For a discussion of Goldhagen's reference to gender via the "rhetoric of pornographication," see also Wenk, "Rhetoriken der Pornografisierung," 286–90.

32. Jürgen Kocka, quoted in Joffe, "The Killers," 224.

33. The incident is recounted in Ron Rosenbaum, *Explaining Hitler* (New York: Harper, 1998), 338–47. According to Rosenbaum, the moderator was a literary theorist and the historians, with one exception, delivered far more personally and intellectually scathing attacks, overshadowing the moderator's slip. The moderator, Lawrence Langer, has told me that his words were not intentionally or unintentionally hostile, that he has known Goldhagen

for many years, and accordingly addressed him very informally. He thus takes issue with Rosenbaum's account.

34. See Jacqueline Rose's notion of celebrity as "diversion" or "distraction," in "Cult of Celebrity," 15.

35. Caplan, "Reflections," 161.

36. See Saul Friedländer, ed., *Probing the Limits of Representation: "Nazism and the Final Solution"* (Cambridge: Harvard University Press, 1992); Geoffrey Hartman, ed., *Holocaust Remembrance: The Shapes of Memory* (Cambridge, Mass: Blackwell, 1994); Peter Hayes, *Lessons and Legacies: The Meaning of the Holocaust in a Changing World* (Evanston: Northwestern University Press, 1991). More recently see Dominick LaCapra, *History and Memory after Auschwitz* (Ithaca: Cornell University Press, 1998), and *Writing History, Writing Trauma*; Lang, *Holocaust Representation.*

37. I might note, for example, that in Yehuda Bauer's recent overview of work on the Holocaust, *Rethinking the Holocaust,* he does not even cite Dominick LaCapra's work in the bibliography, let alone integrate it into his general discussion. Yet LaCapra has written three of the most important and widely cited books addressing the vexed subject of "Holocaust representation."

38. See V. R. Berghahn, "The Road to Extermination," *New York Times Book Review,* April 14, 1996; Stern, "Goldhagen Controversy," 128–38.

39. Christopher Browning, "German Memory, Judicial Interrogation, Historical Reconstruction," in *Probing the Limits,* ed. Friedländer, 27. See also his *Ordinary Men: Reserve Police Battalion 101 and the Final Solution in Poland* (New York: Harper Perennial, 1992), 188 ("The behavior of any human being is, of course, a very complex phenomenon, and the historian who attempts to 'explain' it is indulging in a certain arrogance").

40. Michael Marrus, *The Holocaust in History* (New York: Penguin, 1987), 7.

41. Stanley Milgram, *Obedience to Authority: An Experimental View* (New York: Harper and Row, 1974).

42. See, among others, the collection edited by Ulrich Herbert, *National Socialist Extermination Policies,* where the notion that murder became "abstract" for those who participated predominates (esp. 33–34, 117, 122, 288); Browning, *Ordinary Men;* and Wolfgang Sofsky, *The Order of Terror: The Concentration Camp* (Princeton: Princeton University Press, 1999). Sofsky argues that the terror of the camps is characterized by a model of "absolute power" that is self-sustaining and thus needs no ideological legitimation at all. See also Elaine Scarry, *The Body in Pain: The Making and Unmaking of the World* (Oxford: Oxford University Press, 1985), 57. In a recent essay, Paul Roth points out how much this sort of analysis may also reflect our need to distance ourselves from perpetrators. He argues that Goldhagen is finally as

"functionalist" as those historians he criticizes (since for all his emphasis on how much his perpetrators wanted to do and even liked what they did, they are "conditioned" by a cognitive model that accounts finally for what they do). Paul Roth, "Beyond Understanding," in *The Blackwell Guide to the Philosophy of the Social Sciences*, ed. Stephen P. Turner and Paul Roth (Oxford: Blackwell, 2003), 311–33.

43. Hannah Arendt pioneered this argument in her *Eichmann in Jerusalem: A Report on the Banality of Evil* (New York: Penguin, 1961). Arendt's account underplayed Nazi anti-Semitism in order to criticize the instrumental rationality of the modern social world (and so she writes from a perspective critical of arguments that merely replicate methodologically such forms of rationality), but laid out an influential blueprint for understanding industrialized murder. Zygmunt Bauman famously tries to make an argument for the power of individual agency but only after demonstrating to what extent the Holocaust was a product of "modernity"—that is to say of elaborate processes of dehumanization and depersonalization. Zygmunt Bauman, *Modernity and the Holocaust* (Ithaca: Cornell University Press, 1989). For an elaborated cognitive account from social psychologists' point of view, see the essays in Leonard S. Newman and Ralph Erder, eds., *Understanding Genocide: The Social Psychology* (Oxford: Oxford University Press, 2002).

44. Herbert, ed., *National Socialist Extermination Policies*, 17.

45. Saul Friedländer, *Nazi Germany and the Jews*, vol. 1: *The Years of Persecution, 1933–1939* (New York: HarperCollins, 1997), 2. For a discussion that bears more on this issue somewhat differently, see Saul Friedländer, *Memory, History, and the Extermination of the Jews of Europe* (Bloomington: University of Indian Press, 1993), 64–101; Broszat and Friedländer, "A Controversy," 102–32. Raul Hilberg's treatment of victims in his magisterial work, *The Destruction of the European Jews*, 3 vols. (New York: Holmes & Meier, 1985), is an early and particularly controversial example of this tendency.

46. Friedländer, *Memory, History*, 130–31.

47. Browning, *Nazi Policy*, ix.

48. Inga Clendinnen, *Reading the Holocaust* (Cambridge: Cambridge University Press, 1999); Omer Bartov, *Mirrors of Destruction: War, Genocide, and Modern Identity* (Oxford: Oxford University Press, 2000).

49. See Michael Marrus, review of Bartov, *Mirrors of Destruction, New York Times*, September 10, 2000, sec. 7, p. 40; Eric D. Weitz, *Modernism/Modernity* 8.4 (2001): 694–96; Joseph Robert White, *History: Reviews of New Books* 29 (2001): 69–70.

50. David Cesarani, "Holocaust on the Right Side of Kitsch," *Times Higher Education Supplement*, issue 1443, July 1, 2000, p. 20. I should note that this review is exceptional. Most of the reviews of Clendinnen's book are ex-

tremely positive. For example, a prominent review, by Daphne Merkin in the *New York Times Book Review,* claims the book constitutes a "radical departure point" from which discussion about the Holocaust can begin anew. See Daphne Merkin, "Meditations on the Unthinkable," *New York Times Book Review,* April 11, 1999, pp. 17–18.

51. Clendinnen, *Reading the Holocaust,* 4.

52. Ibid., 111, 104. On Sereny's interviews with Speer and Stangl, Clendinnen writes, for example, "In a morass of self-and-other deceptions and delusions, she keeps her footing. She is neither shocked nor shamed by Stangl's lies: she merely notes them—and bides her time. She has perfect moral pitch" (110).

53. Ibid., 87, 86. She quotes from Friedländer's "On the Unease in Historical Interpretation" reprinted in *Memory, History,* 102–16.

54. Bauer, *Rethinking the Holocaust,* esp. 20–23.

55. Clendinnen, *Reading the Holocaust,* 86.

56. As Clendinnen notes, Arendt discusses the prestige attached to being a *Geheimnisträger*—a "bearer of secrets"—in the Nazi hierarchy, ibid., 85. See Arendt's discussion in *Eichmann,* 27. Yet Arendt's understanding of secrecy is far closer to Friedländer's than to Clendinnen's, who appears to interpret the term instrumentally as a means of promoting internal loyalty within the SS. Such an interpretation still begs the question of how these men could be loyal to, even proud of, the fact that they were murdering millions of human beings.

57. I might note here that Clendinnen refers to the Nazis' initial killings of Polish and Russian civilians as motivated by "pragmatic political motives"—". . . to destroy a future generation of enemies, to increase German living space" (6). It is extremely hard to understand how exactly such motives qualify as "pragmatic."

58. Clendinnen, *Reading the Holocaust,* 72.

59. See also Martin Jay's response to Hayden White's "Of Plots, Witnesses, and Judgments," in Friedländer, *Probing the Limits,* 97–107, for a different discussion of the tendency to level perpetrator and victim in the context of a very different effort to "close the gap between subject and object" (101).

60. This tendency not to see the structural differences between social groups (even as she clearly recognizes that Nazis did evil things and that Jews were their victims) manifests itself in all kinds of less obvious ways. She doesn't, for example, consider that perpetrators' "honesty" with Gitta Sereny has as much to do with Sereny's own identity (she is an Austrian gentile) as with her insistence on treating them as human beings. When one reads Robert Jay Lifton's efforts to interview Nazi perpetrators—doctors who experimented on Jews and gypsies at Auschwitz—we learn as much if

not more from the way in which their suspicion that he might be Jewish colors their testimony. See Robert Jay Lifton, *The Nazi Doctors: Medical Killing and the Psychology of Genocide* (New York: Basic Books, 1986), 131, 333.

61. Clendinnen, *Reading the Holocaust*, 71.

62. Ibid.

63. Ibid., 73.

64. Ibid., 72.

65. Ibid., 45.

66. Tadeusz Borowski, *This Way for the Gas, Ladies and Gentlemen* (New York: Penguin, 1967).

67. Clendinnen, *Reading the Holocaust*, 182.

68. We might note here Lawrence Langer's insistence, after countless interviews with Holocaust survivors, that they cannot and will not generally use a vocabulary of heroism or nobility. See Lawrence L. Langer, *Holocaust Testimonies: The Ruins of Memory* (New Haven: Yale University Press, 1991), esp. 162–205. Of course, this is not necessarily true of all survivors. I thank Ruth Gutmann for her insights.

69. Bartov, *Mirrors of Destruction*, 29.

70. Ibid., 185.

71. Bartov, *Murder in Our Midst*, 198 n. 38.

72. Ibid., 29.

73. Ibid., 62.

74. Bartov, *Mirrors of Destruction*, 116. Bartov, after Saul Friedländer, also addresses the prevalent tendency to write about victims and perpetrators separately in both literary and historical work, as if the meaning of their experiences were not mutually constitutive. He notes too that this segregation enables perpetrators to see themselves as victims, since they are rarely pressured to examine their self-perceptions critically in relation to victims' experiences. See Bartov, *Mirrors of Destruction*, 79, 118, 182–83. See also Bartov's essay "German Soldiers and the Holocaust: Historiography, Research, and Implications," in *The Holocaust: Origins, Implementation, Aftermath*, ed. Omer Bartov (New York: Routledge, 2000), 174–79.

75. Bartov, *Mirrors of Destruction*, 98–99, 106.

76. Ibid., 96. I should note here that Bartov caricatures approaches to the fantasmic elements of genocide (those which move beyond his cognitive emphasis on stereotype) in an uncharacteristically disrespectful and *ad hominem* fashion. Thus Bartov asserts that relativism and postmodernism (which he claims are "common currency in some contemporary intellectual and scholarly circles" without being precise about what circles he means and how they use these terms) are finally complicitous with Holocaust denial ("Holocaust deniers . . . have adopted to their own purposes relativist and postmodern assertions regarding the instability or nonexistence of facts about the past").

Bartov, *Mirrors of Destruction*, 123. There are good reasons to criticize postmodern constructions of memory. But his particular claim about the relationship between postmodern assertions and Holocaust denial has been refuted by others, and some discussion of such views, as well as distinctions between relativism, postmodernism, poststructuralism, and deconstruction, contested and debated as they are even within the circles of their own advocates, might have helped clarify his meaning and made his case stronger. As Geoffrey Hartman puts it, "Quite mistakenly, the vicious ideological turn taken by Holocaust deniers is sometimes associated with deconstruction's care in avoiding premature or forced closure, a care which has no ideological motive but is directed against an anxiety that produces shortcuts to meaning." Geoffrey Hartman, *The Longest Shadow: In the Aftermath of the Holocaust* (Bloomington: Indiana University Press, 1996), 8. On this question, see Pierre Vidal-Naquet, *Assassins of Memory: Essays on the Denial of the Holocaust* (New York: Columbia University Press, 1992), who implicates poststructuralist arguments in strategies of Holocaust denial, but also Lawrence Douglas, *The Memory of Judgment: Making Law and History in the Trials of the Holocaust* (New Haven: Yale University Press, 2001), who claims that in a Canadian trial of one Holocaust denier, the arguments "of revisionists are less suggestive of Paul de Man than of Johnnie Cochran" (237).

77. Bartov, *Mirrors of Destruction*, 142.

78. Ibid., 157, 176. The last phrase ends: "is the lesson that these writers [meaning Jean Amery, Ka-Tzetnik, Tadeusz Borowski] see as the enduring legacy of the Holocaust," and one Bartov sustains in his own work.

79. Ibid., 30. It cannot be a coincidence that Bartov ends with a conditional "if we were willing to face the truth"—a truth we have trouble facing and may not be able to face—and then quotes Primo Levi to the effect that it could all happen again if we are not vigilant (230).

80. Gillian Whitlock, "In the Second Person: Narrative Transactions in Stolen Generations Testimony," *Biography* 24.1 (2001): 204. Here one would have to disagree with Elaine Scarry's insistence that we think of "injuring others retrospectively" with relative ease but not with injuring others "prospectively." She claims this is "especially ironic because we *cannot* intervene and change an injury that has occurred in the past. But we *can* intervene and prevent an injury in the future." Instead, this analysis suggests that we intervene prospectively via the mechanism of retrospective memorialization and that it is a crucial form of defense against future injury. Moreover, at least in the case of the Holocaust, it's not at all clear that thinking about injury retrospectively is so easy. Elaine Scarry, "The Difficulty of Imagining Other Persons," in *Human Rights in Political Transitions: Gettysburg to Bosnia,* ed. Carla Hesse and Robert Post (New York: Zone Books, 1999), 282.

81. Saul Friedländer has identified some of the negative consequences of using the Holocaust as a metaphor for evil more generally. He expresses concern over the potential effects of flattening the Holocaust's significance into a message about good and evil that would permit historical distortion (the presumption, as he puts it, that because the Catholic Church is against "evil in our time," the Pope stood on the side of the victims). See his "History, Memory, and the Historian," esp. 276–78. I will address his own history of Jews in Nazi Germany in Chapter 3. In a related argument, the literary critic Michael André Bernstein protests against the recent treatment of the Holocaust as particularly revelatory of human behavior generally. As he writes, "very little about human nature or values can be learned from a situation *in extremis* except the virtual tautology that extreme pressure brings out extreme and extremely diverse behavior." Michael André Bernstein, *Foregone Conclusions: Against Apocalyptic History* (Berkeley: University of California Press, 1994), 78. Lawrence Langer has perhaps offered the most negative view of any effort to interpret the Holocaust historically; for him there is only the unredeemable devastation of the victims. See Lawrence L. Langer, *Preempting the Holocaust* (New Haven: Yale University Press, 1998).

82. In *Representing the Holocaust, History and Memory after Auschwitz,* and *Writing History, Writing Trauma,* Dominick LaCapra has invoked the concept of the "sublime" (the concept is so central to his work that I do not offer page numbers) to describe the moment this invocation of universalized, needlessly suffering humanity moves beyond empathic identification (and thus appeals to our responsibilities as human beings and citizens) to the ecstatic transfiguration of victims' suffering—to what he terms "sublime" identification—that can lead to morally dubious positions such as the blotting out of the other, a desire to suffer in their place.

83. See Ernst Bloch's discussion of varying constructions of human dignity in *Natural Law and Human Dignity,* trans. Dennis J. Schmidt (Cambridge: MIT Press, 1986), esp. 205–9.

84. It is crucial to distinguish between this notion that extant constructions of humanity have been scandalously betrayed by Auschwitz (the position of George Steiner, for example), and that of Giorgio Agamben, who has recently suggested that humanist constructs of dignity were completely exhausted by Auschwitz, where the degraded image of humanity represented by the "Muslim" (those camp inmates who were alive and yet on the verge of death and could barely hold themselves upright) exceeds normative categories of dignity and indignity. George Steiner, *In Bluebeard's Castle: Some Notes toward the Redefinition of Culture* (New Haven: Yale University Press, 1971), 79; Giorgio Agamben, *Remnants of Auschwitz: The Witness and the Archive* (New York: Zone Books, 1999), esp. 68–72, 80–82.

Agamben uses the "Muslim" as a figure of aporia and entirely underplays the historical context in which "muslims" were actively deprived of dignity by perpetrators. For a negative, thought-provoking assessment of Agamben's book, see Dominick LaCapra, *History in Transit* (Ithaca: Cornell University Press, 2004).

3. INDIFFERENCE AND THE LANGUAGE OF VICTIMIZATION

1. Cynthia Stokes Brown and Herbert Kohl, "Teaching about Conscience through Literature," an excerpt of *Teaching Human Rights through Literature*, http://www.amnesty-volunteer.org/usa/education/lit.html.

2. Michael Ignatieff, "Human Rights as Idolatry," in *Michael Ignatieff: Human Rights as Politics and Idolatry*, ed. Amy Gutmann (Princeton: Princeton University Press, 2001), 79.

3. Elazar Barkan, *The Guilt of Nations: Restitution and Negotiating Historical Injustices* (Baltimore: Johns Hopkins University Press, 2001), 31. Hannah Arendt believed that responses to the refugee crises of the Second World War revealed that dignity was not after all an attribute of a human being, but of a citizen, since stateless persons were not treated with dignity. Hannah Arendt, *The Origins of Totalitarianism* (New York: Meridian Books, 1958), 279–302.

4. John Keane, *Reflections on Violence* (London: Verso, 1996), 182.

5. There are multiple versions of these lines, cited in different ways in a multiplicity of sources, so I offer no particular reference. The reader may go to any website about Pastor Niemöller, which all cite different versions. Most recently, journalist Ted Koppel cited these lines when he accepted a "Humanitarian" award by the Human Rights Campaign in February 2003 (on behalf of gay rights). Unfortunately, Niemöller objected to the Nazis less because they persecuted Jews than because they targeted *converted* Jews. Saul Friedländer, *Nazi Germany and the Jews: Volume I: The Years of Persecution, 1933–1939* (New York: HarperCollins, 1997), 45, 163. See also Richard Gutteridge, *Open Thy Mouth for the Dumb! The German Evangelical Church and the Jews, 1879–1950* (Oxford: Blackwell, 1976), 100–104 on Niemöller's anti-Semitism, and Frank Stern, *The Whitewashing of the Yellow Badge: Anti-semitism and Philosemitism in Postwar Germany* (Oxford: Pergamon Press, 1992), 198–99, 306–8 on his postwar German reception. Niemöller acknowledged his own personal guilt after the war. Hence the comments attributed to him.

6. We might look to the concern of North American and Western European students and intellectuals for the wounds of "others," including victims of U.S. and French imperialism in Vietnam, French imperialism in

Algeria, and Soviet imperialism in Budapest and Prague, as well as their focus on racism, sexism, and homophobia more generally. Moreover, both the Vietnam War and the Holocaust raised questions of collective responsibility for horrific crimes in new ways. American students and others felt they had a moral responsibility to end them. Young Germans began to ask whether their parents were Hitler's victims or his silent accomplices and what responsibility they bore for sustaining the memory of the genocide. For an interesting perspective on the German case, see Dagmar Herzog, "'Pleasure, Sex, and Politics Belong Together': Post-Holocaust Memory and the Sexual Revolution in West Germany," *Critical Inquiry* 24 (Winter 1998): 442–44. Finally, the 1967 Arab-Israeli war raised questions about the moral legacy of the Holocaust by reinforcing new forms of Jewish self-definition underway in the United States. These phenomena are generally distinct from—though they may overlap with—civil rights movements, in which victims of discrimination make claims for themselves and in which others who are not targets of discrimination refuse to be bystanders.

7. Omer Bartov, *Murder in Our Midst: The Holocaust, Industrial Killing, and Representation* (New York: Oxford University Press, 1996).

8. Saul Friedländer, "History, Memory, and the Historian: Dilemmas Responsibilities," *New German Critique,* 80 (Spring–Summer 2000), 5. See also the discussion in Alain Finkielkraut, *The Imaginary Jew,* trans. Kevin O'Neill and David Suchoff (Lincoln: University of Nebraska Press, 1997), 17.

9. The headline reads "Nous sommes tous Américains," *Le Monde,* September 13, 2001, and was penned by editor Jean-Marie Colombani.

10. On collective identity as a fantasmic, often retrospectively forged identification that stabilizes self-definition by erasing historical differences and creating false continuities (in the context of feminist struggle and thus the identity of "woman") see Joan Scott, "Fantasy Echo: History and the Construction of Identity," *Critical Inquiry* 27 (Winter 2001), 284–304.

11. See Michael Staub, *Torn at the Roots: The Crisis of Jewish Liberalism in Postwar America* (New York: Columbia University Press, 2002), 43–47, 52, 119. Staub traces the various shifts in Jewish-Black relations, and demonstrates how complicated was the intra-Jewish struggle to come to terms with Jewish responsibility for racism. In particular he shows how ethnic identities became increasingly linked to ideology as the Cold War developed. Thus, Jewish sympathy for the persecution of African-Americans was increasingly equated with a deficit of Jewish ethnicity, for a weak identification with, even betrayal of, one's Jewish past and future. Among various groups of left-wing Jews, however, the analogy between Jewish and Black suffering, however problematic, remained a crucial element of Jewish self-understanding.

See also the discussion in Finkielkraut, *The Imaginary Jew,* 17–34. Finkielkraut speaks about his ambivalent identification with the slogan 'we are all German Jews,' since he *was* a Jew, and how he found the "protestors' generosity far too facile and flashy" (17).

12. The literature on these topics is voluminous, but see a compelling account of the Nuremberg trials by Lawrence Douglas, *The Memory of Judgment: Making Law and the History of the Trials of the Holocaust* (New Haven: Yale University Press, 2001), 11–94; Amir Weiner, *Making Sense of War: The Second World War and the Fate of the Bolshevik Revolution* (Princeton: Princeton University Press, 2001), 208–35. Jeffrey Herf explains why the emergence of different public memories of the Holocaust in East and West Germany was not a foregone conclusion *(Divided Memory: The Nazi Past in the Two Germanys* [Cambridge: Harvard University Press, 1997], 106–61, 179–266). Henry Rousso, *The Vichy Syndrome: History and Memory in France since 1944,* trans. Arthur Goldhammer (Cambridge: Harvard University Press, 1991), 104. The book refers to postwar anti-Semitism on pages, 132–67.

13. As we've seen, Omer Bartov has discussed this dynamic most extensively in *Mirrors of Destruction: War, Genocide, and Modern Identity* (Oxford: Oxford University Press, 2000).

14. For example, David Engel's successive works, *In the Shadow of Auschwitz: The Polish Government in Exile and the Jews, 1939–1942* (Chapel Hill: University of North Carolina Press, 1987), and *Facing a Holocaust: The Polish Government-in-Exile and the Jews, 1943–45* (Chapel Hill: University of North Carolina Press, 1993). For the war and the postwar period in Poland, see Michael C. Steinlauf, *Bondage to the Dead: Poland and the Memory of the Holocaust* (Syracuse, NY: Syracuse University Press, 1997), 52, and Jan T. Gross, *Neighbors: The Destruction of the Jewish Community in Jedwabne, Poland* (Princeton: Princeton University Press, 2001). Steinlauf notes that between 1944 and 1947 some 1,500 to 2,000 Jews were murdered by Poles in the course of seeking out their families or reclaiming homes and businesses. See also essays by Israel Gutman, "The Victimization of the Poles," Bohdan Vitvitsky, "Slavs and Jews: Consistent and Inconsistent Perspectives on the Holocaust," and Aahron Weiss, "The Holocaust and the Ukrainian Victims," in *A Mosaic of Victims: Non-Jews Persecuted and Murdered by the Nazis,* ed. Michael Berenbaum (New York: New York University Press, 1990), 96–100, 101–8, 109–15, and esp. Vitvitsky's discussion 103–7. For local collaboration in the East (specifically in the second wave of shootings of Jews in Western Belorussia and the Ukraine in the summer of 1942), see Martin Dean, *Collaboration in the Holocaust: Crimes of the Local Police in Belorussia and Ukraine, 1941–1944* (New York: Saint Martin's Press, 2000). More general essays include: István Déak, Jan T. Gross, and Tony Judt, eds., *The Politics of Retribution in Europe: World War II and its Aftermath* (Princeton: Princeton University

Press, 2000); John Dower, "Triumphal and Tragic Narratives of the War in Asia," *Journal of American History* 82 (1995): 1124–35. On Belgium, the Netherlands, and France in the postwar period, see Pieter Lagrou, *The Legacy of Nazi Occupation: Patriotic Memory and National Recovery in Western Europe, 1945–1965* (Cambridge: Cambridge University Press, 2000).

15. This is, as we've seen, fairly standard rhetoric. Note that Bartov, in *Mirrors of Destruction*, makes a similar rhetorical move whose complexity I discussed in Chapter 2. My point is that this particular rhetoric is not confined to bystander history and seems to be part of the more general and difficult problem of how to write the history of the Holocaust.

16. Michael Geyer, "Resistance as an Ongoing Project: Visions of Order, Obligations to Strangers, and Struggles for Civil Society, 1933–1990," in *Resistance against the Third Reich, 1933–1990*, ed. Michael Geyer and John W. Boyer (Chicago: University of Chicago Press, 1994), 332.

17. Geyer, "Resistance as an Ongoing Project," 332.

18. In the vast literature on trauma there is a lot of controversy over what a victim's experience of the Holocaust might have been, so we cannot refer to some universal or real "experience," only a variety of diverse and complex experiences that have been interpreted in various ways. See Cathy Caruth, *Unclaimed Experience: Trauma, Narrative, and History* (Baltimore: Johns Hopkins University Press, 1996), and Dominick LaCapra's criticism of her position in *Writing History, Writing Trauma* (Baltimore: Johns Hopkins University Press, 2001), 181–219.

19. Martin Broszat and Saul Friedländer, "A Controversy about the Historicization of National Socialism," in *Reworking the Past: Hitler, the Holocaust, and the Historians' Debate*, ed. Peter Baldwin (Boston: Beacon Press, 1990), 119–20. Broszat and Friedländer debated whether or not the Holocaust could be conceived "objectively" rather than "only" in relation to the victims' suffering. Friedländer took the view that the victims' suffering was central to the history of the Third Reich, whose history could not be "normalized" as if Jews were not stripped of rights, isolated, and murdered with the knowledge and even support of the general population. Insofar as I am concerned with the way the nonvictim's perspective is inscribed as the norm in most bystander historiography, the concerns of this debate converge with the concerns about indifference I examine here, only with a different emphasis.

20. Important early works include William Sheridan Allen, *The Nazi Seizure of Power: The Experience of a Single German Town, 1930–1935* (Chicago: Quadrangle Books, 1965). Sheridan's work was one of the first of its kind to acknowledge Germans' consent to Nazi policies. But he also stressed that anti-Semitism was abstract for most of them and that they often cooperated out of "self-protection," meaning fear (77, 212). See also the mammoth col-

lection of articles and documents *Bayern in der NS-Zeit: Soziale Lage und politisches Verhalten der Bevölkerung im Spiegel vertraulicher Berichte*, ed. Martin Broszat, Elke Fröhlich, and Falk Wiesemann, 6 vols. (Munich and Vienna: R. Oldenbourg Verlag, 1977–1983); Helen Fein, *Accounting for Genocide: National Responses and Jewish Victimization during the Holocaust* (New York: Free Press, 1979), for a comparative sociological approach that mostly focuses on institutions; Ian Kershaw, *Popular Opinion and Political Dissent in the Third Reich: Bavaria, 1933–45* (New York: Oxford University Press, 1983); Marlis G. Steinert, *Hitler's War and the Germans: Public Mood and Attitude during the Second World War*, trans. and ed. Thomas E. J. De Witt (Athens: Ohio University Press, 1977). Otto Dov Kulka and Aaron Rodrigue have noted that most German historians did not focus on the social history of Germany until the 1970s and that the classic analyses of totalitarianism by Hannah Arendt and Jacob Talmon presumed that popular opinion under totalitarian regimes was necessarily homogenous and saw no need to investigate it. See Otto Dov Kulka and Aaron Rodrigue, "The German Population and the Jews in the Third Reich: Recent Publication and Trends in Research on German Society and the 'Jewish Question,'" *Yad Vahshem Studies* 16 (1984): 422–23.

21. In this chapter I focus exclusively on the work about German public opinion under Nazism, itself voluminous. There also exists a vast literature not only on electoral politics and the coming to power of the Nazis, but on the less ambiguous, active complicity of Germans and also Poles and others in occupied territories who profited directly from the persecution and expropriation of the Jews, as well as on the inaction of German churches, the Vatican, and the Allies themselves, but this work is necessarily beyond the scope of this analysis. In addition to work already cited in note 14, see also Frank Bajohr's essay "No 'Volksgenossen': Jewish Entrepreneurs in the Third Reich," on the expropriation of Jewish businesses in *Social Outsiders in Nazi Germany*, ed. Robert Gellately and Nathan Stoltzfus (Princeton: Princeton University Press, 2001), 45–65; and the essays in Déak et al., *The Politics of Retribution*. See Bob Moore, *Victims and Survivors: The Nazi Persecution of the Jews in the Netherlands, 1940–45* (London: Arnold, 1997), 239–41, for attitudes toward Dutch Jews in Holland. On the churches, see, for Pius XI (1922–39), who sought to protect only Jews in mixed marriages who had wed in church, David Kertzer, *The Popes against the Jews: The Vatican's Role in the Rise of Modern Anti-Semitism* (New York: Alfred A. Knopf, 2001), 264–91. Some of the now voluminous work on Pius XII is discussed in Susan Zuccotti, *Under His Very Windows: The Vatican and the Holocaust in Italy* (New Haven: Yale University Press, 2002). For a sympathetic portrait of Pius XII but not of the German Catholic Church, see Guenther Lewy, *The Catholic Church and Nazi Germany* (New York: DaCapo Press, 2000 [1965]), 242–56; and on the German Protestant churches, see Victoria Barnett, *For the Soul of*

the People: Protestant Protest Against Hitler (Oxford: Oxford University Press, 1992); Robert P. Ericksen and Susanna Heschel, eds., *Betrayal: German Churches and the Holocaust* (Minneapolis: Fortress Press, 1999); and Gutteridge, *Open Thy Mouth for the Dumb*. Bishop von Galen, famous for opposing Nazi policies on euthanasia, "remained in an overall sense loyal to the Nazi state." See Beth A. Greich-Polelle's recent work on *Bishop von Galen: German Catholicism and National Socialism* (New Haven: Yale University Press, 2002), 4–5.

22. Steinert, *Hitler's War and the Germans*, 134.

23. Kershaw, *Popular Opinion and Political Dissent*, 364. In *They Thought They Were Free: The Germans, 1933–45* (Chicago: University of Chicago Press, 1955), Milton Mayer stressed that Germans' "knew" what was happening to Jews, and in this sense the book was ahead of its time. Mayer visited a small town in Germany after the war and befriended ten men to learn how and why they became Nazis and what they saw in Hitler. But Milton was very much of his time when he attributed German behavior to the fact that "men are that way sometimes" and wrote: "I came back home a little afraid for my country. . . . I felt . . . that it was not German Man that I had met, but Man. He happened to be in Germany under certain conditions. He might be here, under certain conditions. He might, under certain conditions, be 'I'" (xix).

24. Sarah Gordon, *Hitler, Germans, and the "Jewish Question"* (Princeton: Princeton University Press, 1984), 301.

25. David Bankier, *The Germans and the Final Solution: Public Opinion under Nazism* (Oxford: Blackwell, 1992); Robert Gellately, *Backing Hitler: Consent & Coercion in Nazi Germany* (Oxford: Oxford University Press, 2001); Eric Johnson, *Nazi Terror: The Gestapo, Jews, and Ordinary Germans* (New York: Basic Books, 1999); Otto Dov Kulka, "The German Population and the Jews: State of Research and New Perspectives, in *Probing the Depths of German Antisemitism: German Society and the Persecution of the Jews, 1933–1941*, ed. David Bankier (New York: Berghahn Books, 2000), 271–81. The collection by Jörg Wollenberg, ed., *The German Public and the Persecution of the Jews, 1933–1945*, trans. and ed. Rado Pribic (New Jersey: Humanities Press, 1996 [1989]), 3, insists that Germans had "welcomed and tolerated" the Kristallnacht pogroms some fifty years prior. On Austria, see Evan Burr Bukey, *Hitler's Austria: Popular Sentiment in the Nazi Era, 1938–1945* (Chapel Hill: University of North Carolina Press, 2000). For a succinct summary of this view, see Philippe Burrin, "Régime Nazi et société allemande: les prismes de l'acceptation," in *Stalinisme et nazisme: Histoire et mémoire comparées*, ed. Henry Rousso (Paris: Éditions Complexes, 1999), 185–98. This volume demonstrates to what extent studies not only of Germany but also of Eastern Europe under Nazism and Stalinism have begun to explore popular complicity with the Soviets as well as with the Nazis.

26. This trajectory also characterizes historiography on Allied bystanders to the Holocaust. Studies of Allied attitudes to the Holocaust in the aftermath of the Eichmann trial have offered important revelations about anti-Semitism and refugee policies in Britain and the United States, as well as often scathing assessments about what could have been done for Jewish refugees and the impact of anti-Jewish feeling on Allied policy. Many focus on how domestic considerations and American and British anti-Semitism rendered policy-makers indifferent to the fate of European Jews, and reveal the extent of Allied knowledge about mass murder. They also assess the response of Jewish communities in the United States, Britain, and Palestine to the Jewish crisis in occupied Europe, in particular the relative paralysis of (British and American) Jewish communities' response to domestic anti-Semitism. Among others in a voluminous literature, see Arthur Morse, *While Six Million Died: A Chronicle of American Apathy* (New York: Random House, 1968); Henry Feingold, *The Politics of Rescue: The Roosevelt Administration and the Holocaust, 1938–1945* (New Brunswick: Rutgers University Press, 1970); David Wyman, *The Abandonment of the Jews: America and the Holocaust, 1941–45* (New York: Pantheon, 1984); Bernard Wasserstein, *Britain and the Jews of Europe, 1939–1945* (Oxford: Oxford University Press, 1988); Dina Porat, *The Blue and Yellow Stars of David: The Zionist Leadership in Palestine and the Holocaust, 1939–1945* (Cambridge: Harvard University Press, 1990). On what and how the Allies knew about the mass murder of European Jewry, see in particular Walter Laqueur, *The Terrible Secret: The Suppression of the Truth about Hitler's Final Solution* (Boston: Little, Brown, 1980); Martin Gilbert, *Auschwitz and the Allies* (London: Michael Joseph, 1981). See also Michael Marrus, ed., *The Nazi Holocaust: Historical Articles on the Destruction of European Jews*, vol. 1, *Bystanders to the Holocaust* (Westport, CT: Meckler, 1989). For a recent assessment, see David Cesarani and Paul A. Levine, *"Bystanders" to the Holocaust: A Re-evaluation* (London: Frank Cass, 2002); Tony Kushner, *The Holocaust and the Liberal Imagination: A Social and Cultural History* (Oxford: Blackwell, 1994).

27. Kulka and Rodrigue, "German Population and the Jews in the Third Reich," 430, 434.

28. Bankier, *Germans and the Final Solution,* 73–74.

29. Nathan Stoltzfus, "The Limits of Policy: Social Protection of Intermarried German Jews in Nazi Germany," in *Social Outsiders in Nazi Germany,* ed. Gellately and Stoltzfus, 117.

30. Gellately, *Backing Hitler,* 263.

31. Ian Kershaw, *The 'Hitler Myth': Image and Reality in the Third Reich* (New York: Oxford University Press, 1987), 40–42. For the army, see Omer Bartov, *Hitler's Army: Soldiers, Nazis, and War in the Third Reich* (New York: Oxford University Press, 1991).

32. Doris L. Bergen, *War & Genocide: A Concise History of the Holocaust* (Boston: Rowman & Littlefield, 2003), 67. On ideological indoctrination generally, see Gellately, *Backing Hitler.*

33. Hans Mommsen, glossed in Frank Trommler, "Between Normality and Resistance: Catastrophic Gradualism in Nazi Germany," in *Resistance in the Third Reich,* ed. Geyer and Boyer, 130.

34. Trommler, "Between Normality and Resistance," 130. See also Peter Longerich, *Politik der Vernichtung: Eine Gesamtdarstellung der nationalsozialistischen Judenverfolgung* (Munich: Piper, 1998), 109.

35. Kershaw, *Popular Opinion and Political Dissent,* 273; Bankier, *Germans and the Final Solution,* 129–30.

36. Gellately, *Backing Hitler,* 51–69; Kershaw, *Popular Opinion and Political Dissent,* 73. Camps on German soil for the most part held Jewish inmates primarily after the *Kristallnacht* pogrom and at the very end of the war, but the general population knew that people of all sorts were arrested and sent to camps without trial. Ulrich Herbert, Karin Orth, and Christoph Dieckmann, "Die nationalsozialistischen Konzentrationslager: Geschichte, Erinnerung, Forschung," in *Die Nationalsozialistischen Konzentrationslager: Entwicklung und Struktur,* ed. Ulrich Herbert, Karin Orth, and Christoph Dieckmann, 2 vols. (Göttingen: Wallstein Verlag, 1998), 1:17, 28–32.

37. Gellately, *Backing Hitler,* 204–23. Also, countless memoirs recount Germans' negative attitudes toward prisoners with whom they had contact and less often acts of sympathy. See, for example, Charlotte Delbo, *Auschwitz and After,* trans. Rosette C. Lamont (New Haven: Yale University Press, 1995), 183–85.

38. Gordon J. Horwitz, *In the Shadow of Death: Living Outside the Gates of Mauthausen* (New York: Free Press, 1990), 35. Horwitz cites an impressive series of testimonies and documents, including complaints about how the cruelties perpetrated on prisoners were hard on the nerves. He also writes of witnesses to the murder of disabled children at Castle Hartheim close by (58–82).

39. Kershaw, *Popular Opinion and Political Dissent,* 364. Kershaw's opinion about the extent of German knowledge has since been confirmed in ways that call into question his emphasis on Jews being literally out of sight and mind. See, for example, Bankier, *Germans and the Final Solution,* 102–15, 130–38; Dov Kulka, "German Population and the Jews," in *Probing the Depths,* ed. Bankier, 276; Eric D. Weitz, *A Century of Genocide: Utopias of Race and Nation* (Princeton: Princeton University Press, 2003), 135.

40. This is confirmed by the essays in *Social Outsiders in Nazi Germany,* ed. Gellately and Stoltzfus, which also includes an overview by Richard Evans, "Social Outsiders in Nazi Germany: From the Sixteenth Century to 1933," 20–44.

41. For a discussion of the Gestapo's reliance on citizens' denunciations

to control dissidence and spread terror, see Robert Gellately, *The Gestapo and German Society: Enforcing Racial Policy, 1933–1945* (Oxford: Clarendon Press, 1991).

42. Bankier, *Germans and the Final Solution*, 156.

43. Ibid.

44. Kershaw, *Hitler Myth*, 249. See also his *Hitler, 1936–1945: Nemesis* (New York: Norton, 2000), 426, in which he discusses the difference between the population's attitude toward the Party's effort to remove crucifixes from Bavarian schools in 1941 and its attitude toward anti-Jewish policies.

45. Ulrich Herbert, "Good Times, Bad Times," *History Today* 36 (1986): 47.

46. W. G. Sebald, *On the Natural History of Destruction*, trans. Anthea Bell (New York: Random House, 2003), 146. There is a vast literature on postwar German memory and the "inability to mourn." See in particular Charles Maier, *The Unmasterable Past: History, Holocaust, and German National Identity* (Cambridge: Harvard University Press, 1988); Eric L. Santer, *Stranded Objects: Mourning, Memory, and Film in Postwar Germany* (Ithaca: Cornell University Press, 1990); and for an influential earlier account, see Alexander Mitscherlich and Margarete Mitscherlich, *The Inability to Mourn* (New York: Grove Press, 1984).

47. Longerich, *Politik der Vernichtung*, 109. Hans Mommsen, *From Weimar to Auschwitz*, trans. Philip Connor (Cambridge: Polity Press, 1991), 241, also expresses this view.

48. Gordon, *Hitler, Jews, and the "Jewish Question,"* 301; Kershaw, *Public Opinion and Political Dissent*, 269–74. In *War & Genocide*, Bergen claims that "dislike of disorder" predominated over other concerns (88). Bankier, *Germans and the Final Solution*, 87, notes that the chief complaint even of Communists about the pogrom was the "waste of public property." Many historians have noted that we should not overinterpret such expressions of dismay as sympathy for Jews: peasants and businessmen who resisted Nazi policy often did so because they were fearful of the economic consequences of Jewish expropriation, and dismayed responses to *Kristallnacht* may often have had more to do with disapproval of civil disorder and the destruction of property than with sympathy for the plight of Jews.

49. Kershaw, *Public Opinion and Political Dissent*, 273.

50. Hans Mommsen, *From Weimar to Auschwitz,* 225. Here, speaking of soldiers and low-level bureaucrats and others who had participated in or been in proximity to the killing, Mommsen writes, "The crucial question is why they were not aware of what they were doing, or why they were able to suppress with such strange consistency such knowledge as dawned on them."

51. Hans Mommsen, "The Reaction of the German Population to the Anti-Jewish Persecution and the Holocaust," in *Lessons and Legacies: The*

Meaning of the Holocaust in a Changing World, ed. Peter Hayes (Evanston: Northwestern University Press, 1991), 144.

52. Mommsen, "Reaction of the German Population," 150.

53. Gellately, *Backing Hitler,* 251.

54. Bergen, *War & Genocide,* 69.

55. Kulka, "German Population and the Jews," in *Probing the Depths,* ed. Bankier, 277.

56. Bankier, *Germans and the Final Solution,* 130.

57. Gellately, *Backing Hitler,* 264.

58. Deborah Dwork and Robert Jan van Pelt, *Holocaust: A History* (New York: Norton, 2002), 298–300.

59. Mayer, *They Thought They Were Free,* 147.

60. Gellately, *Backing Hitler,* 18. Friedländer has elsewhere criticized the unwitting "pleasure in historical narration" of those historians of *Alltagsgeschichte* (history of everyday life) who would write about how non-Jewish Germans led their lives under Nazism with no particular awareness of the distorting lens through which they consequently view the period, since everyday life was permeated and framed by Jewish suffering, whatever the Germans' relation was to it or whatever their ignorance of it was. It is precisely this narrative pleasure, however, which makes it at once an ideal form for generating empathy with victims (suffering their agonies along with them) and woefully inadequate for that purpose, since, as Friedländer points out, there can be no "pleasure" derived from reading about the kinds of violence perpetrated against Jews that is faithful to their experience. See the exchange between Saul Friedländer and Martin Broszat in "A Controversy about the Historicization of National Socialism," in *Reworking the Past,* ed. Baldwin, 117–18.

61. Marion A. Kaplan, *Between Dignity and Despair: Jewish Life in Nazi Germany* (Oxford: Oxford University Press, 1998), 235.

62. Mommsen, *From Weimar to Auschwitz,* 224–53.

63. Kaplan, *Between Dignity and Despair,* 235. For another mode of posing the same question, see Leni Yahil, "The Double Consciousness of the Nazi Mind and Practice," in *Probing the Depths,* ed. Bankier, 41.

64. Saul Friedländer, "The Wehrmacht, German Society, and the Knowledge of the Mass Extermination of the Jews," in *Crimes of War: Guilt and Denial in the Twentieth Century,* ed. Omer Bartov, Atina Grossmann, and Mary Nolan (New York: New Press, 2002, 27.

65. Friedländer, "Wehrmacht," 26–27.

66. Daniel Jonah Goldhagen, *Hitler's Willing Executioners: Ordinary Germans and the Holocaust* (New York: Vintage, 1996), 440.

67. Philippe Burrin, *Hitler and the Jews: The Genesis of the Holocaust,* trans. Patsy Southgate (London: Edward Arnold, 1994), 151.

68. Raul Hilberg, *Perpetrators, Victims, Bystanders: The Jewish Catastrophe, 1933–1945* (New York: Harper Perennial, 1992), 195–97, 188, and on page 214 he links the positive qualities of Jewish survivors to the positive qualities of those bystanders who did help Jews. Both groups had "inner flexibility" and were quick decision-makers. He thus tends to develop implicit distinctions between the positive qualities of Jewish survivors and the vast majority of their murdered brethren, thereby undermining the forcefulness of the pressure wrought by generalized indifference on all Jews.

69. Bankier, *Germans and the Final Solution*, 77.

70. Of course, the radicalization of anti-Semitism is normally attributed to the war and the opportunities it offered the regime for intensified surveillance, censorship, persecution, and murder. This is certain, and yet we still need to understand how the isolation and persecution of Jews before the war became part of the course of things.

71. Friedländer, *Nazi Germany and the Jews*, 5, 117–18.

72. David Engel, *The Holocaust: The Third Reich and the Jews* (Essex: Longman, 2000), 76.

73. Kushner, *Holocaust and the Liberal Imagination*, 25. Indeed, Kushner's unusual work tries to redefine indifference to Jewish suffering neither as anti-Semitism nor as guilty repression but as the expression of liberalism's limits and for this reason requires some further comment. According to him, British liberalism could acknowledge neither the particularity of Jewish suffering nor the irrationality of Nazi anti-Semitism; it linked anti-Semitism to a reasonable prejudice against unassimilated or "Jewish" Jews and refused to recognize the differences between Jewish refugees and others in the name of universal suffering. Moreover, it rationalized anti-Jewish feeling among Germans by reference to Jewish "domination" of business and professions. Yet in his argument it's not clear if or why liberalism is by definition anti-Semitic: Why can't liberal ideology integrate even the assimilated Jews it emancipated in the first place? In short: from whence comes anti-Semitism and what exactly is the relationship between liberalism and anti-Semitism? For an account of Dutch liberalism and Jewish refugees, see Moore, *Victims and Survivors*, 161–62.

74. Kushner, *Holocaust and the Liberal Imagination*, 127, 133, 137, 225, 273.

75. The book received numerous positive reviews in Britain and the United States, including those by Walter Laqueur, *Los Angeles Times*, February 23, 1997, p. 8; Donald Niewyk, *American Historical Review* 103, no. 3 (1998): 918–19; William Rubenstein, *History Today* 48 (1998): 51–52; Istvan Déak, "Beginning of the End," *New Republic* 217 (1997): 42–46. For an ambivalent reference (he believes that the time has not yet come for the sort of synthesis Friedländer has undertaken), see Christian Ingrao, "Conquérir,

aménager, exterminer: Recherches récentes sur la Shoah," *Annales HSS* 2 (March–April 2003): 435.

76. Friedländer, quoted in Fritz Stern's review, "The Worst Was Yet to Come," *New York Times,* February 23, 1997, p. 12.

After this book went to press, I read Shulamit Volkov's essay "Anti-Semitism as Explanation: For and Against," in *Catastrophe and Meaning: The Holocaust and the Twentieth Century,* ed. Moishe Postone and Eric Santner (Chicago: University of Chicago Press, 2003), 34–48. In an entirely different context, she makes some observations of Friedländer's work that I make here. She argues that Friedländer's text is most profound not when he is speaking of "redemptive anti-Semitism" but when he documents the gradual exclusion of Jews from German life. Obviously, my own argument strongly concurs with hers, however different our frameworks of analysis (43–44).

77. Nancy Scheper-Hughes, "Coming to Our Senses: Anthropology and Genocide," in *Annihilating Difference: The Anthropology of Genocide,* ed. Alexander Laban Hinton (Berkeley: University of California Press, 2002), 369.

78. Hannah Arendt, *The Origins of Totalitarianism* (New York: Meridian, 1958), 87.

79. For a German perspective that uses the diaries as literal evidence of Jewish persecution and German indifference, see Susanne Heim, "The German-Jewish Relationship in the Diaries of Victor Klemperer," in *Probing the Depths,* ed. Bankier, 312–25. For a more subtle view that counters the notion that Klemperer's diaries exonerate Germans, see Omer Bartov, "Jews and Germans: Victor Klemperer Bears Witness," in Omer Bartov, *Germany's War and the Holocaust: Disputed Histories* (Ithaca: Cornell University Press, 2003), 192–215.

80. Victor Klemperer, *I Will Bear Witness: A Diary of the Nazi Years, 1942–1945,* trans. Martin Chalmers (New York: Modern Library, 2001), 40, 197, 328.

81. Ibid., 304, 435, 504.

82. Ibid., 144.

83. Ibid., 118, 493, 429.

84. Kaplan, *Between Dignity and Despair;* Friedländer, *Nazi Germany and the Jews.* See also Monika Richarz, ed., *Jewish Life in Germany: Memoirs from Three Centuries,* trans. Stella P. Rosenfeld and Sidney Rosenfeld (Bloomington: Indiana University Press, 1991): 301–474.

85. Mihail Sebastian, *Journal 1935–1944: The Fascist Years,* trans. Patrick Camiller (Chicago: Ivan R. Dee, 2000), 392.

86. Marcel Reich-Ranicki, *The Author of Himself: The Life of Marcel Reich-Ranicki* (Princeton: Princeton University Press, 2001), 46. Though it is mar-

keted as a Holocaust memoir, the main motif of Reich-Ranicki's work is the problem of Jewish assimilation in contemporary Germany. He bends over backwards to give others the benefit of the doubt but also consistently reports on the difficulty of being a Jew in Germany, then and now. He describes a series of hilarious but also depressing encounters, in which he is mistaken for "Mr Bubis" (the head of the German-Jewish community), is asked in Salzburg if he wants to call Jerusalem when he requests the phone, and is asked by a Frankfurt taxi driver if he were just in from Tel Aviv (212–13).

87. Ibid., 53.

88. Ibid., 51–52.

89. Ibid., 341.

90. Ibid., 342.

91. Ibid.

92. Hannah Arendt first raised the issue of "not thinking" in relation to the Jewish genocide in her discussion of Adolf Eichmann in *Eichmann in Jerusalem: A Report on the Banality of Evil* (New York: Penguin, 1963). She, however, tied banality to the personality of Eichmann and his particular role as a bureaucrat (he becomes an emblem of "mass" society and its capacity for evil). I would prefer to see not thinking as an actively complicit form of perpetration and thus cruelty by even well-intentioned but structurally privileged groups that may take seemingly banal forms.

93. Friedländer, "Wehrmacht," 10.

4. WHO WAS THE "REAL" HITLER?

1. Sebastian Haffner, *The Meaning of Hitler*, trans. Ewald Osers (London: Phoenix Press, 1997), 3.

2. Tucholsky, cited in ibid., 25; Bertolt Brecht, *Journals*, trans. Hugh Rorrison, ed. John Willett (New York: Routledge, 1993), 203.

3. G. M. Gilbert, *The Psychology of Dictatorship: Based on an Examination of the Leaders of Nazi Germany* (New York: Ronald Press, 1950), 33–34.

4. Ernest Jones, "The Psychology of Quislingism," *International Journal of Psycho-Analysis* 22 (1941): 6.

5. As we will see, this understanding of homosexuality as latent, that is, as an unconscious potential in men who may not be homosexual, is crucial to the unfolding of the narrative about Hitler and Nazism. In his discussion of the Frankfurt School and homosexuality, Andrew Hewitt has discussed the pernicious implications of "the disingenuous distinction drawn between repressed homosexuality and homosexuality per se." Following his lead, throughout the text I refer to Nazism and *homosexuality*. See Andrew Hewitt,

Political Inversions: Homosexuality, Fascism, and the Modernist Imaginary (Stanford: Stanford University Press, 1996), 33, 52–55.

6. I don't wish to suggest that there is no relationship between male homoeroticism, homosexuality, and the Nazi *Männerbund*, but to argue that important historical research into how Nazism drew on militaristic, anti-aristocratic, and homophilic associations in *völkisch* culture (including the youth movement of Hans Blueher and the elite Georgekreis—the circle of young men surrounding the poet Stefan George) is far different from the widespread presumption that male homosexuality and Nazism somehow go together.

7. See Alexander Zinn, *Die soziale Konstruktion des homosexuellen Nationalsozialisten: Zu Genese und Etablierung eines Stereotyps* (Frankfurt: Peter Lang, 1997), 37–49; Harry Oosterhuis, "The 'Jews' of the Antifascist Left: Homosexuality and Socialist Resistance to Nazism," in *Gay Men and the Sexual History of the Political Left*, ed. G. Hekma, H. Oosteruis, and J. Steakley (New York: Haworth Press, 1995), 227–57.

8. Although there is still some debate, historians now generally believe that van der Lubbe acted alone. Ian Kershaw, *Hitler, 1889–1936: Hubris* (New York: Norton, 1998), 731 n. 112.

9. See the discussion in Oosterhuis, *Gay Men and the Sexual History of the Political Left*, 232–33.

10. Klaus Mann, *Heute und Morgen: Schriften zur Zeit*, ed. Martin-Gregor Dellin (Munich: Nymphenburger Verlagshandlung, 1969), 137.

11. As Dagmar Herzog has demonstrated, the link between Nazism and homosexuality was forged not in Germany but primarily in the United States after the war both by Americans and by German-Jewish refugees. It is not clear why this was the case. Homophobia was nonetheless vicious in postwar Germany. See Dagmar Herzog, *Sex after Fascism: Memory and Morality in Twentieth-Century Germany*, forthcoming (Princeton: Princeton University Press, 2005). Of psychoanalytic and psychoanalytically inflected studies, see Wilhelm Reich, *The Mass Psychology of Fascism*, trans. Vincent R. Carfagno (New York: Farrar, Straus & Giroux, 1970 [1933]; Erich Fromm, *Escape from Freedom* (New York: Henry Holt, 1969 [1941]); the classic T. W. Adorno et al., eds., *The Authoritarian Personality* (Norton: New York, 1982). On totalitarianism, see Carl J. Friedrich, ed., *Totalitarianism* (New York: Universal Library, 1964), particularly the contributions of Erik Erikson, Else Frenkel-Brunswik, Marie Jahoda, and Stuart Cook, 156–230. Some of these texts—Fromm's, Adorno's, and Friedrich's collections—articulate a "psychological position" which is implicitly homosexual, whereas Reich explicitly makes the association. For a discussion of the connection between latent homosexuality, anti-Semitism, and fascism more generally in some of these texts, see Elizabeth Young-Bruehl, *Anatomy of Prejudices* (Cambridge: Har-

vard University Press, 1996), 60–73. Young-Bruehl's focus is not, however, on homosexuality, but on the development of American theories of prejudice.

12. Alice Kaplan, *The Collaborator: The Trial and Execution of Robert Brasillach* (Chicago: University of Chicago Press, 2000), 162–64. Regarding films, see, among others, Roberto Rossellini's *Rome: Open City* (1946) and *Germany, Year Zero* (1947); Gillo Pontecorvo's *Kapò* (1961); Luchino Visconti's *The Damned* (1970); and Bernardo Bertolucci's *The Conformist* (1971). Lesbianism is also equated with fascism, but intermittently and less pervasively, and mostly in literary and cinematic representations rather than in the psychoanalytic discussions that formed the basis for the more popularly diffused association of male homosexuality and fascism. Female homosexuality does not denote a sexual *identity*, but refers to a set of gender-deviant *behaviors* (inappropriate masculinity or hyperbolic femininity).

13. Arthur Schlesinger Jr., *The Vital Center: The Politics of Freedom* (New York: DaCapo Press, 1988 [1949]), 53; Theodor Adorno, *Minima Moralia* (London: Verso, 1974 [1951]), 46.

14. The term "Hitler boom" comes from Hans Gatzke's important overview, "Hitler and Psychohistory," *American Historical Review* 78, no. 2 (1973): 394–401. Gatzke views psychohistory as relying far too heavily on evidence for which there is no empirical proof and on the whole believes that its practitioners force evidence into preconceived categories.

15. See Peter Loewenberg, "The Unsuccessful Adolescence of Heinrich Himmler," *American Historical Review* 76, no. 3 (1971): 612–41; "The Psychohistorical Origins of the Nazi Youth Cohort" *American Historical Review* 76, no. 5 (1971): 1457–1502; "Psychohistorical Perspectives on Modern German History," *Journal of Modern History* 47, no. 2 (1975): 229–79. We will have occasion to speak of his work further on. For an earlier, important German psychoanalytical (but not psychohistorical) account of what he calls "fatherlessness," see Alexander Mitscherlich, *Society Without the Father: A Contribution to Social Psychology*, trans. Eric Mosbacher (New York: Harcourt, Brace & World, 1969 [1963]).

16. See Zinn, *Die soziale Konstruktion*, for a discussion of the political context and legal status of homosexuals under Nazism. For an overview of the field, see the essays in *Nationalsozialistischer Terror gegen Homosexuelle: Verdrängt und ungesühnt*, ed. Burkhard Jellonnek and Rüdiger Lautmann (Paderborn: Ferdinand Schoeningh, 2001). Lautman also published a short essay in English, "Gay Prisoners in Concentration Camps as Compared with Jehovah's Witnesses and Political Prisoners," in *A Mosaic of Victims*, ed. Michael Berenbaum (New York: New York University Press, 1990), 200–206. For some of the most up-to-date research and thinking in the

field, see Geoffrey J. Giles, "The Denial of Homosexuality: Same-Sex Incidents in Himmler's SS and Police," and Stefan Micheler, "Homophobic Propaganda and the Denunciation of Same-Sex Desiring Men under National Socialism," both in a special issue on "Sexuality and German Fascism" of *Journal of the History of Sexuality* 11 (January/April 2002): 256–90, 95–130. Giles has also published "The Institutionalization of Homosexual Panic in the Third Reich," in *Social Outsiders in Nazi Germany,* ed. Robert Gellately and Nathan Stoltzfus (Princeton: Princeton University Press, 2001), 233–55.

17. Joachim C. Fest, *The Face of the Third Reich: Portraits of the Nazi Leadership* (New York: Da Capo Press, 1970), 143., Bock infers, however unwittingly, that working in a concentration camp somehow belongs together with gender-deviant behavior and thus with female homosexuality—with women who don't marry and supposedly don't have children. Gisela Bock, "Equality and Difference in National Socialist Racism," in *Beyond Equality and Difference: Citizenship, Feminist Politics, Female Subjectivity,* ed. Gisela Bock and Susan James (New York: Routledge, 1994), 109. The assertions are an allusion to Bock's debate with Claudia Koonz over the role of middle-class married women's support for Hitler, and particularly the role played by "separate spheres"—nineteenth-century idealized notions of womanhood and motherhood—in women's complicity. Bock argues that Koonz exaggerates the role of "separate spheres" in ensuring that complicity. In this passage, therefore, she is perhaps somewhat defensive of women who were both mothers and wives. For an exchange between them, see (untitled) *Geschichte und Gesellschaft* 18 (1992): 394–99. In the popular book *The Rise and Fall of the Third Reich: A History of Nazi Germany* (New York: Simon & Schuster, 1960), William Shirer insisted that Ernst Roehm was, "like so many of the early Nazis, a homosexual" (38).

18. See, for example, Fest, *The Face of the Third Reich,* 139, 143; John Lukacs, *The Hitler of History* (New York: Vintage, 1997).

19. Brigitte Hamann, *Hitler's Vienna: A Dictator's Apprenticeship,* trans. Thomas Thornton (New York: Oxford University Press, 1999), 362.

20. Werner Maser, *Hitler: Legend, Myth, and Reality* trans. Peter and Betty Ross (New York: Harper & Row, 1973), 196. Maser is most concerned to dismiss speculations based on a well-known and unreliable account of Hitler by the dictator's friend in youth, August Kubizek, published as *The Young Hitler I Knew,* trans. E. V. Anderson (Boston: Houghton Mifflin, 1955), 236–39. The other major biographers of Hitler mostly ignore the issue by simply presuming his (albeit troubled) heterosexuality. See Allan Bullock, *Hitler: A Study in Tyranny* (New York: Harper, 1960), 359–61; Joachim C. Fest, *Hitler,* trans. Richard Winston and Clara Winston

(New York: Harcourt Brace Jovanovich, 1974), esp. 22–23, 322–23, 523–25; and John Toland, *Adolf Hitler* (Garden City: Doubleday, 1976), 23–24. For an earlier account also responsible for the assertion that Hitler was "sexually frigid," see Franz Jetzinger, *Hitler's Youth* (London: Hutchison, 1958), 113.

21. Michael Burleigh, *The Third Reich: A New History* (New York: Hill and Wang, 2000), 233.

22. Kershaw, *Hitler, 1889–1936: Hubris*, 46, 251. In an earlier work, he noted that jokes about Hitler's sexuality circulated widely until around 1938, when worries about the impending war shifted Germans' focus of concern. Ian Kershaw, *The Hitler Myth: Image and Reality in the Third Reich* (Oxford: Oxford University Press, 1987), 136–37 n. 50.

23. Lothan Machtan, *Hidden Hitler* (New York: Basic Books, 2001).

24. Geoffrey Giles, "Führer Fantasy," *Washington Post*, November 25, 2001, p. 5.

25. Richard Bessel, "The Hidden Hitler," *History Today* 51 (2001): 4.

26. Anson Rabinbach, "Adi's Friends," *Times Literary Supplement*, January 11, 2002, p. 10. Walter Reich's review in the *New York Times* merely notes that "assertions of Hitler's homosexuality, active or latent, are hardly new. They dogged him during his rise to power and after he gained it. They are made in a number of biographies. And they form the basis of occasional images of him to this day." He then situates Machtan's work in the context of such allegations but never comments on the fantasmic nature of the allegations themselves except to say that Machtan can't prove them any more effectively than anyone else. Walter Reich, review of *Hidden Hitler*, *New York Times* December 16, 2001. Not surprisingly, reviews in the gay press consistently addressed the appeal of making the "world's greatest villain" a "gay villain." See Charles Kaiser, "Heil Mary," *Advocate*, November 20, 2001, p. 73; Gabriel Rotello, "Thinking against the Grain," *Advocate*, December 25, 2001, p. 72. This appeal is, of course, exactly what Bessel wants to avoid when he claims he did not want to appear homophobic. That is, by evoking the fear of appearing homophobic, Bessel raises a question about who incites this fear (your conscience? gay friends?) In so doing, he inadvertently reinforces the notion that where there is fear of seeming homophobic, there can be no homophobia.

27. In an important analysis, literary theorist Andrew Hewitt argues persuasively that in various modernist texts homosexuality is an allegory of how we can't pin fascism down: of how fascism constitutes itself as an "unspeakable" myth outside of a linear, productive model of History. In Hewitt's view, several modernist authors constructed male homosexuality homophobically as a defense against the anxiety "about the possibility of

fixing historical phenomenon at all," as the very image of an aporia that they feared might be implicated in modernism itself. Hewitt analyses in detail the works of Theodor Adorno, Alberto Moravia, Wyndham Lewis, Henry Mackay, and Alfred Jarry. Hewitt, *Political Inversions*, 1–37.

28. Historian Dagmar Herzog says this in her critical reading of Klaus Theweleit's book *Male Fantasies*, in which, she claims, he ends up suggesting that there are similarities between gay men and fascists "precisely in the context of trying to *refute* the old canard that all Nazis were gay!" What's fascinating here is that, as Herzog points out, even the most sincere efforts to uncouple homosexuality and Nazism can't help but keep them together. Herzog is concerned with other issues and does not elaborate on this point. Dagmar Herzog, " 'Pleasure, Sex, and Politics Belong Together': Post-Holocaust Memory and the Sexual Revolution in West Germany," *Critical Inquiry* 24 (Winter 1998): 434 n. 99.

29. The literary theorist Laura Frost, who argues that the sadomasochistic eroticism and sexual deviance associated with fascism constitute the unacknowledged fantasy life of liberal democracy, still feels compelled to claim that "eroticized fascism is [not] exclusively a 'gay thing.' " Laura Frost, *Sex Drives: Fantasies of Fascism in Literary Modernism* (Ithaca: Cornell University Press, 2002), 119. Elizabeth D. Heineman has written that "the social-psychological explanation for fascism has kept fascism's possible appeal to the erotic on the intellectual agenda and in the popular imagination." Elizabeth D. Heineman, "Sexuality and Nazism: The Doubly Unspeakable?" *Journal of the History of Sexuality* 11 (January/April 2002): 27. She does not, however, explore this assertion. Heineman's essay does significantly address the importance of the history of sexuality—the persecution of sexual minorities, controlling women's reproduction and heterosexuality more generally—for our understanding of the Nazi regime. Note also the absolute silence on the topic of homosexuality in a recent effort to update old concepts of the "Nazi Personality." Perhaps it is not merely that homosexuality has been thoroughly dissociated from Nazism but that the silence itself bears investigation. The book provides ample evidence for this suspicion. E. Zillmer, M. Harrower, B. A. Ritzler, R. P. Archer, eds., *The Quest for the Nazi Personality: A Psychological Investigation of Nazi War Criminals* (Hillsdale, N.J.: Lawrence Erlbaum Associates, 1995).

30. Ian Kershaw, *Hitler, 1936–1945: Nemesis* (New York: Norton, 2000), 114. Kershaw claims that American journalists originated this rumor.

31. Hermann Rauschning, *Voice of Destruction* (New York: Putnam's Sons, 1940), 263.

32. Rudolf Olden, *Hitler the Pawn* (London: Victor Gollancz, 1936), 315.

33. Rauschning, *Voice of Destruction*, 262.

34. Clifford Kirkpatrick, *Nazi Germany: Its Women and Family Life* (New

York: Bobbs-Merrill, 1938), 104; Frederick L. Schuman, *The Nazi Dictatorship: A Study in Social Pathology and the Politics of Fascism* (New York: Knopf, 1939), 28.

35. Walter Langer, *The Mind of Adolf Hitler: The Secret Wartime Report* (New York: Basic Books, 1972 [1943]), 174. Langer also notes that Hitler's personality seems to be composed of two, irreconcilable halves (127–28).

36. Langer also diagnosed Hitler as a masochist, recounting anecdotes told by Otto Strasser, whose Nazi brother Gregor had been murdered by Hitler in the "blood purge" of 1934 after clashing with Hitler over the direction of the Party. In his published work on Hitler, Strasser seeks to discredit him by calling him a "nihilist"—he is the "incarnation of the principle of destruction"—and by claiming that he is "like a woman" and a *"soubrette."* Otto Strasser, *Hitler and I*, trans. Gwenda David and Eric Mosbacher (Boston: Houghton Mifflin, 1940), 62, 76, 212. For a discussion of the various accounts of Hitler's heterosexual perversions, see Ron Rosenbaum, *Explaining Hitler* (New York: Harper, 1998), 99–117, 138–52. For some reason, Rosenbaum does not mention the pervasive discussions of Hitler's homosexuality, even though many of the texts he cites address it explicitly. He oddly interprets the antifascist *Munich Post*'s publication of a series of revelations about Roehm's homosexuality as a brave effort to reveal the hypocrisy of the Nazis (46–56). Of course it was that too, but its impact derived from the way in which the Left sought to exploit the homophobia of the general population to discredit Nazism, as Mann's contemporary critique of left-wing homophobia and Zinn's account in *Die soziale Konstruktion* make very clear.

37. George W. Herald, "Sex as a Nazi Weapon," *American Mercury* 54 (1942): 658; Lewis Corey, "Marquis de Sade—The Cult of Despotism," *Antioch Review* 26.1 (1966 [reprint of 1952 original]): 25.

38. Strasser, *Hitler and I*; Rauschning, *Voice of Destruction*.

39. Klaus Mann, quoted in Machtan, *Hidden Hitler*, 259.

40. I might add that even the eminent historian Hugh Trevor-Roper plays with the notion of Hitler as a man marked by a "dark angel of destruction" whose fundamental "nature" was nonetheless that of an "Austrian petty bourgeois." He uses the "petty bourgeois" appellation continually throughout his famous book on Hitler's last days (his marriage to Eva Braun, for example, was a "petty bourgeois" gesture) to ridicule the Nazi leader, but he is not particularly interested in interrogating his dual nature, only his "extravagant" side. See Hugh Trevor-Roper, *The Last Days of Hitler* (London: Papermac, 1971 [1947]), 159, 82–83.

41. Wyndham Lewis, *The Hitler Cult* (London: J. M. Dent & Sons, 1939), 79.

42. Ibid., 76.

43. William Shirer, *Berlin Diary: The Journal of a Foreign Correspondent 1934–41* (New York: Alfred Knopf, 1942), 110, 211.

44. Ibid., 363.

45. In many ways, the sociopsychological arguments about Hitler's rise to power made by well-known German critics in exile Konrad Heiden (1901–1966) and Sebastian Haffner (1907–1998) preceded many of these analyses. These two German journalists in exile sought to understand Hitler's pull beyond the terms of reference then proffered by socioeconomic and political analysts, who viewed Nazism in terms of capitalist economic dynamism, German Imperialism, or as the outcome of the State's conquest by a single political party: Hitler was regarded either as a tool of business interests, as a nationalist, or as a political opportunist bent on self-aggrandizement. They also looked beyond reductive psychological accounts of a "neurotic" or a "mad" Hitler and sought to yoke sociohistorical investigation to psychological analysis. They too relied on metaphors of sexual and gender deviance but in a more muted fashion. Heiden claimed that Hitler was not a homosexual but a masochist. He nonetheless claimed that Hitler is special but also part of the atmosphere, which bears an "inner kinship to all disintegration and decay," in which the "perversion" prevailed (homosexuality, he tells us, was "widespread in the secret murderers' army" of the postwar period, and its devotees denied that it was a perversion. They were proud, regarded themselves as "different from the others," meaning better. They boasted about their "superiority.".And Haffner claimed the Germans had been emasculated and sought to compensate via a "fatherland fixation." Konrad Heiden, *Der Fuehrer* (London: Heinemann, 1944), 179, 294; Sebastian Haffner, *Germany: Jekyll and Hyde* (New York: E. P. Dutton, 1941), 143–44. These important accounts form part of this narrative about sexual deviance and fascism but are not sufficiently explicit to be included in more detail in this discussion.

46. Rodney Collin, "Hitlerism as a Sex Problem," *Spectator*, June 19, 1934, p. 7. According to Dagmar Herzog, the German view of Nazis as sexually repressed does not develop until after 1966 and is a retrospective fantasy about Nazism. According to her, Nazism actually challenged strict bourgeois morality while giving lip service to middle-class sexual conventions. See Herzog, *Sex after Fascism*.

47. George W. Herald, "Sex as a Nazi Weapon," *American Mercury* 54 (1942): 657–58.

48. Samuel Igra, *Germany's National Vice* (London: Quality Press, 1945), 10.

49. Ibid., 28, 8.

50. Ibid., 28, 58. I should note that Lothar Machtan makes exactly the same argument in almost exactly the same words in his recent *Hidden Hitler*

(reviews of which were extensively discussed at the beginning of the chapter), demonstrating its continued power. He writes that Hitler "must have felt personally assailed" by the revelations. Machtan, *Hidden Hitler*, 49. Moreover, Machtan cites Igra as if the book were a reliable historical source rather than a synthesis of rumors and unverified and unverifiable evidence (116, 332n).

51. Igra, *Germany's National Vice*, 63.

52. Ibid., 58–59, 63, 67.

53. Eugen Dollmann, *Roma Nazista*, trans. Italo Zingaretti (Milan: Longanesi, 1949). This work is oddly one of Lothar Machtan's most important sources, and he relies as well on some of Dollmann's papers that he found in a private family archive and in one State archive (the original German manuscript seems to be lost). Much if not all of what he finds in these papers appears to be reproduced in the memoirs to which he gives great credence because of the author's high-level contacts ("by his close proximity to the events and matters he describes" [Machtan, *Hidden Hitler*, 133]). Why this should be a guarantee against distortion or fraud is not clear. Moreover, Machtan never informs the reader that Dollmann's memoirs are meant less to inform than to titillate, entertain, and exculpate their author. Instead, he presents the disadvantages of Dollmann's memoirs as advantages, noting that "it was not the scholarly reputation of a trained historian that prompted the publisher to bring them out, but the inside information available to one of the Third Reich's most influential representatives in Rome" (319), and cites a favorable 1950 review of the book from *Corriere della Sera*. This seems to me somewhat disingenuous.

54. Eugen Dollmann, *The Interpreter: Memoirs of Doktor Eugen Dollmann*, trans. J. Maxwell Brownjohn (London: Hutchison, 1967). Almost all explicit references to Hitler's homosexuality were removed. Hence I rely on the Italian edition.

55. For example, in reference to the 1944 Nazi retaliatory massacre of Italian partisans at the Ardeatine Caves, Dollmann claims that he had not been asked his advice, and if he had, he would have recommended against retaliation. Dollmann, *Roma Nazista*, 241–55. This section was also deleted from the English edition.

56. Ibid., 10, 47. He says (47) that Göring was as "fat as a cow and afraid of his own shadow," Goebbels "limped," and Himmler had eyes like a "cold fish" and was almost blind, with "white, feminine skin."

57. Ibid., 33.

58. For discussions of the broader context of this discourse in the works of the Frankfurt School, see Martin Jay, *The Dialectical Imagination: A History of the Frankfurt School and the Institute of Social Research, 1923–1950* (Boston: Little, Brown, 1973), esp. 86–142; Young-Bruehl, *Anatomy of Prejudices*,

58–70. For an overall discussion of evolution and aims of American psychology in this period, see Ellen Herman, *The Romance of American Psychology: Political Culture in the Age of Experts* (Berkeley: University of California Press, 1995). Herman notes that during the war, psychologists began to "understand political ideas in psychological terms" as a way to respond to the conflict (58). On the reconciliation of American psychoanalysis with "received social values," including the stigmatization of homosexuality, Nathan Hale, *The Rise and Crisis of Psychoanalysis in the United States: Freud and the Americans, 1917–1985* (Oxford: Oxford University Press, 1995), 298–99.

59. Harold Lasswell, "The Psychology of Hitlerism," *Political Quarterly* 4 (1933): 380.

60. Erik Erikson, *Childhood and Society* (New York: Norton, 1950), 290–91. First published as "Hitler's Imagery of German Youth," *Psychiatry* 4 (November 1942).

61. Erich Fromm, *Escape from Freedom* (New York: Henry Holt, 1994 [1941]), 35.

62. Jay, *Dialectical Imagination*, 128; Young-Bruehl, *Anatomy of Prejudices*, 60–61.

63. Wilhelm Reich, *The Mass Psychology of Fascism* (New York: Farrar, Straus & Giroux, 1970 [1933]), 162–63.

64. Ernest Jones, "The Psychology of Quislingism," *International Journal of Psycho-Analysis* 22 (1941): 5.

65. The phrase "identification with the aggressor," widely used at the time, was formulated by Anna Freud in her *The Ego and the Mechanisms of Defense*, trans. Cecil Baines (New York: International Universities Press, 1946), 117–31.

66. Jones, "Psychology of Quislingism," 6.

67. The shift away from an emphasis on national character, especially in psychoanalytic analyses of Nazism and of prejudice more generally, was itself—as I am arguing here—embedded in the dynamics of an explanatory framework that increasingly detached universal psychological patterns from culturally specific ones (such as the German authoritarian family). In the 1970s psychohistorians thus not surprisingly and fruitfully (if often problematically) emphasized the historically and culturally specific expressions of those universal patterns in new terms.

68. T. W. Adorno et al., eds., *The Authoritarian Personality* (Norton: New York, 1982), 406. Young-Bruehl, *Anatomy of Prejudices*, 60–73. Andrew Hewitt most effectively exposes the (not always so implicit) homophobia of this work in *Political Inversions*, 44–54. For a general discussion of the work's genesis, see Jay, *Dialectical Imagination*, 234–52. For a debate about homophobia in Frankfurt School writings see the criticism of Randall Halle,

"Zwischen Marxismus und Psychoanalyse: Antifaschismus und Antihomosexualität in der Frankfurter Schule," *Zeitschrift für Sexualforschung* 9 (1996): 343–57; and Martin Dannecker's defense, "Der Kristische Theorie und ihr Konzept der Homosexualität: Antwort auf Randall Halle," *Zeitschrift für Sexualforschung* 10 (1997): 19–36.

69. Martin Wangh, "National Socialism and the Genocide of the Jews: A Psycho-Analytic Study of a Historical Event," *International Journal of Psychoanalysis* 45 (1964): 388.

70. Ibid., 393.

71. Loewenberg, "The Psychohistorical Origins," 1501. The prolonged absence of the father strengthens closeness with the mother and stimulates incestuous fantasies, thereby intensifying fear of punishment for the "forbidden longings" (1486).

72. Wilhelm Reich, *Sex-Pol: Essays, 1929–1934* (New York: Vintage, 1972), 297.

73. Gilbert, *The Psychology of Dictatorship*, 155.

74. Ibid., 64.

75. Ibid., 149.

76. Ibid., 279–80.

77. Wangh, "National Socialism," 393.

78. Lowenberg, "The Psychohistorical Origins, 1495.

79. Wangh's reference is disturbing, since it was already well known that Hitler's speech accusing the SA and its leaders of "immorality" (homosexuality) was aimed simply at justifying the illegal, illegitimate, and brutal murders of his political rivals. Geoffrey Giles claims that Hitler was concerned about homosexuality tarnishing the image of the Party even before the Roehm putsch, and how extensive the persecution of gay men was after 1934 in the Party, the SS, and the population in general. Giles, "Institutionalization of Homosexual Panic," 236–40.

80. J. R. Rees, ed., *The Case of Rudolf Hess: A Problem in Diagnosis and Forensic Psychiatry* (New York: Norton, 1948), 203.

81. Henry V. Dicks, *Licensed Mass Murder: A Socio-Psychological Study of some SS Killers* (New York: Basic Books, 1972), 110–11, 124, esp. 253. He articulates the "psychological position of the homosexual" as a crucial factor throughout the book to explain the behavior of various Nazis without calling it that explicitly, frequently leaning on Wangh's analysis.

82. Douglas Kelley, *22 Cells in Nuremberg: A Psychiatrist Examines the Nazi Criminals* (New York: Greenberg Press, 1947), 212–13.

83. Loewenberg, "Himmler," 625. "Homosexual Panic" was a diagnosis pioneered by American psychologist Edward Kemp in 1920 to describe the anxiety generated by a struggle between the "uncontrollable, perverted . . . craving [homosexual desire] struggling with the socialized affective cravings, the

ego, in the same personality." Edward Kempf, *Psychopathology* (St. Louis: C. V. Mosby, 1921), 479–80. Homosexual panic was included in the *Diagnostic and Statistical Manual* of the psychiatric profession in 1952 and removed in 1980 for lack of coherence, and though it was rarely used as a medical diagnosis, it became a widespread legal defense for men accused of murdering men who were (or who the defendant perceived to be) gay (most recently, in the murder of Matthew Shepard). Eve Kosofsky Sedgwick addressed the concept as a way of exposing the structure of homophobia more generally in *Epistemology of the Closet* (Berkeley: University of California Press, 1990), 19–21. The term is used so often and with so little explanation that it seemed important to add clarification. Loewenberg's usage is a good example of the generally irresponsible invocation of an incoherent term.

84. Langer, *Mind of Adolf Hitler,* 174.

85. Haffner, *Germany: Jekyll and Hyde,* 15.

86. I hope I have by now clarified the importance of attending to the specific role played by homosexuality in fantasies about fascism. Laura Frost, who rightly argues that sexual deviance and fascism enjoy a broad cultural association that works as a projection of democratic societies' anxiety about sexuality onto "abnormal" sexual practice, doesn't differentiate between homosexual and heterosexual deviance—indeed she is at pains to demonstrate that fascist eroticism was not, as she puts it, a "gay thing." But she thereby tends to downplay the way in which critics have used male homosexuality to *account* for fascism as a historical phenomenon. She mentions Reich, Adorno, Fromm, and even William Shirer as alluding to perversion more generally when they speak of fascism, but she fails to note that each of these thinkers at some point explicitly linked sadomasochism to homosexuality (to regression) and identified Nazis as overt or latent homosexuals. Thus while she rightly stresses the general association of perversion and fascism and the way in which it works as a projection of anxiety among nonfascists, she fails to address the peculiarly privileged status accorded to homosexuality as a "perversion." This may be because she doesn't address the extent to which homosexuality has been conflated with sadomasochism itself in most of these accounts. She does not, for example, engage Hewitt's extremely subtle reading of Adorno, where he takes the great thinker to task for equating homosexuality with sadomasochism and relying on a heteronormative model of the psychological growth of the oedipal subject. Frost, *Sex Drives,* 119, 28–32.

87. Gershon Legman, *Love and Death: A Study in Censorship* (New York: Hacker Art Books, 1963), 13.

88. Eric Larrabee, "Pornography Is Not Enough," *Harper's Magazine* 221 (November 1960): 96.

89. Abram Kardiner, *Sex and Morality* (New York: Bobbs-Merrill, 1954), 171, 189.

90. Erikson, *Childhood and Society,* 284; see also Erik Erikson, "Wholeness and Totality: A Psychiatric Contribution," in *Totalitarianism,* ed. Carl J. Friedrich (New York: Grosset & Dunlap, 1964), 168–69.

91. Wangh, *National Socialism,* 394; Kelley, *22 Cells,* 12. In 1964, the psychiatrists Maria Jahoda and Stuart W. Cook sought to examine "ideological compliance" that permitted unparalleled aggression against others no longer as "a phenomenon appearing in political dictatorships only. . . . We are about to demonstrate that it is not uncommon in this country [the United States] whose democratic institutions are intact." Marie Jahoda and Stuart W. Cook, "Ideological Compliance as a Social-Psychological Process," in *Totalitarianism,* ed. Friedrich, 204.

92. Gilbert, *Psychology of Dictatorship,* 279.

93. Legman, *Love and Death,* 13, 16–17.

94. Ibid., 40–41.

95. Ibid., 43. Legman's critique of Superman was taken up later by others. By 1966, for example, the anti-comic-book crusader Fredric Wertham insisted that Hitler was "like a comic-book hero" and that sexual abnormality was linked to the "moral disarmament of comic books" which express "a blunting of the finer feelings of conscience, of mercy, of sympathy for other people's suffering." Fredric Wertham, *A Sign for Cain: An Exploration of Human Violence* (New York: Macmillan, 1966), 74. See also Wertham, *Seduction of the Innocent* (New York: Rinehart, 1953), 90–91.

96. Haffner, *Germany: Jekyll and Hyde,* 126–27.

97 This isn't to say that if (externally induced) repression didn't exist there would be no more homophobia, since latent homosexuality is intrinsic in oedipal formation. Nevertheless, oedipal formation is itself conceived in heteronormative terms that might be challenged.

98. A perfect and concise example of this reasoning is Robert G. L. Waite's widely quoted *The Psychopathic God: Adolf Hitler* (New York: Basic Books, 1977), 235: "A different kind of evidence indicates that Hitler was personally concerned about latent homosexuality and struggled against it. There is a remarkable similarity between his attempts to deny any suggestion of homosexuality and his efforts to prove that he could not possibly be tainted by Jewish blood. In both cases he used the same defense: he denied that he was Jewish by persecuting the Jews; he denied that he was homosexual by attacking homosexuals." This ambivalent construction of homosexuality as both a sexual preference and the repression of that same preference is also signaled by Hewitt in his analysis of Adorno, Frenkel-Brunswik, Levinson, and Sanford's *The Authoritarian Personality* and throughout Adorno's work. In such texts, Hewitt writes, "homosexuality is always already repressed and self-repressing: or, more accurately, it is capable of drawing pleasure from a structure of repression experienced as submission. Consequently, the

argument that it is not homosexuality per se but merely repressed homosexuality that is authoritarian no longer holds: homosexuality is at home in its repression. Structured as it is around a fundamental submission, homosexuality experiences the renunciation of its desire as desirable; and homosexuality—as a potential identity structure—is based on an authoritarian repression of the desires it supposedly denotes." Hewitt, *Political Inversions*, 54.

99. Gitta Sereny, *Into That Darkness: An Examination of Conscience* (New York: Vintage, 1974), 325.

100. Erich Fromm, *The Anatomy of Human Destructiveness* (New York: Henry Holt, 1992), 456.

101. Victor Bromberg and Verna Volz Small, *Hitler's Psychopathology* (New York: International Universities Press, 1983), 2.

102. Ibid., 244–45. The list of such examples is endless. One judicious account that avoids these patterns is Frederick C. Redlich, M.D., *Hitler: Diagnosis of a Destructive Prophet* (New York: Oxford University Press, 1999), esp. 280–86.

103. Machtan, *Hidden Hitler*, 321, 317.

104. Haffner, *Germany: Jekyll and Hyde*, 126–27.

105. The assertion of the homosexual origins of Nazism is surely, as Hewitt argues, anxiety about the loss of the productive, meaning-bearing temporality—homosexuality as an allegory for an ungraspable location beyond history, which is represented by fascist myth-making. But I am interested in how critics created a narrative about numbness to suffering that formed the specific context within which more general anxieties about the ontological foundations of "History" and selfhood were articulated. Hewitt notes that he is not a historian and is thus not concerned with the specific questions in which this discourse was embedded. His main goal is to demonstrate how the homophobic construction of the relation between fascism and homosexuality works rhetorically to deny the potential affinities between fascism and modernism, and to show how the latter is grounded unwittingly in a symbolically heterosexual paradigm of generation and productivity. Hewitt's insightful analysis tells us much more about the generalized anxieties of modernists than it does about the context in which those concerns were embedded. The rhetorical association between homosexuality and fascism works to serve particular cultural aims that remain almost totally abstract in Hewitt's account, mostly because he is concerned not with a narrative that seeks to address fascism's challenge to civil society but one that addresses its challenge to certain notions of selfhood and temporality. For example, Italian fascism was far less likely to be equated with homosexuality than Nazism (with the exception of Bertolucci's *The Conformist*). Italian neorealist films tend to equate Nazis with homosexuality, and most references to homosexuality and fascism assimilate images originally derived from

Nazi Germany. The pressing historical question, if one seeks to understand the rhetorical association between fascism and homosexuality, thus becomes "Why Nazi Germany?"

106. We might now see more clearly that Foucault's concept of power mirrors the rhetorical function of homosexuality and pornography. Recall that Foucault figured power in modern democracies in the counterimage of sexual pathology—as a force that shapes and inhabits bodies but that can never itself be located, one that mutates with no aim that can be grasped, and exercised, to paraphrase a famous line from *The History of Sexuality*, but never possessed. Hayden White argued long ago that Foucault's work employed the trope of catachresis. Arguably both pornography and homosexuality, as examples of how Foucault allegorizes power, are "undecidable" because they also refer to more than one referent, and that is what gives them the rhetorical power they enjoy in the cultural context to which I've been referring. It's also important, however, to sustain a focus on what makes them powerful cultural explanatory tools in a detailed and rigorous fashion. Hayden White, "Michel Foucault," in *Structuralism and Since*, ed. John Sturrock (Oxford: Oxford University Press, 1979), 81–115.

EPILOGUE

1. Lawrence L. Langer, *Preempting the Holocaust* (New Haven: Yale University Press, 1998), 193.

INDEX

Adorno, Theodor, 109, 121, 134
African Americans. *See* Black-Jewish relations
Agamben, Giorgio, 7, 168n83
Agee, James, 20–21
Alphen, Ernst van, 30–31
Amnesty International, 1, 76–78
Anti-Semitism: Clendinnen on, 63–64; and the Dreyfus Affair, 96, 97; and the "eliminationist mind-set," 46, 93; Gordon on, 81; and historical knowledge, 45–48, 63–64, 66; and Hitler's psychological makeup, 107, 121, 127, 133; and indifference, 81, 83–86, 89–90, 92–100, 102, 104; and Nazi bureaucrats, 46–47; and pornography, 35, 36; redemptive, 94–95
Arendt, Hannah, 58, 61, 164n42, 181n92; on the Dreyfus Affair, 96, 97; and the problem of "ordinary monsters," 64
Auschwitz, 9, 14, 21–22, 25, 42; Clendinnen on, 63–67; failure of the allies to bomb, 4, 139n16; and the Jewish Museum of New York exhibit, 28. *See also* Concentration camps
Austria, 80, 84, 112
Authoritarian Personality, The (Adorno, Horkheimer, and Frenkel-Brunswick), 121
Authoritarianism, 121–23, 126, 129

Balzac, Honoré de, 2, 3
Bankier, David, 82, 85, 87, 93
Barkan, Elazar, 11, 76
Barnett, Victoria, 25
Bartov, Omer, 43, 60, 68–78, 157n4, 166n75

Baudrillard, Jean, 8, 14, 143n35
Bauer, Yehuda, 48, 62, 163n37
Bauman, Zygmunt, 164n43
Berenbaum, Michael, 32
Bergen, Doris, 87
Berghahn, Volker, 57
Berlin, Isaiah, 4
Berliner Tageblatt, 112
Bessel, Richard, 110, 134
Betroffenheit (affectation of dismay), 49
Birkenau, 65–66. *See also* Concentration camps
Birn, Ruth Bettina, 50
Bitburg, cemetery at, 146n54
Black-Jewish relations, 78, 170n11
Bloomsbury critics, 6
Bock, Gisela, 109
Bodeman, Michael, 34
Boltanski, Luc, 143n36
Borderline personality disorder, 132
Borowski, Tadeusz, 66
Bosnia, 69–70
Bourgeois class, 2, 119–20
Boyarin, Jonathan, 9
Brasillach, Robert, 108
Braun, Eva, 26
Brecht, Bertolt, 106
Britain, 4, 93
Bromberg, Norbert, 132
Broszat, Martin, 80–81, 89
Browning, Christopher, 57–59
Buchenwald, 26, 27. *See also* Concentration camps
Bulgaria, 11
Bureaucracy, 46–48, 58
Burleigh, Michael, 110

Hitler's psychological makeup, 108, 131; and indifference, 84, 92, 93, 96, 99; international, 76; and pornography, 19–22, 33–39, 41
Moscow Declaration (1943), 80
Murder in Our Midst (Bartov), 68–69, 77–78
Museum of Modern Art (MoMA), 8
Mussolini, Benito, 117

Narcissism, 13, 14; and Hitler's psychological makeup, 126, 127, 132–34; and pornography, 31, 41
Nazism, 80; bureaucracy of, 46–48, 58; and historical knowledge, 44–47, 53, 58, 61, 63, 67–69; and Hitler's psychological makeup, 107–9, 111–12, 116, 118–19, 122–26, 128–33, 134; and homosexuality, 4, 136, 194; and humanism, 44; and indifference, 81–83, 87–89, 93–95, 99; and pornography, 19, 22–23, 30–31, 35–36, 39, 45–46. *See also* Hitler, Adolf
New-York Historical Society, 1, 24
Niemöller, Martin, 77, 169n5
"Night of the Long Knives" massacre, 133
Nochlin, Linda, 28, 30
Normalcy, 90, 99
Novick, Peter, 11
Numbness, 1–2, 4–6, 136; challenge of, to the liberal ideal of empathy, 5; and complicity, 87; and historical knowledge, 45, 51, 54, 67, 73–75; and pornography, 16, 18, 29, 36, 41. *See also* Indifference
Nuremberg Laws, 92, 93
Nuremberg trials, 2, 4, 78, 123, 139n14

Obedience, 57
O'Connor, John, 22
Oedipal conflicts, 120, 124
Office of Strategic Services (OSS), 112–13
Olden, Rudolf, 112
"Ordinary Germans," role of, 45–46, 57, 64, 75, 84
Other, 5, 36; obliteration of, 36; self and, boundaries between, 9–11, 14; space of, Boyarin on, 9

Paget, Violet. *See* Lee, Vernon
Painted Bird, The (Kosinski), 24
Passion, prosecutorial, 52, 53

Peep shows, 32–33
Pelt, Robert Jan van, 88
Philo-Semitism, 102
Poland, 12, 80, 84, 96, 101–2
Pontecorvo, Gillo, 109
Pornography, 4, 15, 16–42, 136; advent of, after the Great War, 20; Agee on, 20–21; Gorer on, 21; and historical knowledge, 45–55; and homosexuality, 131; Jameson on, 18; Lissner on, 18–19; MacKinnon on, 17–18; respectable, notion of, 29; use of the term, 16
Pornography of Power, The (Rubinoff), 21
Posen speech, 61–63, 68
Postmodernism, 43, 166n76
Power, Samantha, 140n19
POWs (prisoners of war), 80
Propaganda, 28, 85, 87, 90, 121
Protestantism, 77, 119

Racism, 83
Radicalization, cumulative, 46
Rage, 96, 98, 121, 122
Rationality, 41, 63
Rauschning, Hermann, 112, 113, 114
Reading the Holocaust (Clendinnen), 60, 63–64
Reagan, Ronald, 13, 146n54
Reddy, William, 140n18
Redemption, 7, 94–95
Reductio ad absurdum, 13
Reich, Wilhelm, 108, 119–20, 123
Reich-Ranicki, Marcel, 96, 101–4
Reichstag fire, 108, 115
Relativism, 166n76
Repression, 67, 107, 119–20, 129, 131, 134
Revisionism, 44
Riccoboni, Madame, 2, 9
Riess, Volker, 50
Rodrigue, Aron, 82
Roehm, Ernst, 108, 112, 122, 124–25, 132–33
Roehm (or Röhm) episode, 122, 125. *See also* Roehm, Ernst
Roma Nazista (Dollmann), 117
Romantic tradition, 14
Rosen, Roee, 26
Rosenbaum, Ron, 53–54, 162n33
Rosenfeld, Alvin H., 12, 22, 25
Rosensaft, Menachem, 26–27
Rosler, Martha, 153n62
Rossellini, Roberto, 108